Samson of a Man

Samson of a Man

saved soul, wasted life

Kevin McDowell

WINEPRESS **WP** PUBLISHING

WinePress Publishing (PO Box 428, Enumclaw, WA 98022) functions only as book publisher. As such, the ultimate design, content, editorial accuracy, and views expressed or implied in this work are those of the author.

Unless otherwise noted, all Scriptures are taken from the New King James Version, © 1979, 1980, 1982 by Thomas Nelson, Inc., Publishers. Used by permission.

ISBN 13: 978-1-57921-887-4
ISBN 10: 1-57921-887-3
Library of Congress Catalog Card Number: 2006938207

TABLE OF CONTENTS

Acknowledgements

This book is dedicated to my Lord and Savior Jesus. Without His saving grace there would be no reason . . .

And to His servant Pastor Matthew "Chik" Chikeles, whose influence in my life can be found on every page.

To all those who have at one time or another cared about me, especially my family: I'm sorry, please forgive me. The pain and suffering I caused you was not intentional.

Foreword

This book is going to save lives.

If our lives are the only book someone reads what will they see? Would the reader see the hand of God or the futility of man? Kevin's life has been set to print for all to see. Yet this is not simply an account of a wasted life. It's about God's grace and mercy, a testimony to His forgiveness, reconciliation and restoration. Kevin took his life to the depths of despair and made it back alive (burnt, beat, and bloodied). Now he shares the biblical insights and divine truths that brought victory and healing.

This book is desperately needed in today's wicked and perverse world. Violence, drug abuse, and sexual perversion headline the news. The Church is not immune. Reports of Christian men and women falling victim to sexual sin are epidemic. It affects all of us. Lives are being destroyed. Marriages are failing. Families are crushed. Children are being robbed of their innocence. All the while believers do nothing. It's as though the church is blind to the holocaust. We don't want to know that the person next to us is secretly struggling. Most believers live in the shadows, hiding in fear that their secret sin may be discovered.

The Bible says Christians should be open and honest with one another. They are to ask for forgiveness, pray for each other, counsel one another and be accountable to each another. Church should be a place where believers deal with sin and work out their salvation. Yet sex is rarely discussed. It's a sensitive and embarrassing topic. Sex is a powerful force. It has great potential for blessing and for harm.

Understand this, God created sex. Every believer has, has had, or will have sexual thoughts and desires. God wants His children to enjoy healthy sexual relations within the secure boundaries of His Word. However every believer's thoughts, desires, and actions will at some point violate God's standards (sin).

All too frequently I've witnessed pastors and church leaders who struggle with sexual sin quickly discarded by the church without any possibility of reconciliation or restoration. Church leaders are not immune to temptation. Pastors are above all sinners saved by God's grace. Forgiveness is just as available to church leaders as it is to all of God's children. When a leader is cast aside, all it does is cause others struggling to draw further into the darkness. Seeing others treated without mercy, they recoil in fear that their sin will be discovered. Consequently the sinful cycle is perpetuated and God's children live hopeless secret lives. The Bible makes it clear that we are *all* sinners in need of God's forgiveness. Silence is our enemy. It keeps us in bondage, strains our relationship with God, and limits our fellowship with other believers. Not until we walk in the light will we enjoy the fullness of being one of God's children.

Extremes characterize Kevin's life. No one I know has traveled to the depths of despair as Kevin has and made it back. I have known Kevin since 1985 and I've witnessed his struggle with sin and been privileged to be a part of God's reconciliation and restoration in his life. Kevin is a precious brother in the Lord and a man of God. I'm honored to count him as one of my most trusted and close personal friends.

Yet this book isn't just about sex or Kevin's sin. God has equipped Kevin with biblical wisdom and the ability to communicate spiritual truth. Consequently this book is full of biblical teaching on numerous subjects critical for believers today. It contains valuable insight on parenting, marriage, leadership, church discipline, fundamentals of Christianity, and much more. Most important it's a book about God's love and just how far He will go to redeem His children.

Every believer should read this book. I admit I'm biased. But I'm thoroughly convinced that this book is going to save lives! Do you want to overcome sin in your life? Read this book. Do you want to help others overcome sin in their lives? Read this book. Do you want to see a dramatic example of Gods love? Read this book. Church leader? Pastor? Parent? Husband? Wife? Friend? Read this book!

My prayer is that through this book you discover God's love and experience the wonder of His Word. May you receive with great joy the hope of God's love, grace, and redemption and, if needed, His restoration. Furthermore I pray that God will reveal to you the truth of Romans 11:29 *"For the gifts and the calling of God are irrevocable."* No one has fallen so far that they cannot be restored.

Hey, you're here now. May God bless your socks off.
In His Grip!

Chik Chikeles
Senior Pastor, Calvary Chapel Saint Paul
Saint Paul Police Department Chaplain #9
Ramsey County Correctional Facility Chaplain
A vomitus, carnal, flesh-bag of pus, saved by the grace of God

Introduction

Of making many books there is no end . . .

—Ecclesiastes 12:12

Most books should never be written . . . I wish this were one of them. Above all I wish I wasn't the author. There is no glory in this writing, only great sorrow and tears. Any glory belongs to Jesus—He is the hero. If it were not for Him there would be no reason for this writing.

This book is not a labor of love; this is an act of obedience. My story, as dark as it is, needs to be told. The church is in crisis. We are living in an immoral and perverse world. Darkness threatens to overcome us. It's time to wake up.

Mine is a life of extremes, full of contradictions. I once heard a paradox defined as two opposites that are both 100 percent true. My life is full of paradoxes. Even I find it perplexing that the main character and the author of this book are the same person; it just doesn't seem possible.

I hate this book! It's hideous. Disgusting! This is an account of human depravity and self-indulgence, a true-life horror story. This alone should make for interesting reading. Even the most timid are drawn to the macabre. Who wouldn't slow down to observe a train wreck? This is a story of multiple train wrecks.

WARNING! This book is for mature audiences. It contains accounts of sexually perverse behavior. Every effort has been made to present these events tastefully and without elaboration. It is not my intent to shock; I'm not purposefully trying to disgust the reader. However, the very mention of such things has the potential to offend.

This book is not just a testimony. *I hate testimonies!* Too many Christian testimonies are sensationalized tales of immoral exploits with an understated climax about how God rescued them. Been there—done that—won't do it again. In this book I examine my life through the lens of Scripture every step of the way. My story is merely a vehicle to show the practical application of God's Word. Consequently this book is full of Bible references and teaching. The biblical applications are the heart of my message; my story apart from God's Word is meaningless.

This biography is totally biased. It's also brutally honest. Imagine a subjective mirror, not a fun-house carnival mirror that distorts the image. No, this mirror presents an accurate but selective reflection: instead of reflecting the whole, it shows only the parts important to the message. My story is told through my eyes with a biblical world-view. If someone else were to write this account I'd expect it to be similar yet different. And if authored from an alternative worldview it would be very different. At one time I seriously considered writing a purely secular account of my life. Most of what is in this writing would be excluded and the rest would be scripted to make me appear the hero (or at least a likeable character). Instead of a biblical per-spective, the story would be told through the lens of contemporary 1970s music. Thank God He spared me from my folly.

"Does this story have a happy ending?" God's grace and mercy throughout my life are beyond comprehension. My pastor (who has witnessed my life for over twenty years) once told me that I'm a model for God's grace. He said that no one he's ever known has abused God's grace more, yet amazingly God's hand remains on my life. That alone should inspire and encourage. The fact that I'm still here, still growing, and am still one of God's children defies human logic. Happy ending? While there is joy and happiness in my life I'd have to say I'm still looking forward to the happy ending. Yet I'm not chasing it anymore, I'm simply enjoying the journey. I know beyond a doubt that a happy ending is coming. God promised. If I've learned anything, it is to trust God's promises.

> *That which has been is what will be, that which is done is what will
> be done, and there is nothing new under the sun.*
>
> —Ecclesiastes 1:9

There is nothing in my life that has not been experienced by others. It's just that my life is full of extremes. My pastor once put it this way, "When Kevin came clean and confessed, there was nothing I hadn't heard before. Only I'd never heard it all come from the same person." It's doubtful that anyone reading this will share in my life experiences. The lives of most readers will be far different from mine. It doesn't matter. *There is nothing new under the sun.* While aspects of my life may be strange to you, they are not new to mankind, and they are most definitely not foreign to God. One of the few things God can't do is be surprised. He knows everything.

Eliciting empathy from the reader is not my goal and I certainly don't want your sympathy or pity. I share my story only as a way to exemplify the message. The biblical wisdom and insights apply to all believers. What you choose to do with them is what matters, and that is totally dependent on you.

> *For it is shameful even to speak of those things which are done by
> them in secret. But all things that are exposed are made manifest by
> the light . . .*
>
> —Ephesians 5:12,13

> *For there is nothing covered that will not be revealed, nor hidden that
> will not be known. Therefore whatever you have spoken in the dark
> will be heard in the light, and what you have spoken in the ear in
> inner rooms will be proclaimed on the housetops.*
>
> —Luke 12:2,3

One day all secrets will be revealed. This will be a troubling day for most people. As for me I'm going to get it out of the way and start now.

To my shame and embarrassment, this is my story.

SECTION ONE

Age of Innocence . . . NOT!

chapter 1

childhood folly

It was strangely quiet, birds chirping, a distant car, insects in flight. My senses were on high alert, aware of every sight, sound, and smell—eucalyptus tainted by the odor of rotten citrus, the faint smell of the ocean on a gentle breeze. The sky above the coastal mountains was a blue canvas dotted with clouds. The white trail of a distant jet could be seen on the horizon. It was a sensual summer afternoon in 1968; my twelfth birthday had just passed. These were the innocent days of youth: totally unaware of the adult world of war and social unrest.

Carefully I made my way through the orange grove: hiding behind trees, watching, expecting, pretending. It was quiet, too quiet. I knew they were out there waiting for me to make a mistake. Heavily armed and alert, I was ready for them. I stood lifeless and still for what seemed an eternity, acutely aware of every sound, every movement . . . nothing. Maybe they had moved on to seek some other prey. They must have moved on. Relieved, and disappointed, I stepped out from behind the tree. Still nothing. I stood there contemplating my next move. Then it happened. I was hit, hit hard in the face. I fell to the ground in pain.

Holding my wounded face I cried and swore. Instantly they were upon me, but the game was over. "Are you OK?" "I didn't mean to hit you in the face." Chris was visibly concerned. I looked up and saw him and his two sisters standing over me. Chris still had several hard green oranges in his hands. Not wanting to appear weak in front of the girls I got up and viciously confronted Chris. Swearing and pushing him I challenged him to fight. It was all show. He would have

1

pulverized me. He was older and bigger. Chris was mentally challenged. He had few friends and was not about to lose my friendship. I suspect he knew I hung out with him because I liked his sister.

We moved to the Ojai Valley several months earlier in spite of my protests. I didn't want to leave Arizona. I liked living in Prescott with its rich Wild West history and imagery. It fueled the imagination of a boy raised on 1950s westerns. My parents' business was located in a nineteenth-century hotel. The rooms on the upper floors were untouched, complete with their original furnishings. I explored those rooms for hours, imagining, pretending. We lived outside of town on fifteen acres overlooking two lakes and next to an Indian reservation. I had my own horse. Why would I want to move to California?

Ojai is the home of celebrities, writers, artists (not starving), eastern gurus, television and movie producers. Private boarding schools, world-class tennis tournaments, and a transcendental meditation retreat contribute to Ojai's mystique. It was a world vastly different from the simplicity of Prescott.

We made our way to their house, laughing and joking. Chris and his sisters lived in an abandoned western movie set converted into rentals. It was a complete western town hidden among the orange groves in the Ojai foothills. The first floors of the buildings were finished while the second floors were only fronts. Chris and his family lived in the sheriff's office. I spent a lot of time that summer with Chris.

It was a long walk home. We lived near the top of a steep road lined with eucalyptus and oak trees. It was a very peaceful neighborhood with nice houses on large wooded lots, gated estates, and a private boy's camp. Few cars would pass. If a car did come by it was likely to be an exotic luxury or sports car. A husky twelve-year-old boy with a buzz hair cut, western shirt, and cowboy boots would have been a strange sight.

Walking home I passed the time in the playground of my mind. Stopping to rest I'd contemplate what lay beyond the iron gates of a private estate. Maybe it was the home of some celebrity or other icon. I could only imagine what life was like behind the stone walls. In Ojai the possibilities were endless. Later I'd discover that one of our neighbors was a television producer while another was the mother of a popular rock and roll star. My imagination may have been closer to reality than one would think.

Much of my childhood was unsupervised. Even at a young age I was allowed to go off by myself or with a friend for long periods. In Arizona I'd explore the town or countryside, catch crawdads or water snakes in the creek, go horseback riding, swimming, or fishing. By the time we moved to Ojai, it was nothing for me to be gone for the whole day. My parents both worked long hours, so at home I was still usually alone. Even when I was with my family there was isolation. My father was very quiet and withdrawn. I could spend the whole day with him in silence. My mother was more expressive but very busy. My older sister was an important presence, but she was living her own life.

Both Prescott and Ojai were safe places to live, insulated from a dark and cruel world. All I knew of the social unrest and war that plagued our country was what I saw on television. I knew nothing of poverty, gangs, drug addiction, hate, or prejudice. This wasn't the streets of Los Angeles or New York. It was white middle-class America.

My family loved and cared for me. All my material needs were met. There were family activities and vacations. My parents did their best to give me every opportunity possible. They just didn't talk to me, at least not about real life issues. Family problems, social ills, and world affairs were never discussed. I can't remember ever witnessing my parents working out a life problem, even a simple one. I grew up in a vacuum.

One consistent message I heard growing up was that I was special. Which I interpreted "I'm better, smarter, and more deserving than anyone else." No one had to come right out and say it, I knew the truth—the universe revolves around me. This may sound funny, but it was very serious. In my teen years I'd be confronted with the truth that there are billions of people on this planet; I was no more special than anyone else. The image of being just a speck in a sea of humanity created in me a sense of despair. I became bitter and angry at the world.

My childhood was severely lacking in life instruction and discipline. I was rarely held accountable for my actions. It's difficult to know what a child has been up to when left unsupervised for long periods of time. To complicate matters, I mastered the art of deception at an early age. Cover up the evidence then lie with a straight face; deny all charges; minimize the consequences; remain silent—skills I'd use throughout my life.

I had my share of bad behavior, yet I wasn't thought of as a problem child. Whenever I was caught behaving badly, adults would be surprised. "He's such a nice boy." I wasn't like Dennis the Menace or Bart Simpson who were expected to behave badly (although I did share their mischievousness). I also wasn't the innocent boy who fell in with the wrong crowd (although that would frequently be used to explain my actions). I was generally thought of as a well-behaved child who occasionally got into boyish trouble.

Some have suggested that my bad behavior was a cry for attention. I wish it were that simple. From a young age I've had an attraction to the forbidden, the taboo, the dangerous. If it made my heart race, I was interested. I'd provoke scorpions, tarantulas, and rattlesnakes to see if I could get them to strike. With the help of a friend we killed a rattlesnake with rocks. I threw rocks at a wasp nest then tried to outrun them the mile back to the house (only got stung five times). I'd climb tall trees, jump across the tops of buildings and off rock cliffs into a lake. I'd sneak into a friend's house uninvited while they were home; I'd see if I could make my way through the entire house undetected. I started grass fires, then put them out before they became out of control.

Then there was the truly forbidden—

When I was six or seven, at the prompting of older female children, I took off my clothes for them to look at me. Around the same age, my father caught me lying naked on the ground behind the house. It's a sensual childhood memory. The warm sun, the breeze, the thrill was intoxicating. The tragedy is that my parents did nothing. My father sent me to my room while they discussed the matter. Ultimately nothing was ever done; not a word was said to me about the incident.

At ten I was visiting a neighbor girl my same age. We took off our clothes and fondled each other. We attempted intercourse, but there was no penetration because I was not capable of an erection. When I was eleven I stayed with a male friend my same age. We experimented with masturbating each other. None of these encounters were sexual. The attraction was the thrill of the forbidden, the taboo.

Growing up no one talked about sex (at least no adults). There was a class in school in the eighth grade but they didn't address my struggle. The answers didn't come from church. The closest my parents came was to have me read a short pamphlet on sex and ask me if I had any questions. They seemed quite relieved that I didn't. I was on my own.

Some people attribute early sexual encounters to innocent childhood curiosity. Sadly, some would consider them healthy. But forty years later I can trace a life of struggle back to the sins of my youth.

The best I can figure, the move to Ojai was my parents' attempt to fulfill some fantasy of success. We didn't fit in, didn't belong. To maintain this standard of living my mother worked long hours. My father became more isolated. They both drank. They tried to maintain some semblance of family. We attended church where my father was the treasurer and my mother helped lead the youth group. My father was an Assistant Scout Master. I was active in the school band, drama, Boy Scouts, and church. My time was filled with activities: hobbies, Boy Scouts, church camps, concerts, vacations, and outings.

> . . . *those who desire to be rich fall into temptation and a snare . . .*
> —1 Timothy 6:8,9

In Ojai I was surrounded by worldly success. We lived in a nice house in an upscale neighborhood. Many of my friends came from wealthy families; trust fund kids who were financially set for life. Exotic sports cars, servants, private estates complete with riding stables, tennis courts, and swimming pools—it was a world that most people can only imagine. Unfortunately I got a first-hand look at this world at a very impressionable age. This only raised my already unrealistic expectations. I became covetous. I wanted the life I saw around me. I believed that I deserved that life. After all I'm supposed to be special. It affected me deeply. Throughout my life I've lived under a mysterious cloud of discontentment: never satisfied, always looking for something more.

Let your conduct be without covetousness; be content with such things as you have . . .

—Hebrews 13:5

I grew up with the notion that I was destined to greatness. Of course greatness in my mind meant wealth, accomplishment, and the esteem of others. It never occurred to me that a simple quiet life lived in obscurity could be meaningful. The message I heard was that I could be and do anything. However this message was never qualified; it was without limitation. No one said anything about hard work or perseverance. I wasn't warned that others would be competing with me. My expectation was for great rewards with minimal effort. This became another source of frustration and anger. It was a rude awakening when I realized the world was not going to be handed to me on a silver platter.

The seeds of sin were planted, watered and rooted in my life at a young age. By age twelve I was already in bondage to sin. Yet another seed had also been planted and was taking root, the good news of salvation. My parents failed in many ways, as do most. But they did take me to church and send me to Vacation Bible School. At age eleven in Prescott, I responded to the prompting of the Holy Spirit and received Jesus as my Savior. My understanding of God was limited. But clearly the Holy Spirit had begun a work in my life.

In Ojai I participated in the church youth group. It was a typical group, social activity with a touch of religion to give credibility. For my part I learned how to look and sound spiritual while entertaining lustful fantasies of the girls in the group. Group events were opportunities for sexual exploration. I remember one trip to Disneyland spent heavy petting under a blanket in the back seat of my parents' car. The girl and I were the elected leaders of the youth group! After letting it go on for a long time my father finally told us to stop. But nothing else was ever said and her parents were never told about our behavior.

In spite of this, God was laying a foundation in my life. I can recall church summer camps where God moved mightily. I attended a home fellowship not associated with any church; the focus was worship, study of God's Word, and prayer. By the time I was a freshman in high school, I was on fire for God. I carried my Bible to school and shared my faith at school events.

God had started a work in my life that He intended to finish. Satan had no intent of releasing his stronghold. The battle had begun. Little did I know at the time just how great a battle it would become.

chapter 2
Teach the children

"Created in the image of God" implies moral responsibility. Mankind, unlike any other living creature, is expected to make ethical judgments. No other earthly being contemplates the meaning of life or wrestles with issues of right and wrong. The rest of creation makes decisions based on instinct and experience; they are driven by their environment and genetics. Domestic animals may be described as obedient or disobedient. Animals in the wild follow established patterns of behavior. Yet neither deals with issues of morality.

Navigating the treacherous waters of life requires a keen eye and a steady hand; many vessels have been shipwrecked along the way and no one makes it through unharmed. Everyone comes into this world with an innate knowledge of right and wrong.[1] While a person's conscience may provide a basic sense of moral direction, it isn't enough to successfully navigate life's obstacles. It takes wisdom to live a life of integrity in an increasingly immoral world.

Children come into this world ready to learn. They are like a dry sponge ready to soak up knowledge. It's the responsibility of parents to teach their children. They need to be taught basic survival and social skills. They need an education that will prepare them to be productive members of society. But even more than this, children need to be taught about life. They need a moral compass that will guide them through treacherous waters.

Parents who believe in God must impart their faith to their children. It is far more important for children to have a personal

---

[1] Romans 1:20; 2:15

relationship with God than it is for them to achieve worldly success. "Get an education so you can get a good job and live a happy life." Unfortunately this lie has infiltrated the thinking of believing parents. Education, employment, and financial security are not the path to happiness. Only a personal relationship with God will bring fulfillment. If you want your children to live a happy life then teach them this:

> *Blessed [happy] is the man who walks not in the counsel of the ungodly, nor stands in the path of sinners, nor sits in the seat of the scornful; but his delight is in the law of the LORD, and in His law he meditates day and night.*
>
> —Psalm 1:1,2

> *Blessed [happy] is he whose transgression is forgiven, whose sin is covered.*
>
> —Psalm 32:1

Contemporary western culture has taken the pursuit of happiness to the extreme. We are constantly bombarded with the newest secret to fulfillment. A fundamental tenet of advertising is to create a need (real or perceived) then fill that need; make people think they can't live without your product. I grew up discontented and very unhappy. The few happy moments I did have were fleeting; I was quickly off on the next pursuit. No one taught me the secret to happiness. Of course you can't teach what you don't know.

"Train up a child in the way he should go, and when he is old he will not depart from it" (Proverbs 22:6). This is an exhortation to godly parenting; your efforts will be rewarded. Yet an equally valid translation of this passage would read, *"train a child after the manner of his own way . . ."* or *"let a child train himself."* Then when he grows old he will have difficulty departing from the sinful habits he has developed. I was left to train myself, and the consequences have been devastating.

My parents were nice, respectable people; they would be considered "good" by the world's standards. They were law-abiding, hard-working, and generous. However, I can't say that I grew up in a godly home. The things of God were not discussed. I have no memory of my parents reading the Bible or praying. I never heard them seek God's direction or ask for His forgiveness. We went to church, but it was merely Bible stories. I wasn't taught repentance, accountability, or how to live an open and honest life. If anything, the world I grew up in taught me the exact opposite—to hide and lie about my sin.

Chasten [teach, instruct, rebuke] your son while there is hope, and do not set your heart on his destruction.
—Proverbs 19:18

Fathers (and single parent mothers), you are the prophet and priest in your children's lives. It's your responsibility to teach your children to know God; not just know about God, but to have a personal relationship with Him. Let them see Jesus working in you and through you. Lead them to salvation through Jesus, then disciple them to become godly men and women. Raising your children is the most important responsibility you have. To fail is to *"set your heart on their destruction."*

And you, fathers, do not provoke your children to wrath, but bring them up in the training and admonition of the Lord.
—Ephesians 6:4

I've seen parents who intentionally provoke their children. They belittle them and tear them down instead of encourage them and build them up in their faith. It's sad. Yet I've discovered another way to provoke children to wrath—ignore them. Or worse yet, build them up with unrealistic expectations, but don't give them any instruction; simply let them face life completely unprepared. This certainly worked to provoke me to wrath.

Volumes of books have been written on raising children. I suggest reading some of them; which ones to read is a matter of opinion. Ask your pastor or a trusted friend for recommendations. Of course the first book you should read, and arguably the most important book on the subject, is the Bible. As far as I'm concerned, any other book you read should be based on strict biblical teaching. Whenever I consider reading a book, I check to see if the Bible is the author's primary source. I've seen too many so-called 'Christian' books that fail to use God's Word as their foundation. Meanwhile here are some thoughts on raising godly children:

➤ Teach children the Bible. Not just Bible stories, but the practical application of God's Word (all of it). Children who grow up in my church today have studied through the entire Bible (Genesis to Revelation) by the time they are twelve years old. It's amazing to see what this foundation can do in the life of a young person.

➤ Teach them the "fear of the Lord" (study for yourself what it means to fear God, it's not what you might think)— *"Come, you children, listen to me; I will teach you the fear of the Lord"* (Psalm 34:11).

➤ Children should know the character of God— *"merciful and gracious, slow to anger, and abounding in mercy"* (Psalm 103:8).

➤ Confront and correct their sin— *"He who spares his rod hates his son, but he who loves him disciplines him promptly"* (Proverbs 13:24).

➤ Raise them to know the joy of the Lord—

Oh come, let us sing to the LORD!
Let us shout joyfully to the Rock of our salvation.
Let us come before His presence with thanksgiving;
Let us shout joyfully to Him with psalms.
For the LORD is the great God,
And the great King above all gods.

                                  —Psalm 95:1–3

> Teach them to see themselves through the lens of Scripture, not through the eyes of the world, that they would embrace the great commandment[2]

Hear, O Israel: The LORD our God, the LORD is one! You shall love the LORD your God with all your heart, with all your soul, and with all your strength.

And these words which I command you today shall be in your heart. You shall teach them diligently to your children . . .
—Deuteronomy 6:4–7

Satan is committed to the destruction of children. He hates the innocence and simple faith of a child. History is littered with attacks on children. Pharaoh ordered the destruction of male infants at the time of Moses' birth.[3] Herod made a similar proclamation at Jesus' birth.[4] Hitler destroyed children. Abortion has destroyed millions of innocent children. Children have been prostituted, tortured, and even executed in religious ceremonies.

Satan is an expert in human behavior and the sinful nature of mankind, which he skillfully uses in his attacks on humanity. However, the only influence he has is what we allow him to have. His primary tools are deception and disguise. He speaks lies, innuendo, and half-truths. If Satan can get us to believe his lies, he can manipulate our behavior. The innocent heart and curious mind of a child is fertile ground for Satan to gain a stronghold.

Unfortunately most believers reject or minimize the demonic. Even if they believe it exists, they don't comprehend its influence. To most believers the spiritual world is surreal. It's easier to focus on the physical world that we can touch, taste, and smell, and in which we believe we have some control. Yet the spiritual is just as real as the physical; actually it's more real when you consider that only the spiritual is eternal.

---

[2] Matthew 22:36–39
[3] Exodus 1–3
[4] Matthew 2

For we do not wrestle against flesh and blood, but against principalities, against powers, against the rulers of the darkness of this age, against spiritual hosts of wickedness in the heavenly places.
—Ephesians 6:12

This passage couldn't be clearer. If you believe the Bible, then there is no other conclusion than we live in a spiritual world that includes the demonic. Children aren't immune from the war that rages around us. Satan's strategy is to trap them while they're young and keep them off balance. Parents need to protect and educate their children. Children need to know how to recognize the enemy and be equipped with the biblical tools to defend themselves. Today we teach children to be safe around strangers. Why don't we teach our children to protect themselves against an even greater threat?

Some might complain that it's inappropriate to discuss these things with children; it will steal their innocence and frighten them. Actually Satan is the one who is out to steal the innocence of children. If anything, equipping them with biblical tools serves to protect their innocence. Certainly there are age-appropriate ways to address these subjects. Fear should never be the outcome of any discussion about spiritual warfare (no matter what the age). The demonic is not to be feared by believers. Satan has no power when we protect ourselves with truth. Children need to learn the truth about themselves and the world in which they live.

Then Jesus said to those Jews who believed Him, "If you abide in My word, you are My disciples indeed. And you shall know the truth, and the truth shall make you free."
—John 8:31,32

Most children are not adequately prepared for adult life. I know I wasn't. The mentality is that parents need to protect children from life issues. The concern is that children will grow up too fast. Consequently many don't grow up at all. I'm not suggesting that children be expected to function as adults. I am saying that parents have a responsibility to equip their children to become adults. By the time a child enters adolescence he should be ready to start taking on adult responsibilities.

Between age twelve and fifteen was the coming of age in ancient times. It was the period that boys became men. They took on adult responsibilities. They were held accountable for their behavior. This is the way in many parts of the world today. Until recently this was true in the United States. The Bible doesn't speak of adolescence. Adolescence is a modern invention that attempts to explain a period of transition from child to adult. Unfortunately, it is mostly used to excuse rebellion and bad behavior.

Dr. Spock and his hands-off philosophy of parenting was the standard when I was growing up. Provide children with a safe, healthy environment, then let them raise themselves. This philosophy is based on the premise that people are born naturally good, that children given the right environment will learn for themselves necessary social skills and make morally correct decisions. It doesn't work! Children need instruction, structure, and discipline.

chapter 3

Rebellion... or is it witchcraft?

For rebellion is as the sin of witchcraft, and stubbornness is as iniquity and idolatry.

—1 Samuel 15:23

Ratty long hair, scruffy beard, earring, tie-died shirt, ragged bell-bottom button-down Levis covered with patches, worn biker boots complete with a buck knife and a bag of pot hidden inside—it was the 1970s and I looked the part.

Walking into the living room I hardly noticed or appreciated how privileged my life had been. The spectacular view of the mountains through a wall of glass no longer impressed me. I was on a mission, ready to implement a carefully-rehearsed deception.

"I need to use the car. Dave had a fight with his mom and he needs me." My words flowed with confidence, I could have just as easily been asking, "What's for dinner?" It was a false confidence; I knew my request would be challenged; all trust between my parents and me had long since been destroyed.

"It's a bad idea. You just got your license and we haven't had a chance to put you on the insurance." It seemed as though my mother was expecting such a request. That didn't stop me. I turned up the heat. She put up a good fight but she didn't stand a chance. Her fatal error was, and always has been, that she saw me as a good boy at heart. She wanted to believe me. "I'll be careful, I promise." It was a lie.

As I drove out to the rural park to meet Dave on that summer day I could already feel the effects of the Valium I had stolen from my aunt. Dave had a case of beer and some weed. My mom should have followed her first instinct. Unfortunately I could be a very convincing liar.

My sophomore year in high school was tumultuous. Seemingly over night I threw myself headlong into wickedness, rebellion, and sin. I had struck a friendship with Steve who joined me in my pursuit of self-destruction. Steve and I had met the previous year when I witnessed to him about Jesus at a school event. Later that night he accepted Jesus as his Savior. The next week he found me and told me what he had done. We became instant and inseparable friends. After a wonderful summer of walking in fellowship with God we walked away from the Lord together.

During that year I gave myself over to every thrill I could experience. We'd take any drug that was available. We'd even take drugs stolen out of medicine cabinets without knowing what they were. But our drugs of choice were pot, speed, and LSD. This is when I first used a needle to inject drugs, speed, and LSD.

As an act of self-abuse I would inject myself with an empty needle, pumping my own blood in and out of the syringe for the thrill. This was done under the guise that I was learning how to inject myself without assistance. We cut ourselves with razor blades and broken glass. We burned ourselves intentionally with cigarettes. Somehow there was a perverse pleasure derived from these acts of self-abuse.

We broke into houses for the thrill. The biggest thrill was entering a house that was occupied. The motive wasn't theft, although if there were something worth stealing, we'd take it. The motive was the thrill of not getting caught. We destroyed property, smashed windows and played with explosives. We borrowed cars without asking, driving recklessly at high speeds. I was suspended fourteen times from school until they finally expelled me, then I dropped out of a second high school when they tried to suspend me.

Steve and I had scored a case of beer. On the way home, we met two girls from school, girls who had a reputation for being easy. Back at Steve's we engaged in sex with the girls. This was the first time for both of us. We did it on the floor of his bedroom, one couple on each side of the bed so we didn't have to see each other. It was anything but romantic. Actually it was disgusting. The girls found it quite funny when they discovered it was our first time. They noised it around school, but we denied it. For the most part, I don't think anyone believed them. Somehow I thought the real thing was going to be much better. I had an ultra rich fantasy life; this was a big let down.

During the winter of my sophomore year I ran away. My parents had separated intending to divorce. Steve had been sent to live with his father in Oregon. Dave had become my new best friend. Along with Dave and a girl I'd recently met, we hitchhiked up the coast to see Steve. It was an epic adventure. We met interesting people, faced physical challenges and danger. There was the ride that refused to pull over until I flashed the handgun in my bag. Little did they know that the gun didn't work and wasn't loaded. There was romantic intrigue as Dave and I traded off who was with the girl. There was controversy when she chose not to return with us to Ojai. There was the tension as police searched the bus we were on from Oregon back to California. They missed us only because we were not sitting together (I sat in the back of the bus pouting that Dave had taken the girl).

I came home from my Oregon adventure on the condition that I could live with my sister in Ventura. Things only got worse: more drugs, vandalism, and crime. My sister became afraid to come home because of my friends. It came to a head when she found my marijuana plants and paraphernalia. In a fit of rage she chased Steve, now back in California, down the street hitting him with a broom.

These were the days of the hitchhiker. They were everywhere. Hitchhiking therefore became my primary form of transportation. My parents had approved of my hitchhiking since I was thirteen or fourteen. On a couple of occasions men who picked me up paid me to let them perform oral sex. They tried to get me aroused but it didn't work. I found the experience repulsive, which in a strange way made it exhilarating. It left me feeling intense guilt. I told no one about the experience.

Steve and I had just come back into the house after smoking a joint. We were at my parents' house that day visiting with my sister and her family. Then all of a sudden it happened, my mild-mannered father lost it. The guy who had nothing to say to me for fifteen years chose that moment to unload. "Hippie," "No good long hair," "Lazy bastard," every derogatory remark he knew. Stoned and confused I got up and left the house. He followed. The verbal barrage continued in the driveway until I finally responded with the customary middle finger and exclamation, "F## you!" He went ballistic. I've never seen anything like it. This is a man who lived through two world wars and the Great Depression now having a total melt down over his teenage son. It was time to teach me a lesson. He told me so while standing in a 1920s boxing stance. I didn't know what to do. Everyone was watching. I wanted to laugh he looked so funny. Then to my surprise he hit me . . . so I hit him back. Next thing I know he's laying on the ground, glasses broken. I looked at Steve, Steve looked at me, I said, "Run!" and we both took off.

With the blessing of my family, I went to Arizona for a couple of months. I hitchhiked all over Arizona. I was fifteen, but looked much older. It was a reckless time. I spent time in Prescott looking for something I'd lost; I didn't find it. I hung out with kids I had known in my youth. They didn't recognize me. I left an overweight child with a crew cut, western shirt, and bolo tie. I returned a young man with long hair, a beard, a pierced ear, wearing full hippie regalia.

Looking for drugs to take back to Prescott, I hitched to Tucson. There I met up with two older guys with a woman; they gave the appearance of being on the run. I would spend the next week traveling with them around Arizona. That first night sitting around a campfire in a park they told me a story. They said that each night at dusk homosexual men would arrive in the park looking for sex. It was suggested that a guy could make some quick cash by pretending to be one of them. Once they made a sexual advance a person could extort money from them under the threat of bodily harm or exposure. Since I could use the money and I didn't believe them I'd give it a try.

True enough at dusk guys began arriving in the park. Walking down a secluded trail I observed a man sitting by himself. I found a place to sit nearby, within sight. He came and sat next to me; after some small talk he made sexual advances. I didn't resist, so he took me farther into the park to a secluded area. It was here that I made my move, but not until after we had engaged in perverse homosexual activity. Suddenly, when he was most vulnerable, I began hitting him in the face demanding he give me money. Ultimately it took over an hour of my threats and driving around in circles in his car that I finally got some money out of him.

My assault on this man stirred my emotions on many levels. There was no sexual attraction; I wasn't aroused. I was both disgusted and stimulated by the perversion. I was high on adrenaline for the rest of the night. Back at the camp we smoked pot and drank. I had endeared myself to my new companions. Of course, they didn't hear the whole story. I conveniently left out the part where I engaged in homosexual activity. I would tell this story many times in the years to come, always leaving that part out.

My sixteenth birthday was approaching, so I decided to return to California to get my driver's license. It took me a couple of attempts to pass the exam. My difficulty with the test may have resulted from all the LSD I'd been taking. Finally I passed the exam. Sounded like as good an excuse as any to party. All I had to do was convince my mom to let me borrow the car so I could meet up with Dave.

Dave and I sat in that park for hours and got stoned. Dave tried to get me to let him drive. He knew I was too loaded. I would have none of it. As we turned a corner I passed out at the wheel. When I woke the car was totaled and Dave was screaming at me to get out before the police came. I tried to drive away with the hood smashed into the windshield and the tires screeching against metal. At Dave's insistence we abandoned the car, still running in the middle of the street, and ran.

Dave and I made our way through the riverbed and gullies to his girlfriend Linda's house. Between us we knew every back road and path in the Ojai Valley. Linda's house was just up the street from my parents. By the time we had arrived we had a plan . . . a stupid plan. I was going back to Arizona and Dave was coming with me. The following is a summary of the remainder of that day.

➢ It was decided that Linda could come with us. Dave was eighteen and Linda was fifteen.
➢ We stole merchandise and money valued at over $10,000 from Linda's house.

- ➤ My girlfriend, Renee, decided she was going with us.
- ➤ Friends of Dave, and older couple, agreed to hide us until morning.
- ➤ I proceeded to drink too much then got sick all over everyone.
- ➤ Dave called the police from a pay phone to find out the charges—felony hit and run, grand theft, statutory rape, kidnapping.
- ➤ Dave made arrangements to return what we stole (minus one bottle of liquor) and sent Linda home.
- ➤ Renee refused to go home, she was leaving with or without us.
- ➤ Ojai is a small, elite town. Dave and I already had bad reputations. This was a big deal. There were police roadblocks at all three exits from the Ojai Valley.

The next morning we made our way out of town, past the road-blocks, by way of the railroad tracks. We were on our way to Arizona. Hitchhiking, waiting for a ride, I heard a voice that said, "You are not going to Arizona. The next ride will drop you off at your sister's house in Palmdale. You will return to Ojai and turn yourself in to the Police. Everything will be all right." I kept it to myself. Sure enough the next ride took us to Palmdale and dropped us off a couple of blocks from my sister. After a couple of weeks in Palmdale, my sister convinced me to go back to Ojai and turn myself in.

My father and I rode in silence to the police station. The past couple of weeks were a blur. It didn't seem real. I held back an overwhelming compulsion to flee. The officer on duty stared at me intently for what seemed an eternity. Not a word was spoken; he knew who I was. Gradually a smile came over the officer's face, and then he laughed. "How did you get past the roadblocks?" he questioned. Cautiously, timidly, I explained our route down the railroad tracks. He asked me about the time of day, and then exclaimed, "I knew it. I was right behind you."

In conclusion, the charges of statutory rape, kidnapping, and grand theft were dropped. The charge of hit and run was reduced to a traffic violation. I was issued a ticket, which was thrown out upon completion of traffic school. My parents' auto insurance covered the damage.

Diving headlong into manure, then coming up smelling like a rose was common during this period of my life, too common to be a coincidence. Caught red-handed by the police on several occasions with drugs, but not charged. The police would look right at the drugs, then act as though they didn't see them. But who was protecting me? I used to believe it was God, but I've come to believe that it was the god of this world, Satan.

God rarely removes the consequences of our sin. God forgives us, restores us, walks through the fire with us, uses our failings for our benefit and to further His plan, but He doesn't usually remove the consequences. Getting off the hook is more consistent with Satan's tactics. If there are no consequences we are more likely to continue in sin.

> *His own iniquities entrap the wicked man, and he is caught in the cords of his sin. He shall die for lack of instruction, and in the greatness of his folly he shall go astray.*
> —Proverbs 5:22,23

By age fifteen I was thoroughly confused. I grew up in a void, ill equipped to face life. My spiritual and moral foundations were weak. I was driven by my emotions and passions. The cords of my sin were drawing me further and further into bondage. Satan has had a stronghold in my life from a young age. Satan doesn't know all things, and he can't read our minds yet he's a master of human behavior and knows how to manipulate our sinful nature. The power he has in the life of a believer is the power of deception.

Satan is an expert at imitating God, *"For Satan himself transforms himself into an angel of light"* (2 Corinthians 11:14). He is out to devour and destroy, *"your adversary the devil walks about like a roaring lion, seeking whom he may devour"* (1 Peter 5:8). Satan cannot touch our salvation in Jesus. Satan cannot possess or inhabit a believer; we are God's possession inhabited by the Holy Spirit. Satan cannot force us to do anything against our will. But if he can get us to believe a lie, he can manipulate our behavior.

Satan doesn't have supernatural insight into the future. His ability to predict the future is limited to insider information. He is a diligent student of the Bible, history, and human behavior. He also has a sophisticated network of operatives and informants. He has access to information and conversations. This explains how Satan may have been the voice I heard hitchhiking to Arizona. Satan's informants could have had inside information that the police charges were being dropped. He could have known that the driver had a disposition to pick up hitchhikers and was going to Palmdale. Satan knew my sister had an influence on me.

Don't misunderstand. Going back to Ojai and turning myself in was the right thing to do. God's hand was clearly guiding the situation. The event would play a role in bringing me back to God. It is possible that God was exercising mercy in keeping me from the consequences of my sin. But ultimately my not being held accountable contributed to a false sense of security, my misunderstanding the nature of God, and future bad behavior. I'm not saying conclusively whose influence was at work in getting me off the hook. Obviously both God and Satan were at work in my life. I have learned that just because a situation seemingly works to my advantage, it doesn't mean that it was God's will.

> *. . . being confident of this very thing, that He who has begun a good work in you will complete it . . .*
> —Philippians 1:6

God was protecting and preserving me. In the midst of the drugs, rebellion, and perversion, God was speaking to me. He was calling me back to Him. He began a work in my life that He intends to finish. Don't mistake God's patience for permissiveness. God is sovereign; He can do whatever He wants. What He wants is to have a personal, intimate, loving relationship with his children. Our response to God is an act of our free will. He never forces us to love Him. But He will do what it takes to get our attention.

I moved in with the couple that let Dave and me stay the night when we were on the run. My parents had sold their house and moved into a trailer. There was no room for me with them. I went back to school in Ojai. Outwardly it appeared that I was making an attempt, but little had really changed. I was still doing drugs and running the streets. There was a deep dissatisfaction and emptiness in my spirit. God was warning me of the path I was on and was calling me back to him.

I started my junior year of high school in Ojai. By now I had a bigger-than-life reputation. Not just with kids my age, but with parents, teachers, and the police. Most people kept their distance or dealt cautiously with me. The truth was serious enough; but the stories about me were beyond belief. I encouraged the exaggerations. I liked to tell edited or exaggerated accounts of my escapades. (For the record, this account is not exaggerated.)

A couple of weeks into the school year, I came under investigation for selling drugs. A kid at school was arrested with marijuana I sold him. It was a small amount. I wasn't much of a drug dealer. I've never been very good at selling drugs. Suspecting that the kid had turned me in, I disposed of my stash. The next day the police met me at school with a search warrant. I was totally clean. They were very upset. They laid into me hard, but I denied everything and kept my mouth shut. They didn't know it, but the event and their words shook me. I began to consider the path I was on.

Dave and I were sitting in a park smoking pot and waiting to come on to the LSD we had taken. I was bragging about all the drugs I had done. The drugs I'd taken the past year, especially the LSD, were taking their toll. My mental capacity was diminished; it was difficult to think. But as long as Dave was OK, I assumed I was OK. Dave was a couple of years older and claimed to have done more drugs for a longer time. I had often boasted that when I see Dave overdose, I would know that it's time to quit. I made that boast that day. Coming on to the LSD Dave called me aside. He confessed that he had not done as many drugs as I thought. Upon comparison I had done far more LSD than he had. It scared me. I was messed up. Within the week I checked myself into Teen Challenge.

chapter 4

Play another love song

The solitude of my childhood produced in me a rich imagination. To occupy the countless hours I spent alone I'd role-play heroic fantasies. In my private world I was the center of attention; I could be whoever I wanted—the hero, the villain, or even the victim. When life became uncomfortable I'd simply escape to my inner sanctuary. The hours I spent entertaining these self-indulgences had a significant effect on my personality. I became increasingly self absorbed, indrawn, and introspective.

Fantasies weren't confined to the playground of my mind; they took form, influencing my behaviors. When I ran away at ten years old, I wasn't unhappy or seeking attention, I was living out an adventure fantasy. Or, when I would sneak into someone's house while they were home attempting to make my way around undetected I was engaged in a spy fantasy. Early in my life a connection was made in my inner being between my fantasy life and the thrill of adventure.

As I entered my teens, my imagination turned to romantic infatuations: I was in love with the idea of being in love. Boy meets girl and they live happily ever after. No struggle, no work; they just magically live a happy life. (These were the days before reality television.) Many people might say that this is perfectly normal for a young man. OK, if by normal you mean what is common, not what is healthy. Contrary to popular opinion, romantic fantasy is unhealthy. It's self-indulgent, selfish, and vain. The goal of romantic fantasy is to stimulate the emotions for self-gratification, a skill I mastered at an early age.

I was obsessed with sex. Go ahead and say it, "Of course you were. All teen-age boys are obsessed with sex." But how many thirteen-year-old boys have masochistic fantasies involving humiliation and abuse? From where do you suppose those fantasies came? At thirteen I knew nothing about such perversions, and no, I was not sexually abused as a child. I'm convinced that these thoughts had demonic origins. Satan used my fertile imagination to get his hooks into me and lead me down a path of destruction. I'm not blaming Satan; I take full responsibility for my actions. However, I'm more than willing to give credit for the influences in my life.

Satan has made it his business from the beginning to pervert the good things of God. But he doesn't stop with creation; he seeks ways to pervert the very nature and character of God. God is love.[1] Not the fuzzy kind of love based on emotions and self-delusion we call romance. God's love is pure and true, God created humanity with a deep desire for this love. Romantic infatuation is one of Satan's deceptions designed to keep people from knowing the joy of real love.

Modern romance has its origins during the renaissance as a pastime of nobility. Romantic intrigues were pursued apart from marriage and had nothing to do with selecting a mate. Romance was a form of entertainment where the emotions were manipulated through fantasy, suspense, and intrigue. The focus was not sexual conquest; it was a game of the heart. At the core of romance is the notion of unrequited or unfulfilled love, a fantasy not intended to be fulfilled. As long as a distance was kept between the romantic lovers, the fantasy could continue; but if the fantasy were ever consummated the romance would be destroyed.

Fast forward to modern times. Falling in love. Falling out of love. Finding love. Being in love. Love has become a mystical enchantment that happens to people seemingly against their will. It's portrayed like a disease that is caught when least expected and at the most inopportune times. "They couldn't help it, they fell in love." Never mind that he (or she) was already married with a family. Or when a marriage is failing, the popular defense has become, "They're just not in love with each other anymore."

---

[1] 1 John 4:8,16

There is nothing loving or godly about romance—falling in and out of love, seeking self-fulfillment at the expense of another person, using deception and manipulation to attract a mate (dating). Modern romance is a major contributor to high divorce rates and the destruction of the family. Sadly romance has become a standard of western culture so ingrained in western thinking that to speak against it is cultural heresy.

God's Word tells us that there is a more excellent way.[2]

> *Love suffers long and is kind; love does not envy; love does not parade itself, is not puffed up; does not behave rudely, does not seek its own, is not provoked, thinks no evil; does not rejoice in iniquity, but rejoices in the truth; bears all things, believes all things, hopes all things, endures all things. Love never fails.*
>
> —1 Corinthians 13:4–8

God's love is far superior to romance. It's honest and true. While a godly love deeply touches the emotions, it's not emotional. Real love is an act of the will, a conscious choice to think and act in the best interest of another person especially when the person doesn't deserve it. It's to love a person in spite of their failings, warts and all, or in spite of how you feel about the person at the time. Real love requires personal sacrifice. The ultimate example of real love is found in God sending His Son to die so that we could live.

> *For God so loved the world that He gave His only begotten Son, that whoever believes in Him should not perish but have everlasting life.*
>
> —John 3:16

There is nothing more beautiful than when God brings together two of His children in marriage and makes them one. It's also beautiful to see God redeem and restore a troubled marriage—to see a godly man set aside his own personal interests and needs and lay his life down for his wife—to see a godly woman respond to the love of her husband. There is compassion and tenderness. The couple encourages each other, defends each other, and completes each other.

---

[2] 1 Corinthians 12:31

This is not idealistic. It is within the grasp of all believers. It should be the norm in a Christian marriage.

Godly marriages should begin with believers committed first to their relationship with God. Marriage is not a fix for problems in an individual's life. Whatever struggles a person has single will be compounded when he is married. Unfortunately many singles look to marriage to fill the void in their lives. The Bible clearly portrays marriage as a great blessing, *"He who finds a wife finds a good thing, and obtains favor from the Lord"* (Prov. 18:22). Yet being single is not a curse; it is equally honored. Finding a mate should not be made the most important issue in a believer's lives. Learning to walk close to Jesus should be the first (and only) priority. If you walk close to God you won't have to search far for a mate, God will bring the perfect companion into your life.

> *Then Isaac brought her into his mother Sarah's tent; and he took Rebekah and she became his wife, and he loved her.*
> —Genesis 24:67

Isaac didn't select Rebekah as his wife; she was selected for him. Abraham sent a servant hundreds of miles to his homeland to find a wife for his son Isaac. It was a classic arranged marriage with a twist; God, not Abraham or the servant arranged the marriage.[3] Isaac could love Rebekah with confidence because he knew God ordained it. He trusted God and was submitted to God's plan for his life. What would be so bad in letting God choose your mate? God loves you. He wants the best for you. You can trust Him. He placed the desire for a mate in you. Why not let Him fulfill that desire? Of course that means you have to learn to hear and obey the voice of God.

At the very heart of love is commitment, not emotions. This truth has been so often cited in writings about marriage that it's become cliché. But it's true. Take for example God's love for us. It's demonstrated by the great sacrifice that Jesus made on the cross. At the heart of this sacrifice is God's commitment to restore His relationship with mankind. It took a couple of thousand years for God to set up and

---

[3] Genesis 24

implement the first stage of His plan (from the fall of man to the cross). It's been another couple of thousand of years since the cross and God is still working out His plan. Why so long? Because God is patient and desires that none should perish.[4] Patience and diligence, along with sacrifice and commitment, are attributes of a godly love. God placed the desire for marriage in each one of us; we can trust that He will fill that desire in His time if we let Him.

Now Jacob loved Rachel; so he said, "I will serve you seven years for Rachel your younger daughter." . . . So Jacob served seven years for Rachel, and they seemed only a few days to him because of the love he had for her.

—Genesis 29:18,20

Jacob's life is one of turmoil. He was not a man of good character or reputation. He was deceitful. Yet Jacob knew God; he walked with God; he even wrestled with God and lived to tell about it. As a result, he became known as Israel, a man ruled by God.[5] One constant in Jacob's life was his love for Rachel. Jacob served his devious uncle Laban fourteen years for her to be his wife. While many of the lessons from Jacob's life are about what not to do, one good lesson is that anything worth having is worth waiting for. Are you willing to wait for what God has for you? Or has your passion created urgency? Hasty marriages founded on passion have problems.

Jacob wasn't inactive while he waited. He labored for Rachel. It may be stretching the account a little but I see a parallel to singles preparing themselves for marriage. Too often singles spend their time and energy lamenting about being single, or worse, fantasizing about being married (romanticism). Instead, they should be preparing themselves for marriage. Marriage is a blessing that comes through much trial and suffering. It is a battleground for spiritual warfare. It's not for the weak or timid. To quote a wise man and close friend, "Those who sweat in training, bleed less in battle."[6] Being single is

---

[4] 2 Peter 3:9
[5] Genesis 35:9
[6] Pastor Matthew "Chik" Chikeles, Calvary Chapel St. Paul

a blessed time to grow in your relationship with Jesus and prepare yourself for marriage.

Scripture is rich with instruction about love and marriage. After all, love is fundamental to God's character and He is the originator of marriage. On the other extreme, the Bible contains descriptive accounts of romantic infatuation. Each one is self-centered, deceptive, manipulative, and destructive. Examples include how David committed adultery with Bathsheba, then arranged to have her husband killed in battle.[7] Or, how Samson, ruled by his passions, allowed Delilah to deceive him into divulging the secret to his great strength.[8] Yet the most horrifying account in Scripture of romantic infatuation gone awry is Amnon and Tamar.

> *Amnon was so distressed over his sister Tamar that he became sick; for she was a virgin. And it was improper for Amnon to do anything to her. . . . Amnon said to him, "I love Tamar" . . . he took hold of her and said to her, "Come, lie with me, my sister." But she answered him, "No, my brother, do not force me . . ." However, he would not heed her voice; and being stronger than she, he forced her and lay with her. Then Amnon hated her exceedingly, so that the hatred with which he hated her was greater than the love with which he had loved her. And Amnon said to her, "Arise, be gone!"*
> —2 Samuel 13:3,4,11,12,14,15

This perverse behavior is not what comes to mind when we think of romance. Admittedly this is an extreme example. Most romantics simply suffer through a series of failed relationships, scared emotions, and broken marriages. Some marriages that begin with romance survive. They grow past the infatuation. But there is usually a struggle reconciling fantasy with reality. Unfulfilled expectations, a sense of loss and a general dissatisfaction often haunt these marriages. There may be an ongoing effort to "keep the romance alive." Others will become cynical and disenchanted.

---

[7] 2 Samuel 11 & 12
[8] Judges 16

Romantic fantasy without constraint can turn to obsession and a compulsion for self-gratification. Left unchecked, it can produce bizarre, psychotic, and criminal behavior. This was the case with Amnon and Tamar. It would happen in my life. Heroic fantasy became romantic fantasy; romantic fantasy became sexual fantasy; sexual fantasy became increasingly perverse. The lines between fantasy and reality blurred as I increasingly turned inward. The more I indulged my fantasies, the more difficult it became to distinguish what was real and what was my imagination.

The 1960s and 1970s were a time of exploration. A whole generation believed that God was dead. Social constraints were abandoned. We experimented with sex and drugs. We attempted to expand our minds through science and godless philosophies. Contrary to popular opinion, the result has not been an enlightened generation. The result is a generation that is more perverse than any that has gone before.

> *And even as they did not like to retain God in their knowledge, God gave them over to a debased mind, to do those things which are not fitting; being filled with all unrighteousness, sexual immorality, wickedness, covetousness, maliciousness; full of envy, murder, strife, deceit, evil-mindedness; they are whisperers, backbiters, haters of God, violent, proud, boasters, inventors of evil things, disobedient to parents, undiscerning, untrustworthy, unloving, unforgiving, unmerciful; who, knowing the righteous judgment of God, that those who practice such things are deserving of death, not only do the same but also approve of those who practice them.*
> —Romans 1:28–32

Sexual perversion in the world today is ponderous. Pornography has become a multi-billion-dollar global business. Sexual situations, dialogue, and images in the media have increased exponentially since the 1960s. The news is inundated with sensational accounts of promiscuity. We are no longer a nation of virtue and innocence. Mankind today is ruled by emotions and imaginations. Godly convictions have been abandoned. All this is the result of not retaining God and God's Word in our lives. The consequence has been that

God has turned a whole generation over to *". . . a debased mind, to do those things which are not fitting."*

Criminal sexual behavior has become epidemic. In the 1970s the big issue for law enforcement was drugs. There were occasional accounts of sex crimes or sensational murders in the news. Child molestation was common; it just wasn't being dealt with. Today the media is dominated with accounts of rape, torture, and child abuse. The common assumption is that these are crimes of anger and hate. This may be true in many cases. However I'm convinced that the heart of the matter is an unrestrained fantasy life. These are men (and increasingly women) who have lost themselves in the playground of their mind. They've become enslaved to the wickedness they have entertained in their hearts; their fantasies have taken action.

> *But each one is tempted when he is drawn away by his own desires and enticed. Then, when desire has conceived, it gives birth to sin; and sin, when it is full-grown, brings forth death.*
> —James 1:14,15

". . . drawn away by his own desires and enticed." All sinful behavior begins as a thought. The initial thought is not sin. But when that thought is left unchecked, or worse it's nurtured, it produces sin in our lives. The battle over sin is waged in our hearts and minds. Our actions are merely the fruit or outcome. Jesus brought clarity to this when He said, *"Whoever looks at a woman to lust for her has already committed adultery with her in his heart"* (Matt. 5:28). In a nutshell Jesus is telling us that if we meditate on that sinful thought, even for an instant, it's the same as if we've done it. The battle over sin is a battle in our soul.

Some (including myself) have erroneously argued that since they're getting full credit for the sin anyway, they may as well cash in with their actions. This is fuzzy logic. Sinful actions cause much greater damage and the consequences are more severe. There are two significant points to this passage. First, every person who has ever lived except Jesus, no matter how "good" they appear to be, has sinned against God. Second, the place to do battle with sin is in our hearts and minds, not in our actions. That's not to say that we don't put boundaries and controls on our actions. Socially we dedicate significant resources to restricting behavior. It's why we have prisons.

Among the failings of the church today is that we've not involved ourselves in peoples lives. As believers we should have an influence on our brothers and sisters in the Lord. We should love each other enough to get involved, and help one another overcome sinful behavior and grow to spiritual maturity, and, when needed, set boundaries around those whose lives are out of control.

> . . . *the carnal mind is enmity against God; for it is not subject to the law of God, nor indeed can be. So then, those who are in the flesh cannot please God.*
>
> —Romans 8:7,8

Any attempt to overcome sin by merely controlling our actions will have limited success. It is not what God desires; it doesn't deal with the problem. His desire is for us to have victory over sin. This will happen only when we've gained victory over our thoughts. God isn't in the business of merely fixing broken lives. He's all about making a whole new creation, *"Therefore, if anyone is in Christ, he is a new creation; old things have passed away; behold, all things have become new"* (1 Cor. 5:17). The problem is that our old carnal nature doesn't go away without a fight. Yet God's Word gives us all the instruction we need to win this battle.

> *For the word of God is living and powerful, and sharper than any two-edged sword, piercing even to the division of soul and spirit, and of joints and marrow, and is a discerner of the thoughts and intents of the heart.*
>
> —Hebrews 4:12

> *Therefore gird up the loins of your mind . . .*
>
> —1 Peter 1:13

Gird: to surround or enclose; to prepare for action; to equip with power; to prepare for something requiring strength or endurance.

You can't win this battle as an armchair warrior. It will require an effort on your part. Whether you like it or not, when you accepted God's gift of salvation by asking Jesus into your heart, you enlisted as a soldier in a spiritual war. As soldiers we need to prepare ourselves for the battle. We need to build up our strength and endurance and prepare for action. Success depends on our being closely connected with our comrades at arms (other believers) and in constant communication with our supreme commander (Jesus).

> *Stand therefore, having girded your waist with truth, having put on the breastplate of righteousness, and having shod your feet with the preparation of the gospel of peace; above all, taking the shield of faith with which you will be able to quench all the fiery darts of the wicked one. And take the helmet of salvation, and the sword of the Spirit, which is the word of God; praying always with all prayer and supplication in the Spirit, being watchful to this end with all perseverance and supplication for all the saints*
>
> —Ephesians 6:14–18

If you want victory in your life, master this passage of Scripture. Don't just study it, but learn how to apply it in your daily life. These verses are not passive; notice the call to action. God's Word isn't meant to be merely read; it's meant to be lived. God has provided us with all the tools necessary to succeed. It's up to us to don our gear and engage the enemy. Unfortunately, too many believers run naked into the battle—ouch! The result is that many believers needlessly spend their spiritual lives beaten and defeated.

> *And do not be conformed to this world, but be transformed by the renewing of your mind . . .*
>
> —Romans 12:2

From the moment we were born we began a process of being conformed to this world. By the time Jesus gets a hold of us our lives are weighed down with bad habits and incorrect thinking. While our external world may (or may not) seem ordered and functional, our private world is in chaos. Like a civilian becoming a soldier, we need to be stripped of our selves and retrained. Soldiers have to master and maintain military disciplines so not to fall back into civilian habits. Likewise believers have to exercise godly disciplines so they don't fall back into the patterns of this world.

Set your mind on things above, not on things on the earth.
—Colossians 3:2

Soldiers and athletes alike understand that they can't afford to be distracted by their surroundings. They must set their minds on the challenge before them if they hope to succeed. Alternatively, most believers are much too easily distracted. Our thoughts are frequently consumed with our temporal lives. Our affections and interests are given over to useless idols. We forget who we are and lose sight of our eternal hope. This doesn't mean that we should neglect the practical matters of life. Quite the opposite, believers should be adept at dealing with the issues of this world. However we are citizens of God's kingdom. Let's not forget it.

. . . put off, concerning your former conduct, the old man which grows corrupt according to the deceitful lusts, and be renewed in the spirit of your mind, and that you put on the new man which was created according to God, in true righteousness and holiness.
—Ephesians 4:22–24

chapter 5

Prodigy or prodigal?

God used David Wilkerson in the 1950s to reach New York gangs with the gospel. The book and movie, *The Cross and the Switchblade,* are accounts of what happened. Mr. Wilkerson trusted God and walked by faith. God used his obedience to accomplish a miraculous work. The early days of Teen Challenge were a testimony of one miracle after another: a testimony of obedient men and women being led by the Holy Spirit.

> *Are you so foolish? Having begun in the Spirit, are you now being made perfect by the flesh?*
>
> —Galatians 3:3

Every great work of God that uses people to accomplish His purpose eventually dies. What starts in simple faith is soon corrupted. Man attempts to harness God. Programs are developed that mimic the work of God. Committees are formed and technical manuals are written. Organizations and denominations emerge. The original work and its founders are memorialized. As the work begins to die, we prop it up with human effort. By this time God has long since moved on.

God establishes works of ministry to fill a specific purpose in his plan. We mistakenly assume that God expects every work to continue indefinitely. Once God's objective has been accomplished, the ministry is no longer needed. Furthermore, any work established by God has to be done God's way. As soon as we muck it up with human philosophies it's over. God looks for others who He can use to accomplish His purpose.

God may abandon the original work, but He doesn't abandon His children.[1] God is doing a work that is not dependent upon mankind, a work that will last—the work of redemption. He is doing a work in the life of each believer that He promises to complete.[2] Where there is one believer trusting God, ministry will continue. But God isn't necessarily blessing the ministry; He's blessing the faithfulness of His children.

By the time I arrived, Teen Challenge was a shadow of the original work of God. Ministry was still happening. God was still using Teen Challenge to accomplish a purpose. But it was no longer operating in simple faith and the power of the Holy Spirit. It had been taken over by a large denomination with its own agenda.

The doctrine at Teen Challenge was in the Pentecostal tradition. The emphasis was on experiencing God, not on knowing God. Generating an emotional response and exercising the gifts of the Spirit dominated the meetings. Bible teaching was limited to passages that supported charismatic doctrine. Salvation was uncertain. Assurance of salvation was achieved through good works and the gifts of the Spirit, specifically the gift of tongues.

This was far from my Baptist roots. The churches I had previously attended de-emphasized the supernatural work of the Holy Spirit. They believed that once the Bible was complete, the gifts of the Spirit ceased. They believed once saved, always saved—period. As long as someone had prayed to accept salvation, it didn't matter what he or she did afterward. Today I see that both extremes are wrong. The truth lies in the middle. God's Spirit is alive and active. The gifts of the Spirit are meant for today; however, they must be exercised biblically. Believers can have total assurance of their salvation based on their relationship with Jesus, not on some past event in their lives.

I was attracted to Pentecostalism. Believing that God worked supernaturally was exciting. It created expectancy for God to do great things. Seeking an emotional experience through prayer and worship

---

[1] Deuteronomy 31:6; Joshua 1:5; Hebrews 13:6
[2] Philippians 1:6

suited me. All my life I had stimulated my emotions through fantasy, drugs, and extreme behavior. Now I could produce an emotional high through God. But with each high came the low. In the midst of all the excitement and hype something was still missing in my life. My spiritual growth was stunted. I learned how to put on a good show. I could look and sound spiritual, but secretly I was struggling with my old nature.

God used Teen Challenge in my life as a safe house. I was away from the drugs and evil influences. The LSD had affected my mind. For the first couple of weeks it was difficult to frame a cohesive thought. Recall was impaired. When asked my name, I would draw a blank for several seconds. This would improve in time.

I left Teen Challenge after only a couple of months. The program was supposed to be a minimum of one year. At the time I was convinced it was God's will for me to leave. I don't know if it was or not; it's hard to envision how things might have turned out had I stayed. All I know is that I was anxious to get on with my life. Intent on living a godly life, but still ill equipped to face the challenges ahead, I moved to Lancaster, California to live with my sister.

In Lancaster I attended an alternative high school. In spite of my past, I was not behind in my studies. In fact, because of the academic structure of my previous school I was ahead. The work at the alternative school was easy, and students worked at their own pace on assignments. Consequently I finished high school in six months at age sixteen.

I attended the Four Square Church in Palmdale, California. I was sixteen years old, on fire for the Lord, coming out of Teen Challenge—just what every church needed, a poster child. I was immediately thrust into ministry: counseling troubled youth, teaching junior high Sunday school, speaking at juvenile corrections, homeless shelters, and street evangelism. My flesh loved the attention. Being set apart from others as special fit my delusion that I was unique. I bought into the propaganda. However, I also had an honest desire for ministry. I wanted the things of God in my life. I began making plans to attend Life Bible College.

Behind the scenes I was struggling. Other than smoking pot one time, I didn't do drugs. But lustful thoughts, romantic and sexual fantasies continued. Additionally my flesh found new entertainment. On a couple of occasions I went out into the desert, took off my clothes, and masturbated.

As usual I didn't tell anyone about these struggles. Once again I was in a church that didn't function biblically. Godly counsel and discipleship was lacking. The teaching was inadequate. There were no examples of godly men honestly working out their salvation.

I experienced intense guilt over my sin. My response was to vow never to sin again. Then I'd try harder. I would go out street witnessing in an attempt to make amends. I would vow to read my Bible and pray more. When I'd fail to meet these self-imposed expectations, I'd become angry with myself. On several occasions I physically beat myself with a belt in an effort to bring my body into submission. After all in 1 Corinthians 9:27 Paul spoke of disciplining his body, and 1 Peter 4:1 tells us *"for he who has suffered in the flesh has ceased from sin."* On top of this, Jesus told us to *"be perfect, just as your Father in heaven is perfect"* (Matt. 5:48).

I couldn't reconcile that I wasn't perfect. There was no doubt in my mind that all the answers to life were in Jesus. I very much wanted to live completely surrendered to God. I believed it was possible; I still do. I took the warning about being lukewarm seriously, *"So then, because you are lukewarm, and neither cold nor hot, I will vomit you out of My mouth"* (Rev. 3:16). I had a genuine heart for God. But I also had a sin nature, and Satan had a stronghold in my life.

The previous passages that motivated me to self-abuse are taken out of context. A verse out of context is a pretext; you can make the Bible say anything you want. *"A feast is made for laughter, and wine makes merry; but money answers everything"* (Eccles. 10:19). It's in the Bible. It must be true. In context this passage is the ramblings of a carnal believer. By the end of the book. Solomon comes to his senses. *"Let us hear the conclusion of the whole matter: fear God and keep His commandments, for this is man's all. For God will bring every work into judgment, including every secret thing, whether good or evil"* (Eccles. 12:13,14). This is why it's so important to study the Bible in context. What is the entire passage saying? How does it fit with other passages? God doesn't contradict Himself. The Bible is God's Word. The Bible doesn't contradict itself.

In retrospect this period offered the greatest opportunity for others to influence my life. It would have been the time for someone to disciple me. Had the Bible been taught and used to counsel, the errors in my thinking could have been corrected. If others around me were openly dealing with life issues, I may have been motivated to also be open and honest.

Believers who are biblically ignorant and don't walk with God lack wisdom and discernment. They make poor judgments. That's right, we are to make judgments about one another. *"Judge not, that you be not judged"* (Matt. 7:1) is one of the most abused verses in the Bible. Do a study for yourself. Throughout Scripture we are called on to make judgments. Jesus goes on to give instruction on making judgments in Matthew 7. He tells us *"First remove the plank from your own eye, and then you will see clearly to remove the speck from your brother's eye"* (Matt. 7:5). Jesus also tells us *"Do not judge according to appearance, but judge with righteous judgment"* (John 7:24). In 1 Corinthians 5:5 Paul tells us not to keep company with an immoral brother, to *"deliver such a one to Satan for the destruction of the flesh, that his spirit may be saved in the day of the Lord Jesus."* Sounds like someone is making judgments.

We are expected to make judgments, but we are not to pass judgment. The difference is in our motivation, in the attitude of our heart. *"Open rebuke is better than love carefully concealed. Faithful are the wounds of a friend"* (Prov. 27:5,6). We are to love one another enough to confront sin. Sometimes we have to deal harshly with each other out of love. The motivations for Paul's exhortation in 1 Corinthians 5:5 is the salvation of the offender and the protection of others. We are to defend one another from harm. On two occasions Jesus threw tables and dealt harshly with the merchants in the temple because they were keeping people from worshiping God. Jesus was harsh with His disciples when they tried to keep the children from coming to Him.

We don't like to be confronted with the truth so we use *"Judge not lest you be judged"* to cry foul. The same verse is used as an excuse to not get involved in someone's life. We don't want to hurt their feelings. "It's none of my business." "That's between them and God." The truth is that we don't want to be put out or we don't want the person to think badly about us. We love our pathetic selves more than we love others. Or, we're steeped in our own secret sin and are afraid of being discovered.

I learned early how to look good. I was taught to show my best side and to hide my failings. God equipped me with gifts, talents, and abilities (as He has all believers). He has a call on my life. This was evident at age sixteen. Compared to those around me, I had an above average knowledge of Scripture. Throughout my life people have equated gifts, talents, abilities, and biblical knowledge with spiritual maturity. They are not the same.

Our struggle with sin doesn't go away when we put our faith in Jesus: the spiritually mature struggle with sin. Paul wrote about his struggle with sin. *"For what I am doing, I do not understand. For what I will to do, that I do not practice; but what I hate, that I do"* (Rom. 7:15). If anything, the more we grow in our relationship with God, the greater the struggle. We all need the counsel and fellowship of other believers. We need spiritually-mature believers willing to invest themselves in our lives. We need to invest ourselves in the lives of others.

At age sixteen I was infatuated with marriage. I'm not sure why. I suppose it was an extension of romantic fantasy and my desire for a sexual relationship. I believed marriage would fill the void in my life and cure my lust. It doesn't. Our sinful nature follows us into marriage. If believers aren't content in the Lord as singles, they won't be content married. I was ignorant about marriage. I had no idea what was involved in a successful godly marriage. Biblical principles of marriage weren't taught, and there were no examples for me to follow.

I became close friends with a lady in the church. She was twenty-five years old with two children when I was sixteen. We thought we fell in love. We fell into something, but it wasn't love. I'm not saying we didn't care for each other. But neither of us knew anything about love or marriage. That didn't stop us, we decided to get married. So with my parents' permission, we were married a couple months after I had turned seventeen. We couldn't get married in the church because she was divorced, so we got married by the youth pastor in a friend's backyard. Dave, my former drug buddy, was the best man.

A lot of people from the church attended the ceremony and reception. It was a cloudy day, but the clouds cleared and the sun shown through as we were taking our vows. The pastor declared it was a sign from heaven of God's blessing on the union. He proclaimed that it was as though the Holy Spirit had descended on us.

Let's see, how many things are wrong with this picture? Thirty years later the whole thing is inconceivable to me. Today this would be the making of a television movie. Were people that deceived to think that this was appropriate? The only person I recall challenging this decision was my sister. Who listens to their sister? Where was the church? I don't get it. There is no way this would happen in the church I attend today.

As far as I'm concerned, everyone dropped the ball on this one. Thirty years later I have a lot of regrets. I often play the woulda, shoulda, coulda game. "If I would have . . ." or "I should have . . ." or "I could have . . ." It's a useless and unhealthy game. It accomplishes very little, and I don't recommend it. There is absolutely nothing we can do to change our past. Even if we could go back we would most likely screw it up in some other way. But if there were one point in time that I could go back and change, this would be it.

As much as I'd like to blame others for this tragedy, I can't. It's my own fault. God was speaking very clearly to me that this was not His will. I chose not to listen. I wrote it off as cold feet. But truthfully I didn't want to look bad. It would have been embarrassing to say I'd made a mistake. The good news is that God wasn't surprised at my choices, He knew from the beginning of time exactly what I'd do. He still chose to love me and adopt me as one of His children. Yet by not being obedient to God's voice, I would cause needless suffering and set myself on a long and destructive path.

Marriage didn't make my life better. Lust didn't go away. I was still given to sexual fantasy. I had no idea how to be a husband and father. I had no friends, no fellowship. Friends my age didn't know what to do with me. Friends my wife's age didn't know what to do with me. My wife's family didn't know what to do with me. Plans to go to Bible College were canceled. I couldn't find a job that would support a family. And surprise—my wife was pregnant!

I joined the Army.

chapter 6

The secret ingredient

The nation of Israel was in trouble. The enemy had them out-
manned, out-gunned, and surrounded. The Philistines possessed an arsenal of the most advanced weapons of the day while
the Israelites were fighting with sticks and rocks. Unity among the
twelve tribes that made up the nation was tenuous at best. Many
had defected to the enemy or were hiding in caves. Their leader, king
Saul, was self-absorbed and arrogant. The whole army could collapse
at any moment. These were desperate times.

Early in the morning Jonathan, Saul's son, lay awake considering
their plight. Yet something was different about Jonathan. He wasn't
at all like his father. He didn't share in the pessimism that plagued his
comrades. Jonathan didn't fear the Philistines. In his twilight medita-
tions Jonathan had a revelation, *"nothing restrains the Lord from saving
by many or by few"* (1 Sam. 14:6). God didn't need an army to defeat
the Philistines. So while his father and the rest of the army of Israel
fretted over what to do, Jonathan decided to take a venture of faith.

With his armor bearer at his side, Jonathan approached the Phi-
listine camp. He then revealed his revelation and bold plan. (I find
it intriguing that the armor bearer trusted Jonathan's leadership to
the extent that he would follow him without question.) Jonathan's
plan was to take on the Philistines single-handed from a position of
strategic disadvantage. Read the account for yourself in 1 Samuel 14.
Jonathan was either a megalomaniac with a death wish, or he was a
man who put his faith in God.

Faith is fundamental to humanity. Faith is not complicated or
mysterious. It's actually quite simple. Without faith, society couldn't

exist. There would be total anarchy. Faith produces great power and is the key to the miraculous. By faith mountains are moved and the sick are made well. Faith is the door to the supernatural. By faith we have access to God. Therefore believers need to understand what it means to *"walk by faith, not by sight"* (1 Cor. 5:7).

> *Now faith is the substance of things hoped for, the evidence of things not seen. For by it the elders obtained a good testimony. By faith we understand that the worlds were framed by the word of God, so that the things which are seen were not made of things which are visible.*
> —Hebrews 11:1–3

Faith is simply belief in action, *"the substance of things hoped for, the evidence of things not seen."* We exercise faith hundreds of times each day. Sitting, driving, walking, eating, even sleeping require faith. When drinking a packaged beverage most people don't stop to analyze the contents. They put faith in the manufacturer and our system of food processing. People normally don't stop at green lights to see if the cars coming from the other direction have a red light. They have faith in our traffic control systems and the skill of other drivers. Faith is exercised when someone sits in a chair, turns on a light, places a phone call, takes a drink of water, rides a bus, flies on a plane, and on and on and on.

Personal experiences affect our faith. Most people exercise caution when first introduced to something or someone new. Trust grows with experience. I wouldn't lend my car to a stranger, but I would lend my car to most of my friends. I don't think twice about drinking a name-brand beverage, but I would be hesitant to drink something with a foreign label. If trust is violated, faith is shaken. Your faith would be shaken if you took a drink of your favorite beverage and found it had gone bad. Most of us have learned the hard way not to assume the milk in the refrigerator is good. You will be cautious at traffic signals if you've been in an accident.

Parents, friends, schools, government and the media influence our faith. We are taught to trust and distrust, what to believe and what to reject. The problem is that people are often wrong. At one time tobacco was prescribed for medicinal purposes. Hitler deceived millions of people in WWII. People believe what they are told if they trust the source. People also tend to believe what they want to hear. It can be difficult to let go of a closely-held and popular ideal. Evolution is an excellent example. There is no scientific evidence to support the theory of evolution. Scientific evidence actually refutes the theory. However, it is still held as fact by many people.

The future is uncertain. Every person puts his or her faith for the future in something. They seek a "higher power" to guide them, to give them hope. Many people today place their hope in mankind. People believe that man can solve the problems of the universe. Man has become his own god. Humanism has become the prominent religion.

The problem is not that people lack faith. Everyone is seeking somewhere to place his or her trust. The problem is that the objects of our faith are flawed. We live in an imperfect world. Everything human will ultimately fail. Government will fail. Society will fail. People fail. But God never fails. He never changes; His character is consistent throughout the ages. *"Jesus Christ is the same yesterday, today, and forever"* (Hebrews 13:8). God is the only perfect object for our faith. He will never let you down. You can totally trust Him.

> *But without faith it is impossible to please Him, for he who comes to God must believe that He is, and that He is a rewarder of those who diligently seek Him.*
>
> —Hebrews 11:6

Without faith it is impossible to please God: but not just any faith—faith in God. Many churches emphasize the need for faith. There are faith meetings and faith movements. But it's often not faith in God that's promoted; it's faith in faith. The presumption is that if we believe hard enough and pray long enough we can make things happen, that we can obligate God to do our will. Faith doesn't bring God in line with our will, quite the opposite. Faith aligns us with God's will. Real faith in God produces obedience to God.

> *Therefore we conclude that a man is justified by faith apart from the deeds of the law.*
>
> —Romans 3:28

Religion is an attempt to be acceptable to God through good works and moral excellence. But the Bible tells us that our best is not good enough. *"But we are all like an unclean thing, and all our righteousnesses are like filthy rags"* (Isa. 64:6). Mankind can never be right before God through religion. This includes the Christian religion. Good works and religious ceremony are not enough. It is only by faith that we can have a right relationship with God.

> *For by grace you have been saved through faith, and that not of yourselves; it is the gift of God, not of works, lest anyone should boast.*
> —Ephesians 2:8,9

There is absolutely nothing that we can do to earn our salvation. Our salvation is completely dependent upon God and God alone. The only requirement is to believe in—place our faith in—Jesus. God has done everything. He gets all the credit. And to make sure we can't boast . . . even the faith is a gift of God.

> *But as many as received Him, to them He gave the right to become children of God, to those who believe [have faith] in His name:*
> —John 1:12

What an incredible example of God's grace. We have all sinned and have fallen short of God's standard. We deserve to be eternally separated from God; we deserve hell. But God doesn't give us what we deserve. Not getting what we deserve is mercy. Getting what we don't deserve is grace. God doesn't just save us from hell; he adopts us as His children. He justifies us and makes us righteous in His sight. He blesses us and gives us new life.

> *But someone will say, "You have faith, and I have works." Show me your faith without your works, and I will show you my faith by my works.*
> —James 2:18

It's not good enough to just believe something; you have to act upon that belief.[1] *"You believe that there is one God. You do well. Even the demons believe—and tremble!"* (James 2:19). Satan and the demonic believe in God. Just believing something is not enough. If I really believe something of importance, it will affect how I live. This is the premise behind James 2:17, *"Thus also faith by itself, if it does not have works, is dead."* Faith is nothing more than empty words if it doesn't affect your actions. In the case of faith, actions definitely speak louder than words.

Faith in God is not wishful thinking and it's not blind. Faith is rooted in truth. It's based on evidence. When we first meet someone new or try a new product, our faith is limited. Our faith grows as we get to know the person or we have experience with the product. Our faith in God grows as we grow in our knowledge and relationship to God. *"So then faith comes by hearing, and hearing by the word of God"* (Rom. 10:17). Little knowledge of God equals little faith. A weak relationship with God results in weak faith. If you want to increase your faith, then grow in your knowledge of Scripture and your relationship with God. Then strengthen your faith by acting on what you know. At first, stepping out in faith may seem difficult. You may doubt the truth of Scripture and the goodness of God. But the more you exercise trust in God, the easier it becomes.

Faith in God provides protection against the attack of Satan, *". . . taking the shield of faith with which you will be able to quench all the fiery darts of the wicked one"* (Eph. 6:16). In the midst of the battle it is critical that we hold our position, that we maintain confidence in God. No matter what the enemy throws at us, by faith we can stand firm. We know that God is in control even if we are not. The Roman shield used alone provided limited protection, but when it was linked with the shields of other soldiers it became a powerful defense against the enemy. Believers need each other. We need to encourage each other and provide protection for each other against the enemy.

Faith is our shield against the enemy. The shield is a defensive weapon that is only effective when used in an offensive posture. The shield is useless when retreating. When our back is turned away from

---

[1] James 2:18–26

the battle we become an easy target. By faith we take a stand against the enemy. *"Therefore submit to God. Resist the devil and he will flee from you"* (James 4:7). We don't resist Satan in our own strength. We resist by submitting to God.

Satan uses doubt to shake our faith. If he can get us to doubt the truth he can get us to abandon our convictions. He's been doing it from the beginning. In the garden he cast doubt on God's words, *"Has God indeed said, 'You shall not eat of every tree of the garden?'"* (Gen. 3:1). Then he goes on to cast doubt on God's character, *"You will not surely die. For God knows that in the day you eat of it your eyes will be opened, and you will be like God, knowing good and evil"* (Gen. 3:4,5). All believers struggle with doubt and have lapses of faith. God forgives and restores. Salvation is in the hands of the Lord, it's not up to us, and there is nothing we can do to screw it up. We simply need to repent and keep going. Like the man in Mark 9:24, we, too, can cry *"Lord, I believe; help my unbelief!"*

It is not necessary to know everything about God to have faith in God. *"For My thoughts are not your thoughts, nor are your ways My ways,"* says the Lord. *"For as the heavens are higher than the earth, so are My ways higher than your ways, and My thoughts than your thoughts"* (Isa. 55:8,9). Through His Word God has given us everything we need to know to have faith in Him. The Bible contains all the answers to life and godliness; it never purports to contain everything there is to know about God. Only when we go to be with Him will we understand the rest of the story. *"For now we see in a mirror, dimly, but then face to face. Now I know in part, but then I shall know just as I also am known"* (1 Cor. 13:12).

People put their faith in many things they don't fully understand. I can't explain how an airplane can fly, but I'm still willing to travel by air. Some might argue that although I might not understand the principles of flight, someone does. That's true. But it's also true with God. Although I might not understand everything about God, He knows everything. And with God there is no human error, no design flaws and no accidents. Believers are constantly confronted with questions and circumstances that are beyond our knowledge. It may be that the knowledge is available to us; we simply need to dig deeper into God's Word. Or, it may be that it's beyond finding out. In either case, when you come against what you don't know, fall back on what you do know. Hold tightly to the simple gospel (Good News) of salvation. Remember, "God is good all the time . . . and . . . all the time God is good."

> *"I have been crucified with Christ; it is no longer I who live, but Christ lives in me; and the life which I now live in the flesh I live by faith in the Son of God, who loved me and gave Himself for me."*
> —Galatians 2:20

The Old Testament prophet Elijah was a man of faith. Many incredible things happened when he was around. At his word the rain stopped. Jars of oil and flour miraculously replenished themselves. The widow's son was raised from the dead. By faith Elijah stood up to the wicked king Ahab.[2] In 1 Kings 18, Elijah challenged the priests of Baal and Asherah. With all Israel watching, Elijah proposed a contest. They would each construct an altar then pray to their god to bring down fire from heaven to consume the sacrifice.

The priests of Baal and Asherah went first. They danced and prayed fervently for hours. They cut themselves, as was their custom. But nothing happened. Elijah mocked them. *"Cry aloud, for he is a god; either he is meditating, or he is busy, or he is on a journey, or perhaps he is sleeping and must be awakened"* (1 Kings 18:27). Still nothing. When it was Elijah's turn, he prepared the sacrifice. Then he thoroughly drenched it with water. Elijah called on the name of the Lord. *"Then the fire of the LORD fell and consumed the burnt sacrifice, and the wood and the stones and the dust, and it licked up the water that was in the trench. Now when all the people saw it, they fell on their faces; and they said, 'The LORD, He is God! The LORD, He is God!'"* (1 Kings 18:38,39).

The priests of Baal and Asherah were exercising faith. The problem is that their faith was misplaced; the objects of their faith were inadequate. The priests put on quite a show; they worked themselves into an emotional frenzy. Unfortunately many believers do the same. They mistakenly believe that they have to work themselves into an

---

[2] 1 Kings 17&18

emotional frenzy as an evidence of their faith. On the other hand Elijah remained calm. He maintained a quiet yet bold confidence in God.

Elijah's secret is that his faith was in God and God alone. Elijah was a man who walked with God by faith, day-by-day, moment-by-moment. Elijah lived a life surrendered to God. He didn't just exercise faith in God when faced with a challenge. He knew that God had led him to this challenge and that where God guides, God provides. There could be no doubt in Elijah's mind that God was going to come through.

> *". . . let it be known this day that You are God in Israel and I am Your servant, and that I have done all these things at Your word. Hear me, O LORD, hear me, that this people may know that You are the LORD God, and that You have turned their hearts back to You again."*
> —1 Kings 18:36,37

Many people are looking for God to perform the miraculous. They want to see a show. Jesus warned, *"An evil and adulterous generation seeks after a sign . . ."* (Matt. 12:39). God doesn't perform parlor tricks to entertain us. God acts in supernatural ways to get our attention. The motive for Elijah was that the people would know that Jehovah is God and that they would turn their hearts back to Him.

Elijah was just a man. Elijah didn't do anything miraculous. God did all the work, and He deserves all the glory. The only thing Elijah did was walk by faith; he trusted God. He was available for God to use. Many believers whine that if they only had the faith of Elijah they could do great things for God. If they just had more faith they could overcome sin and live a godly life. Read on in 1 Kings 19. Shortly after Elijah called fire down from heaven, we find him hiding in a cave in fear for his life: Elijah, the great man of faith feeling sorry for himself. Trust God, walk with God. Who knows? You, too, could be a great man of faith like Elijah.

SECTION TWO

Path of Destruction

chapter 7

In the Army now

God intended Israel to be a great nation. They were God's chosen people. He gave them His commandments and established an everlasting covenant with them. Israel was to be a testimony to the world of the nature and character of God. He chose them to bring the Good News of salvation to mankind . . . they failed. They turned their back on their God and served false gods. Wickedness and perversion were everywhere. Government was corrupt. The biblical headline read, "They did evil in the sight of the Lord."

God was patient. He gave Israel countless opportunities to repent and return to His loving arms. They refused. God had no choice but to discipline His children. To not discipline would have been contrary to God's character. God loves His children too much to let them continue in rebellion. God repeatedly warned Israel that there would be consequences. They ignored the warnings.

It was during these difficult times that Daniel was raised. Evidently Daniel was of noble heritage, possibly a descendant of David. As such he would have lived a privileged life. Yet Daniel wasn't influenced by his status or the corruption that surrounded him. When Nebuchadnezzar conquered, he took the best and brightest back to Babylon. At a young age, probably in his late teens, Daniel found himself in Babylon, far from the constraints of family and friends. He could have lived his life any way he wanted. He could have pursued the luxuries of Babylon. But Daniel chose to honor God instead.

But Daniel purposed in his heart that he would not defile himself with the portion of the king's delicacies . . .

—Daniel 1:8

Daniel grew up to be a godly man of integrity and courage. This didn't happen by chance. There were obviously godly influences in Daniel's life. Someone taught him about God; someone discipled him and encouraged him to trust God. God can rise up godly men and women in the midst of wickedness and sin without any help. But God prefers to work through others. Whenever you see a young man or woman living a godly life you can be certain someone influenced them. We don't know who influenced Daniel. I'm looking forward to hearing more about his life when I meet him in heaven.

Every person who has ever lived has had the opportunity to choose to follow God. Just because children have been taught godly virtues and values doesn't guarantee they will live a godly life. Daniel made a conscious choice to follow God and not defile himself with the luxuries of Babylon. He chose to stand firm in his faith in spite of the consequences. Daniel was expected by his captors to live as the Babylonians. But Daniel feared God more than he feared Nebuchadnezzar. Daniel's love of God compelled him to reject the king's portion.

Who a person is in private is who he really is. We find out what a man is made of when he is separated from his family, friends, and community. I found out what I was made of when I went into the Army. I enlisted in November 1974 at age seventeen. In Louisiana I could be anyone I wanted to be. I was free of the constraints of being a husband and father. I was no longer under the microscope of church and family. The minute the plane landed in Louisiana for basic training I threw myself headlong into sin. I drank and smoked pot. On weekend pass I went to strip clubs. I joked and swore. I left my faith and godly convictions back in California.

After basic training I moved my family to Seaside, California for my first duty station at Fort Ord where I was stationed for over two years. We lived in Seaside for a short time, then settled in Moss Landing, a small community away from the base. My first son was born in 1975, two days before I turned eighteen. When I was eighteen I legally adopted my wife's two children.

It was the end of the Vietnam War. Fort Ord, previously a training base, was to be the home of the Seventh Infantry Division. I arrived during the transition. Training had ceased and the Seventh Division had not yet arrived. The base was very quiet and the duty was easy. There was a lot of downtime. We worked half days for several months. Afternoons were spent playing cards, smoking pot, and drinking beer.

Gradually the Seventh Division began to arrive. The men coming back from Vietnam had seen a lot of action. It was a difficult transition for most of them. Many were drug addicts. My company commander was recovering from heroin addiction. The first sergeant, a decorated war hero, was eventually busted to a private. Last heard he went AWOL and was riding with a biker gang. One guy claimed to have a collection of ears he had taken from dead Vietnamese soldiers. His plan was to make a lampshade out of them. I was shown a bag of what looked like human ears. It could have been a hoax, I can't say for certain. But from what I heard and saw I can say it's not beyond belief. I do know that these guys came back messed up. It was obvious that Vietnam had deeply affected them.

As the soldiers arrived, so did the drugs, exotic drugs from all over the world: high potency marijuana, hash, hash oil, opium, LSD, mescaline, peyote, PCP. I'm sure there were many others; these are the ones that I indulged. I smoked pot and drank beer daily. It didn't matter if I was on duty or not. For over a year I was assigned as the driver for the battalion commander, a Lt. Colonel. I'd be high on drugs driving. When I had duty that required me to stay on base, I would indulge in LSD and PCP (angel dust). I remember standing guard duty over an ammo dump with a loaded shotgun, high on LSD and PCP. I was good at covering up the evidence and any sign that I was high. I was never caught or to my knowledge suspected of using drugs.

At home I was a different person. I was a father and husband. We went on outings and generally behaved like a family. Most of our friends were in their late twenties or thirties and were not associated with the military. We didn't tell people my age. I was believed to be in my late twenties or early thirties. I didn't use drugs at home; at least not that anyone knew about. We drank, mostly beer and wine coolers. I'd sneak out and smoke pot. No one knew; I was obsessed with covering up the evidence. I'm certain my wife didn't know, because she was very upset when she found out.

You have heard that it was said to those of old, "You shall not commit adultery." But I say to you that whoever looks at a woman to lust for her has already committed adultery with her in his heart.
—Matthew 5:27,28

During this two-year period I only had sexual relations with my wife, yet I wasn't a faithful husband. I went to a strip club a couple of times and I saw my first "X" rated movie. Sexual fantasies dominated my thoughts. The more I gave myself to sexual fantasy the more I wanted, the more intense and prolonged the next fantasy. The psychedelic drugs I took heightened the experience and increased my desire for more.

As long as I can remember I have been attracted to thrills. Many times in my life I've put myself in physical danger doing things that produce an adrenaline rush—heart-stopping over-the-edge experiences, reckless behavior that produced raw fear. I discovered that a similar rush could be achieved by shocking people, doing things to get people's attention and produce a reaction. It didn't matter if the reaction was disgust.

At age eighteen I would drive around town naked. When I'd see a girl walking in a somewhat secluded area I'd get out and walk with her. I didn't make any sexual advances. If I said anything at all I'd initiate an innocent conversation. Eventually I was arrested and charged with indecent exposure. I played it off as an innocent prank that only happened one time. The judge required me to see a psychologist. I met once with the psychologist. He decided that further treatment wasn't necessary and the case was dropped. My wife was fully aware of the event. But nobody knew that this behavior had been going on for a while and that this was not the only occurrence. Once again I had escaped the full consequences of my actions.

In the midst of it all God was still speaking to me, calling me back to Him. On at least two occasions I made an attempt to get my life right with the Lord. We went to church; I read my Bible, prayed, and tried to overcome sin and live a godly life. Part of me still wanted the things of God. The Holy Spirit had given me a glimpse of what it could be like to live a life surrendered to Jesus. I wanted what God had for me, but it seemed out of reach, unattainable. The more I tried, the harder it seemed to get. I was stuck in Romans 7:15 *"For what I am doing, I do not understand. For what I will to do, that I do not practice; but what I hate, that I do."* I hadn't moved on to the victory, *"O wretched man that I am! Who will deliver me from this body of death? I thank God—through Jesus Christ our Lord!"* (Rom. 7:24).

Paul speaks of hating the sin that he continues to practice. To be completely honest I didn't hate sin. I didn't like the consequences, but I liked sin. With little restraint I had fed my imagination and passions. I had developed a massive appetite for fleshly pleasures. On the other hand I had a deep desire for the things of God. This has created an intense conflict throughout my life. It contributes to my tendency for extremes. When I'm attempting to live a godly life I become fanatical. When I walk away from God I throw myself headlong into sin and degradation. It's all or nothing.

There is nothing more dangerous than a backslidden Christian. If believers in Jesus won't listen to God, they're not going to listen to man. When people accept Jesus as their Savior, the Holy Spirit comes into them and gives them new life. The Holy Spirit works in believers to lead them into a deeper relationship with Jesus, to grow the believer to maturity. Resistance is futile. The Holy Spirit will not leave. The Holy Spirit will complete the work He has started.[1] Resistance just creates pain and suffering for the believer and those he comes into contact with. Backslidden Christians have to work harder to drown out the voice of God and sear their conscience. This often results in extreme and bizarre behavior. I'm convinced that mental institutions and correctional facilities are full of people who are trying to run from God.

The last six months of my duty at Fort Ord we attended an independent church. I was making an effort to live a godly life. I resisted sin, read my Bible, prayed, even took a couple of correspondence

---

[1] Philippians 1:6

Bible courses. Yet once again I wasn't being honest about my past or the struggle I was having with sin.

I knew I was in serious trouble as soon as I received the orders sending me to Korea. My walk with the Lord was weak. I didn't have victory over drugs. Sexual fantasy continued to dominate my thoughts. I immediately initiated a campaign to get out of going. My pastor wrote a letter. I pleaded with the Red Cross to intervene. I tried to convince a psychologist that I was unfit. I sought counsel from an attorney on ways to get an early discharge. I knew that I didn't have the moral integrity or the backbone to survive a year in Korea. Unfortunately I was right.

Wine is a mocker, strong drink is a brawler, and whoever is led astray by it is not wise.
—Proverbs 20:1

Korea was a moral train wreck. From the minute I landed I threw myself headlong into sin. I drank to excess. It was in Korea that I developed a taste for hard liquor. Marijuana was illegal in Korea, but there were plenty of other drugs that were legal. Many bars were adjacent to drug stores. Along with your drink you could order a shot of codeine (liquid codeine in a shot glass). We'd drink beer with codeine chasers, or codeine boilermakers. At my worst I woke up in a gutter on a busy street covered in my own vomit. To finance my binge I would run black market commodities from the base PX or commissary to the local villages.

My son, give me your heart, and let your eyes observe my ways. For a harlot is a deep pit, and a seductress is a narrow well. She also lies in wait as for a victim, and increases the unfaithful among men.
—Proverbs 23:26–28

Prostitution was legal and inexpensive in Korea. Korea was a sexual playground for a twenty-year-old male obsessed with sex and who had abandoned all morality. I regularly engaged the services of the local prostitutes. Not just a few times—weekly, sometimes several times a week. I paid a heavy price for this perversion, contracted gonorrhea three times and crabs several times. But the greatest price was the searing of my conscience and the increase of my sexual appetite.

During my duty in Korea, my wife convinced the Red Cross to bring me home on an emergency leave. She had moved back to Palmdale after my transfer. During the couple of weeks at home I said nothing of my activities in Korea. But I'm sure she knew. I was changed. I was emotionally and spiritually scarred. I don't remember much about the time I was at home except that I continued to drink and smoke pot. By the end of my leave, I came to the decision that I was not going back to Korea. My plan was to wait until I was AWOL, and then turn myself in to the military police at Fort Ord. When the time came, I hitchhiked up the coast to Fort Ord.

When I arrived I spent a few days hanging out with old friends. When I turned myself in, I was informed that they were going to send me back to Korea. The only way they'd keep me is if I was thirty days AWOL, then they'd send me to prison as a deserter. I was only a couple of weeks AWOL at the time so I took off again. I hung around the base and the local communities doing drugs. One night for a place to stay I let a homosexual man pick me up in a park and take me home. After attempting oral sex with me he could tell that I wasn't homosexual. He left me alone and let me sleep there that night. The next morning he was gone and I was alone in his house. I searched the house and found a small amount of cash and drugs, which I stole.

A couple of days before being considered a deserter I turned myself in to the to the military police. To my amazement they gave me a pass and told me to go back to Korea. I was on my own recognizance. I returned to Korea on a Friday night. The first sergeant told me that the captain would deal with me on Monday. Since I had a forged pass, I left base and partied in the local village all weekend. Come Monday, I didn't return to base. Subsequently I went AWOL again for a couple of weeks in Korea. During that time I hung out in the clubs and stayed with the prostitutes at night. When I finally returned, my captain agreed to my request for a discharge—a dishonorable discharge. Personally I didn't care. However, to my surprise and my captain's dismay, when the battalion commander saw that I had been a driver for a Lt. Colonel, he changed it to an honorable discharge.

It was too late; the damage had been done. When I returned home, the perverse behavior continued. I started hanging out with a couple of guys who were into pharmaceutical barbiturates (Quaaludes). On one occasion the police showed up at my house to arrest me for a hit and run. I had passed out at the wheel and hit a car stopped at an intersection. No one was injured. When the police came, I was in the bathtub. They stood at the door trying to convince me to get out of the tub and dressed so they could talk to me. I refused. To my amazement they left. I was sent a ticket in the mail for hit and run and driving under the influence (DUI). The DUI was dropped for lack of evidence and I was given a fine and community service for the hit and run.

The sexual fantasies became less romantic and more perverse. I resumed my habit of stalking girls at high schools and performing acts of indecent exposure. The police questioned me after one such incident. I had learned to keep quiet when being investigated. It's what a defense attorney will tell you. For the most part it worked to keep me from the consequences of my actions. But it also kept me in a place of denial and deceit about what was going on. There was a part of me that desperately wanted to confess. Instinctively I knew that I would not overcome sin until it was brought into the open, yet the guilt was intense and I feared the consequences. I would purposefully suppress these perverse activities. I'd put them behind me vowing to not do them again or to be more careful next time.

It should be no surprise that my marriage didn't survive. My wife suspected I had been unfaithful in Korea. To draw it out, she concocted a story that she had not been faithful while I was gone. When I confessed my sin, she retracted her confession. Within six months of returning from Korea we separated. At first I stayed with two guys from work (the ones with the barbiturates). That was not good so I rented a room in a sleazy motel. After only a couple of weeks I had decided to try and restore my marriage. I had developed an extreme emotional dependence on the children. I can't say it was love. Real love is not measured by emotional intensity, but by action. If you love someone, you will look out for their needs and desires at the expense of your own. My world pretty much revolved around my needs and desires.

I was depressed, despondent, and confused. All I knew was that I couldn't bear not being with the children. That morning I went to work as usual. I was a breakfast cook at a local restaurant. A couple of hours before my shift ended I looked over the counter and to my surprise there was Dave sitting in a booth. Dave was in the Army stationed in Germany. I was ecstatic. My wife had called him when we separated. He immediately took a leave and came back from Germany. My spirits were immediately lifted. At last a friendly face, someone I believed cared for me. I couldn't stop talking; I rambled on and on. I didn't pay any attention to how solemn Dave was. He wasn't saying much. Back at my room I must have talked for over an hour. When I finally ran out of words Dave began.

"What are you going to do about your marriage?" he asked in a serious tone.

"I don't know, Dave, it's so confusing. What's this about?" I finally noticed that Dave was not himself. Then he dropped the bomb.

"I've been here for a week. I came here to try and help. Your wife picked me up at the airport. She was very upset. We stayed up all night talking. One thing led to another and we're together. I love her and want to marry her, I love your children and want to be their father."

The shock paralyzed me. Chaotic thoughts and emotions overwhelmed me. I was speechless. Dave was one of only two guys I considered true friends. We always took care of each other. He was the best man at my wedding. This couldn't be happening. Without saying another word, and without a response from me, Dave got up and left. Come to find out, he had stopped to give me the news on his way to the airport to return to Germany.

Something in me died that day. It threw me deeper into a life of self-destruction. I would know what it was to hate. It would be many years before I would allow myself to become emotionally attached to anyone. Today I know that I'm the only one to blame. It's my sin and mine alone that caused all this destruction and suffering. I'm not the only one who sinned, who behaved inappropriately. But if I had been the man of God I could have and should have been, none of this would have happened.

chapter 8

All is vanity!

Vanity of vanities, says the preacher, vanity of vanities! All is vanity . . .

What has been is what will be, and what has been done is what will be done; and there is nothing new under the sun.
—Ecclesiastes 1:1,2,9

The book of Ecclesiastes is the testimony of a backslidden believer. Solomon, heir to the throne of David, was a man of great wealth and wisdom. He had it all and he did it all. Solomon enjoyed unlimited and unrestrained access to wealth, power, and sensual pleasure. His conclusion, *"All is vanity."* Solomon discovered that a life lived for self is meaningless. Fortunately in the end he came to his senses.[1]

I can relate to Solomon on a much smaller scale. My life has been full of vanities. The pursuit of knowledge didn't fulfill. Money didn't satisfy. Sensual pleasure only produced sorrow. Like Solomon I, too, knew the God of Abraham, Isaac, and Jacob. I had a sense of His greatness and power. I had tasted of his love and mercy. I too chose to walk away from God to pursue my own evil desires and discovered that the self-centered life is meaningless.

To say I was troubled would be an understatement. Twenty years old and I had already destroyed one marriage. My life was consumed by my passions. I was filled with hate for Dave. The emotional pain

---

[1] Ecclesiastes 12:13,14

was intense. Driven by my emotions, I lived in a continuous state of turmoil. It seemed that my life couldn't get any worse . . . I was wrong.

Alex and I were close friends from sixth grade when I moved to Ojai, to the tenth grade when I threw myself headlong into rebellion with Steve. Alex confided that he withdrew from me because it was obvious I was headed for destruction. Alex was no saint. In high school he did drugs, sold drugs, pursued sexual encounters, and vandalized. He was just careful about it. Alex was an all around scam artist. He was small in stature, wiry, fast, and very intelligent. He was a skilled pickpocket and card shark. Alex had a special interest in explosives and firearms. He had gained a reputation for blowing things up—mailboxes, trees, cars, and even buildings.

It had been a long time since I talked to Alex, so I found his number and gave him a call. It was comforting to hear a familiar and friendly voice from the past. He seemed evasive about his life. All I learned was that he had married a girl we both knew in high school and was living in Thousand Oaks, California. He graciously invited me to come visit. Without hesitation I jumped at the chance to get away from my circumstances. Any change was a welcome change.

Driving to Thousand Oaks, I thought about Alex. Our friendship had been characterized by rivalry and competition. We both played trumpet, but he was always the better musician. He had a lot of natural ability. I always had to work harder. But that was true of most everything. Alex was one of those people who didn't have to labor over his accomplishments. They just came naturally. He also had a charisma that made him attractive to women (worldly women). Girls in high school were drawn to him; their mothers doted over him. It drove me nuts (that is it drove my flesh nuts).

Pulling up to a nice house in a middle-class neighborhood, I experienced a renewed envy. Alex greeted me warmly and invited me in. It was early afternoon, his wife was at work, but there was a guy (Mike) and a couple of girls in the living room. It was a large room set up like a lounge. One wall was completely covered by a curtain. We reminisced while the others listened. A couple of times there was someone at the door. Without hesitation or invitation Mike would answer the door and escort whoever it was to a back room. After a while he would escort them out the front door and rejoin us. The phone rang several times. Alex paid no attention. One of the girls or Mike would answer it in the other room. It was all very surreal. I was too naïve or too self-absorbed with my life to realize what was going on.

At one point Alex began bragging about my musical ability. He told everyone how I first taught him to play guitar. I should have known better. I was never very good at guitar and hadn't played in years. He was setting me up. He pulled out a guitar and convinced me to play something. I was terrible. Everyone in the room worked at keeping a straight face. Alex took the guitar and began to play. He was incredible. As it turned out, Alex was a professional musician for a studio in Los Angeles. My pride was wounded and my envy increased.

"Do you still smoke pot?" Alex wasn't sure because he was well aware of my vacillating between Jesus freak and sin freak. Alex, as far as I know, never has been a believer. It puzzled me that he seemed to have no conviction over sin, while my sin produced intense conviction and guilt. It wasn't until years later that I understood it was because I had the Holy Spirit living in me. Mike brought out a tray of pot and we all got high. The guitar incident was mostly forgotten and the party had begun.

As evening approached people began to arrive. Drugs were plentiful: weed and cocaine. Of course Alex was a dealer. The word was (his words) that he was a distributor for an organized crime syndicate. He dealt in large quantities—planeloads. I can't substantiate this either way. I do know that by all appearances this was true. Later I discovered that there were loaded guns hidden everywhere. Additionally, Alex had become a martial arts expert. His entire garage was set up as a martial arts studio. He studied formally to brown belt, then he continued to study privately. He claimed that he didn't pursue a black belt because he didn't want to register with the police. Those who worked out with him credit him as being the equivalent of a fourth- or fifth-degree black belt.

As evening progressed, it was time to play. Alex opened the curtains to reveal tens of thousands of dollars in music and recording equipment. Horns, guitars, amplifiers, mixers, and speakers, he had them all. Alex and a couple of guys played for hours while his guests partied. Most of the guests were high school age. Mike continued to sell drugs while Alex performed. I spent the night and went home the next day.

This visit had a profoundly demonic impact on me. I envied Alex. I wanted what he had. My life seemed boring in comparison.

> *A sound heart is life to the body, but envy is rottenness to the bones.*
> —Proverbs 14:30

This reunion with Alex came before my separation with my wife and the incident with Dave. I returned to visit Alex on a couple of occasions. After the incident with Dave, I had no desire to stay in Palmdale, so at Alex's invitation I moved into his house and became part of his scene. For a couple of months, every day was a party, although you couldn't tell it by looking at me. My bitterness toward Dave grew. I spent hours fantasizing and planning how I would kill him. My heart grew harder and harder each day.

After a couple of months things began to fall apart. Alex was in trouble with his suppliers; he owed them a large sum of money. Rival dealers were threatening his life. He was under a federal DEA investigation. The drugs dried up, Alex lived in fear; the party was over. I made the decision to move to Encinitas, California to live with my parents. Within a couple of weeks after I left, Alex was arrested on drug charges. The account of his arrest tells like an action movie. The police treated him as armed and dangerous. Ultimately he was released for lack of evidence, but he lost everything, including his wife, in the process.

My parents had moved to Encinitas a couple of years earlier. They bought an H&R Block franchise and lived in a one-bedroom apartment on the beach. I slept on the couch. Upon my arrival I began my search for drugs. In the process I met a girl who informed me that the best place to find cocaine was the Hydra Restaurant. So the Hydra is where I went to work. Sure enough on the first day the manager welcomed me with complementary cocaine. For the next eight to ten months I would use cocaine almost every day. Primarily injecting it with a syringe.

Visiting my wife and children was difficult. On one occasion, Dave had the nerve to ask me to let him adopt my children. It was devastating. The emotional pain was so intense I cried almost non-stop for two weeks. I cried myself to sleep and woke up crying in the morning. Something in me died, my heart grew cold; I became despondent, apathetic. To ease the pain I drank, smoked pot, and used cocaine.

To appease my increasing perverse sexual fantasies, I committed frequent acts of indecent exposure. On a couple of occasions, for the thrill, I entered houses in the middle of the night while people were home asleep. On one occasion police interrogated me for this behavior. I kept silent and was released in the morning with no charges. My life became increasingly reprobate; wickedness consumed me.

To the pure all things are pure, but to those who are defiled and unbelieving nothing is pure; but even their mind and conscience are defiled. They profess to know God, but in works they deny Him, being abominable, disobedient, and disqualified for every good work.
—Titus 1:15,16

My life was out of control. I spent all my money on drugs and alcohol. To finance my habit I took out a bank loan to buy a larger quantity of cocaine, hoping to sell enough to cover what I used. Instead, I consumed all of it (with some help from my friends). High on cocaine, I would drive recklessly on busy Southern California freeways (speeds in excess of 100 mph); I would weave through traffic at high speeds missing cars by inches. I would slow down long enough to fix and inject a hit of cocaine while I drove. Then it was back to more high-speed thrills.

To escape the inevitable (or prolong it), I moved to Three Rivers, California with my sister. I had to get away from the cocaine. It was only a matter of time before I was in serious trouble. My brother-in-law had taken a job as a chef for a small mountain resort. He invited me to come and work for him. It was a welcome change. But it didn't take long to find new drug connections and new ways to satisfy my lust.

Three Rivers moved at a slower pace and was a different culture than Southern California. Alcohol was the drug of choice. Marijuana was available, but a person would have to go elsewhere for other drugs. So I drank heavily and continued to smoke pot.

Who has woe?
Who has sorrow?
Who has contentions?
Who has complaints?
Who has wounds without cause?
Who has redness of eyes?
Those who linger long at the wine, those who go in search of mixed
wine. Do not look on the wine when it is red, when it sparkles in the
cup, when it swirls around smoothly; at the last it bites like a serpent,
and stings like a viper. Your eyes will see strange things, and your heart
will utter perverse things . . . When shall I awake, that I may seek
another drink?

—Proverbs 23:29–35

As was my custom I headed to the bar after closing. I had been smoking pot and drinking throughout my shift and already had a "buzz" going. The routine was to drink and play dice until the bar closed. Occasionally I'd go outside to smoke a joint, then return. This particular night the conversation turned to religion. The exact dialogue is lost, but these were guys with no real convictions. It was not a deep or meaningful conversation; I vaguely remember a jumble of unrelated thoughts from eastern religion to aliens. I tried to stay out of it, but I found myself getting increasingly agitated. The truth about Jesus flooded into my thoughts. My heart was torn, my spirit troubled. I drank more and more to drown out the conviction.

That night I was drinking one-hundred-fifty proof rum and was getting seriously drunk. Finally I couldn't take it. I became angry. In a drunken stupor, I made a pathetic attempt to share my faith in Jesus. In turn I was ridiculed and laughed out of the bar. I was so drunk I couldn't open my car door and ended up passed out on the ground covered in my own vomit. A couple of hours later, still blind drunk, I managed to drive myself home. As a result of the alcohol poisoning, I couldn't get out of bed for three days and was not completely recovered for over a week.

The job in Three Rivers ended that fall. The owners wanted to keep us all employed through the winter, but it was not possible. Business was so slow that many nights we had no customers at all. To pass the time we'd drink and smoke pot. From Three Rivers I moved around a lot. From 1979 to 1981 I lived in Visalia, Morro Bay, Huntington Lake, Visalia again, Three Rivers again, back to Visalia, Big Bear Lake, Oceanside, and Vista, California. During the same period I changed jobs at least eight times. I would become bored or would mess up in some way, so I'd move to start over. I was trying to escape, run away. However, I couldn't get away from myself or from God. The drugs and alcohol dulled the pain for a while, but they were not enough to drown out the voice of God.

> *Woe to those who are wise in their own eyes, and prudent in their own sight! Woe to men mighty at drinking wine, woe to men valiant for mixing intoxicating drink . . .*
> —Isaiah 5:22

Marijuana and alcohol were my drugs of choice. I occasionally used other drugs but I smoked pot and drank every day. Drinking and driving were so common to me that I didn't believe there was anything wrong with it. I was arrested twice during this period for drunk driving. One was a misdemeanor; the other was a felony. Drunk and high, I was in a head-on collision driving from Three Rivers to Visalia. There was one passenger in the car I was driving and the driver and one passenger in the other car. Leaving the bar, I pulled into the wrong lane. At the time I let people believe it was just a misjudgment on my part. The truth is that I intentionally pulled into the wrong lane. I was playing chicken with the other car.

When I swerved into my lane the other car swerved with me. Everyone was injured. The guy with me suffered multiple lacerations that required hundreds of stitches. The female passenger in the other car had her leg broken in a couple of places. The driver of the other car suffered minor injuries. I took out the windshield with my face and almost lost an eye. Of course, the car was not insured. Ultimately

I spent four months in a county road camp and had a civil judgment against me for five hundred thousand dollars. Since the car belonged to my sister, she was also sued for the same amount. Subsequently she had to file for bankruptcy to discharge the judgment.

There were numerous encounters with women I met in bars. For several months I maintained an ongoing affair with a waitresses from work who was twice my age. I engaged in sexual activity with any woman who would have me. I wasn't at all discriminating and actively pursued women who had a reputation for being promiscuous. I didn't care if they were married. I didn't care about anything except my own self-gratification.

> *You have plowed wickedness; you have reaped iniquity. You have eaten the fruit of lies, because you trusted in your own way . . .*
> —Hosea 10:13

During this period I got two women pregnant; they gave birth within a couple of months of each other. I was responsible for at least one aborted pregnancy, possibly more. It seems that there was a second abortion but I can't remember for certain. That's the kind of thing a person should be able to remember. The vagueness of my memory is further testimony to the condition of my heart. In the case of the one, I do remember; I drove her to the clinic for the procedure. I stayed in the car drinking and smoking pot. I vaguely remember being so loaded that she had to drive after the procedure.

> *Where can I go from Your Spirit? Or where can I flee from Your presence? If I ascend into heaven, You are there; If I make my bed in hell, behold, You are there.*
> —Psalm 139:7,8

As incredible as it may seem, the voice of God was not silent. Rooted in my heart was a continued desire to get things right. But I didn't know how. The one thing I did know was that the answers would only be found in Jesus. For a short while I attended Visalia Calvary Chapel as well as a young adult ministry hosted by a Baptist Church. I wasn't candid about my life. I only shared what I thought would be tolerated. To be honest, I shared what I thought would impress people.

There were a couple of occasions that I made a limited attempt to get help. These were not made in the shadow of some great consequence. They were motivated by an honest desire to get things right. Afraid to seek help through the church, I met with a secular therapist. He promptly diagnosed my problem as guilt associated with my Christian beliefs. He was going to help me overcome the bondage of my faith. I immediately abandoned that path. Next I started meeting with a "Christian" counselor. He was an ordained pastor and a licensed therapist. He didn't use the Bible. His thing was the book *I'm OK, You're OK* and gestalt therapy. He spiritualized the concepts, comparing the adult, parent, and child to the Father, Son, and Holy Spirit of Scripture. It took a little longer, but I eventually abandoned that treatment.

> *He who sows iniquity will reap sorrow . . .*
> —Proverbs 22:8

In 1981 my father died. He was hospitalized while I was in jail. I was permitted to leave custody for three days to visit him in the hospital. In between visiting my father I spent the three days drinking, smoking pot, and engaging in sexual activity. Upon my release I moved back to the San Diego area to be near my parents. My father died shortly thereafter.

> *And what profit has he who has labored for the wind? All his days he also eats in darkness, and he has much sorrow and sickness and anger.*
> —Ecclesiastes 5:16,17

"Sorrow, sickness and anger" pretty well describes my state of mind after the death of my father. Darkness consumed me. I became despondent; I didn't care about anything. Drinking and drug use increased, and my sexual fantasies grew even more perverse. I committed numerous acts of indecent exposure. For years I had played with fantasies of sexual violence. Now it became an obsession.

In November 1981 I was driving around, drinking and fantasizing about rape. Walking through an apartment complex I saw a woman go into an apartment with a bag of groceries. I slipped into the apartment when she went back to her car for another bag. When she came back into the apartment I grabbed her from behind. She struggled so I immediately let go and fled. Neighbors saw me go into the apartment and called the police. They followed me to the parking lot and restrained me until the police came.

Sow for yourselves righteousness; reap in mercy; break up your fallow ground, for it is time to seek the LORD, till He comes and rains righteousness on you.

—Hosea 10:12

There are consequences for sin. Although serious as my situation was, it could have been a lot worse. God spared me from raping that woman. As soon as I grabbed her, it was as though a cloud was lifted. Up until that moment I was living in a dark fantasy world. A secular therapist would later describe my mental state as psychotic; I had lost touch with reality. I'd say that's an accurate description, with one clarification. My mental state was the result of my sin. I chose to walk in darkness and suffered the consequences.

As would be expected, the episode threw me into a panic. I was in serious trouble and I despised what had become of my life. Filled with remorse and panic, I made a desperate effort at damage control. I denied the attempted rape allegations, claiming my motive was robbery. Once released on bail, I began doing everything I could to minimize the consequences. I hired an attorney, went on Anabuse (a drug that causes nausea when mixed with alcohol), starting seeing a secular counselor and attending church.

Admittedly I was motivated by remorse. I was scared. My life was out of control and I was in serious trouble. Yet God still used the situation to build on the work He had begun. I prayed a lot, not just prayers of desperation, but genuine communication with God. I went to weekly meetings at San Diego Teen Challenge. I began attending Encinitas Calvary Chapel every day! Three home fellowships, church services twice a week, Friday night concerts, I even showed up for worship practice. The last thing I wanted was to deal with this alone; I wanted people involved in my life.

As soon as I turned my life back over to Jesus (even though it was not a full surrender and my motives were not pure), the seemingly impossible happened. The gifts of God and His calling became apparent once again. God provided me opportunities to minister to others. I was able to share insights into God's Word. I didn't understand how this could be; it was a paradox. It was also a stumbling block—I liked the attention. Other believers mistakenly associated gifts and calling with repentance and spiritual maturity.

People knew I was in trouble. They just didn't know the details. I wasn't honest about my circumstances. The prosecutor didn't charge me with attempted rape; I was charged with first-degree burglary. So when asked, I told people about the burglary charges and let them make their own assumptions. I certainly didn't tell people about the rest of my life of perversion. I lived in great fear that people would find out the truth.

My understanding of biblical instruction about confession and accountability was limited. Yet the Holy Spirit began doing a work in my heart, prompting me to be open and honest. Conviction burned in me. It seemed as though I'd explode if I kept all this darkness bottled up inside me any longer. I was on the verge of going into court and confessing the truth. I would simply trust God to work out the details. But first I decided to tell one of the assisting pastors the truth about my arrest. It was obvious that it took him by surprise. Visibly shaken, he was adamant that I should not confess to the courts. His reaction confirmed my concern about how people would react and strengthened my resolve to not tell anyone. Unfortunately it also meant that once again I didn't deal with the sin in my life.

chapter 9

Wicked Ways

Throughout history great minds have attempted to answer the question, "What makes some people good and others bad?" It's a fundamental question of philosophy, sociology, and criminology. If we could isolate the source of bad behavior, we could eliminate crime, prejudice, and war. Imagine what the world would be like if there were only good people! Unfortunately, mankind has made no significant progress eradicating the world of evil. That's the bad news. The good news is that God has a plan that will fix everything, and He's invited us to join Him.

God created man and knows exactly how we function. He's the manufacturer, so why not go to the manufacturer's guide for understanding. The question at hand regards the dichotomy of good versus bad people. Let's see what the guide has to say on the subject.

> As it is written: "There is none righteous, no, not one; there is none who understands; there is none who seeks after God. They have all turned aside; they have together become unprofitable; there is none who does good, no, not one." [1]
>
> —Romans 3:10–12

From this passage it appears that questions regarding good versus bad people are inherently flawed; the basic premise is wrong. According to God's Word, there are no good people. I know this may be hard to accept; you may even find the idea offensive. However, I'm

---

[1] Psalms 14:1–3; 53:1–3; Ecclesiastes 7:20

not the one who said it. God said it and He should know. God is the one who sets the standards. We define what's good and bad relative to ourselves. God defines them relative to Himself.

. . . for all have sinned and fall short of the glory of God . . .
—Romans 3:23

The word sin is an old archery term that simply means to miss the mark. If archers missed the bull's-eye, it was said that they sinned. God, who created man, established the standards by which he should live. Anytime we fail to live up to God's standards, we sin. Every person who has ever lived has sinned (except Jesus). We have all missed the mark according to God's standards.

People aren't born perfect then become corrupt; we are corrupt from our beginning. People are born with a sin nature. From the moment we were conceived, we had already fallen short of God's standards. *"Behold, I was brought forth in iniquity, and in sin my mother conceived me"* (Psalm 51:5). This may be difficult to accept; however it's biblically sound and important to understanding God's gift of salvation.

Adam and Eve weren't born with this sin nature; they were created directly by God.[2] As such they were created without sin. They were completely innocent, without any knowledge of good or evil. All they knew was an intimate fellowship with God. Adam and Eve were created in the image of God, complete with the ability to make moral choices (free will). Then God gave them a command: *"Of the tree of the knowledge of good and evil you shall not eat, for in the day that you eat of it you shall surely die"* (Genesis 2:16).

Adam and Eve may not have been born with a sin nature, yet we discover that they did have the capacity to sin. When Adam and Eve chose to disobey God, they brought death to all humanity. Not just physical death, but more importantly spiritual death. God is spirit and the source of spiritual life; to be separated from Him is to be spiritually dead. Adam's sin separated him from God resulting in spiritual death.

---

[2] Genesis 1,2

When the curse was brought on humanity, the fundamental character of man was forever changed. No longer would man live in innocence; instead, humanity would be enslaved by the knowledge of good and evil. Mankind became an enemy of God. Yet God was merciful. Along with spiritual death, God brought physical death. He blocked the path to the tree of life[3] so that man couldn't live forever separated from God. It may be difficult to view physical death as merciful. However, the pain and suffering death brings to our physical being is nothing compared to the torment of being eternally separated from God.

However, the path to the tree of life would only be blocked until God fulfilled His plan of salvation.[4] From the beginning, God had a plan to redeem mankind. It was an ingenious plan involving the shedding of innocent blood for the remission of sin.[5] Once this plan was in effect, mankind would never again have to be separated from God. Mankind would be able to enjoy an even closer relationship than did Adam and Eve. The incredible part is that God would do all the work; the entire plan would be dependent upon Him. There was nothing man could do to screw it up. All mankind has to do is choose to accept or reject God's plan of salvation.

> For the wages of sin is death, but the gift of God is eternal life in Christ Jesus our Lord.
> —Romans 6:23

Starting with the killing of animals to clothe Adam and Eve, God established the practice of animal sacrifice as a covering for sin. Animal sacrifice continued throughout the Old Testament as part of the Levitical ceremonies. However, the sacrifice of animals was never sufficient to fully restore mankind's relationship with God. God established the practice of animal sacrifice merely to prepare the way for the ultimate sacrifice.[6] Only a man could pay the price required to

[3] Genesis 3:21–24
[4] Revelation 22:1,2
[5] Hebrews 9:22
[6] Hebrews 10

redeem creation. But not just any man; the man would have to be perfect, not corrupted by sin.

Since God is perfect, He can't have a relationship with imperfect sinful man. Sin separates mankind from God (sin also separates man from each other). However God loved His creation and desired to have fellowship with mankind. What a conundrum. The only man who started life not blemished by sin was Adam. We've seen how well he resisted temptation! No, it would take another Adam, a second Adam.[7] Someone not corrupted by sin; someone who had the motivation to resist temptation[8] and a willingness to lay down his life.[9] The answer was that God Himself would become a man and pay the price for sin.

> *For God so loved the world that He gave His only begotten Son, that whoever believes in Him should not perish but have everlasting life.*
> —John 3:16

Jesus is that second Adam. With a heavenly Father and a human mother he was born one hundred percent God and one hundred percent man. Like the first Adam Jesus started life without sin. Yet, unlike Adam, He resisted temptation and kept Himself pure. Then with full knowledge of what He was doing, He willingly allowed Himself to be sacrificed on a cross to pay the price for sin.

> *But God demonstrates His own love toward us, in that while we were still sinners, Christ died for us.*
> —Romans 5:8

God desires to have a personal relationship with each one of us. God's plan of salvation is simple and clear. There is only one way, believing in Jesus.[10] God doesn't desire that any should be lost. He isn't looking for reasons to condemn, he doesn't need to; mankind

---

[7] Romans 5:14; 1 Corinthians 15:22, 15:45
[8] Hebrews 4:15
[9] John 10:15–17; John 15:13
[10] John 6:40

condemns itself. As offensive as sin is to God, He is prepared to forgive. When it comes to salvation, all sin is the same in God's eyes;
there is no sin greater than another. There is no sin that God will not
forgive . . . except one . . . rejecting God's plan of salvation (rejecting
Jesus).

> *For God did not send His Son into the world to condemn the world,
> but that the world through Him might be saved. He who believes in
> Him is not condemned; but he who does not believe is condemned
> already, because he has not believed in the name of the only begotten
> Son of God.*
> —John 3:17,18

We are all sinners; there are no "good" people. Yet, why is it that
one person's bad behavior is different from another's? Some trans-
gress social boundaries while others stay within acceptable norms.
Some people's sin even leads to criminal behavior (mine did). Why
do we each have different limits on what we will or won't do?

My life is one of extremes. I've ascended to the very throne room of
God and descended into the pit of hell. I've tasted of God's goodness,
and I've gorged myself on wickedness. Consequently, I've wrestled
with why I have such an inflated capacity for sin. Frequently others (believers and non-believers) have confronted me with the same
question. By the time you finish this book, it's likely that you will
also be asking this question.

From the moment the sperm enters the egg, humanity is corrupted
by sin. I don't know how this works, only that it's true. Maybe our
sin nature is a corruption of our DNA or a flaw in our spirit or both.
Sinful patterns are passed from one generation to another. The sin
of drunkenness is one obvious example that the secular world recog-
nizes as hereditary (however they would call it alcoholism). Why not
other sinful patterns such as greed, gluttony, lust, or pride?

While sinful patterns have hereditary origins they are also learned
behaviors. Sin is passed from one generation to another through the
complex maze (or haze) of society and culture. We learn how to sin
from our family, friends, and the world around us. We also learn

the boundaries of what is acceptable—how far we can go in our sin before we suffer consequences. Those of us who fail to master these lessons tend to suffer greater and more frequent consequences.

Societal boundaries are rarely consistent with God's standards. For example, in contemporary western culture the consequences for adultery are minimal. While there may be pain and suffering, adultery is not a crime. However, adultery in the Bible was punishable by death.[11] To our modern sensitivities this sounds harsh and unreasonable. However, it clearly demonstrates that God's perspective on marriage is very different from ours. He takes faithfulness in marriage very seriously; after all, marriage is a model of the relationship He desires to have with us.[12]

God enacted the ultimate punishment for adultery, but don't think that He is without mercy or compassion. The book of Hosea uses the example of a husband who remains faithful to an adulterous wife to paint a picture of God's relationship with His people. And don't forget that Jesus didn't condemn the woman caught in the very act of adultery.[13]

Mankind, created in God's image, is responsible for making moral choices (free will). We can choose obedience, which leads to life, or disobedience, which leads to death. Obedience or disobedience to God is the only choice we really have.

Even if we weren't hardwired for sin, then educated in sinful behaviors, we would still sin. Adam did. Adam and Eve were created without sin and they lived in the perfect society. Their disobedience wasn't the result of bad parenting and they didn't live in poverty. When confronted with their crime, they immediately began the blame game (compounding their sin with more sin). Adam blamed Eve. Eve blamed the serpent. Yet they both were actually blaming God. "It's the woman *You* gave me." "It's the serpent *You* allowed in the garden." "Why did *You* create that stupid tree anyway!"

If Adam and Eve were to be honest, they would have to admit that they simply did what they wanted to do. They exercised their right

---

[11] Leviticus 20:10
[12] Ephesians 5:30–32
[13] John 8:1–11

to choose. The bottom line is that people will do whatever they want to do.

So what about my life? What forces came together to form my particular sin nature? I was born a sinner just like everyone else. Most likely my genetic heritage played a part. Sometimes I joke about my ancestry. "I'm Scot, Irish, English and Welsh; no wonder I'm messed up. I'm at war with myself." This quip may actually contain some truth; behavior and personality do seem to be influenced by ancestry. It's easy to see how family and social dynamics have contributed to my sinful behavior. Finally, there is no doubt that the demonic has had an influence in my life.

However all sin ultimately comes down to an act of our will. We are each responsible for our own sinful choices. While I can acknowledge their influence, I can't blame genetics, family, society, the Devil, or God for my actions. When it comes to my sinful behavior, the buck stops with me.

chapter 10

Walking on hot coals

Can one walk on hot coals and his feet not be seared?

—Proverbs 6:28

As I walked to the prison transport handcuffed and shackled, a warm breeze, the distant smell of the ocean, and the sounds of traffic overwhelmed my senses. The last two weeks were spent in total chaos locked up in the San Diego County Jail. The jail had been in a state of unrest for months. Overcrowding pushed the institution's capacity and the inmate's tempers to the limit—one-hundred-twenty guys crammed into a holding tank designed for forty. It was a constant battle for self-preservation. I coped by keeping to myself, staying up all night and sleeping all day. Of course, the pot I smuggled into the jail took the edge off. I also prayed a lot, read my Bible, and even witnessed to a couple of the less-threatening inmates. I'm glad God is patient.

The judge allowed me a couple of months to finish the semester before beginning a four-year sentence for first-degree burglary. When I committed the offense I had been attending junior college. I continued my studies while on bail. After this semester I would receive an Associates Degree in Business. Off and on since I had left the military I had attended college classes motivated by the veterans' benefits. The VA covered my educational expenses and provided me with a monthly income. Prior to committing the offense, I attended class high on drugs and alcohol; I put in a minimal effort but still managed to achieve passing grades. Occasionally I speculated what I could do sober.

After sentencing, I let down my guard. I didn't completely abandon my renewed faith, but since I was going away for a while, I let myself have a last fling. I stopped taking the Anabuse so I could drink. I smoked pot and even tried shooting heroin for the first time. I liked it; I liked it too much. That was one drug I knew I had to stay away from.

A brother from church was transferred to San Francisco and needed someone to bring him his motorcycle. I was happy to volunteer. It was a memorable excursion. I visited friends and family, stopped to see my wife and children, attended a service at Calvary Chapel San Francisco, and went to a secular concert. Then I flew back to San Diego to turn myself in to begin my sentence.

Before turning myself in, I swallowed a balloon packed with marijuana. Smoking it was tricky with all those guys around, but I managed. I can be very clandestine when I want to be. Two o'clock in the morning, most everyone asleep, I'd mix it with tobacco and smoke it under an air vent like a cigarette.

Riding in the transport van I thought about my future. I was scared. I could only imagine what lay ahead. In jail guys encouraged me that prison time was a lot better than spending time in county jail. I was certain that just about anything would be better than county.

About half way to the state prison in Chino, California, I was transferred to a prison bus from San Diego. Walking onto the bus I couldn't help notice the faces of the other guys. They looked scared, angry, and mean. No one looked happy. But there was one guy who stood out—big, burly, and mean. He was wearing paper clothes that the jail provides prisoners who don't have clothes of their own. It was a hot summer day and he was soaked in sweat, his arms and shoulders ripping through the paper. Sitting behind him, watching him, I prayed "Lord, please keep me far away from that guy."

When we arrived at Chino, the tedious process of induction began. The closest experience for me would be the Army, but without the honor. At one point we were all required to strip naked. Our clothes were taken from us and we were left for a long period of time waiting for our prison issue clothing. I was very uncomfortable sitting in a room with a hundred naked prisoners without even a towel to cover myself. One by one our names were called and we were issued clothing. It seemed to take forever. The anxiety grew the longer I sat there. Mine was the last name to be called.

Being naked in a group of convicted felons doesn't make a person feel very secure. I was feeling very vulnerable. Scrambling to get my clothes on, I heard an unexpected voice calling my name. My heart shot into my throat when I looked up to see who was talking. It was the guy on the bus, the one who I wanted to stay away from. He again called my name. Timidly I responded that he had the correct guy. To my amazement he exclaimed in a booming voice, "Praise the Lord! I've heard about you."

God has a sense of humor. I learned a lesson that day about jumping to conclusions and making assumptions about people. Prior to his sentencing, Keith had been attending meetings at Teen Challenge in San Diego. I, too, had been attending meetings at Teen Challenge, but on different days. The guys had told Keith about me. There are no coincidences in God's economy. It was no accident that God had brought Keith into my life. For better or worse, I would spend the next two years with Keith.

After a short stay in maximum security, I was transferred to the medium security yard. Chino was where most everyone from Southern California was first sent upon entering the correctional system. From Chino guys were sent to various prisons around the state to complete their sentences. I desperately wanted to stay at Chino. I was close to family and friends. People from church came to visit. True to my nature, I did everything I could to manipulate the circumstances to stay at Chino. God had other plans.

Chino offered excellent opportunities for spiritual growth and Christian fellowship. I made an effort to be open about my faith, sharing the gospel with other inmates. There was an active Bible study. Guys were getting baptized. Darrel Mansfield, a Christian musician, performed a concert on the yard. When I was attending Encinitas Calvary Chapel, he performed almost every Friday night at the church. Darrel came to Chino with a heart to share the gospel. By the end of the event, hundreds of guys had made commitments for Jesus

I lost the battle to stay at Chino and was transferred to the prison in Soledad, California (the middle of nowhere as far as I was concerned). After a short stay in maximum security, I was moved to the minimum-security yard. Upon arrival, I was assigned to the "quiet dorm." There is not much privacy in a prison dorm; there's a lot of tension, noise, and chaos. The "quiet dorm" was reserved for inmates who worked odd hours. Lights out twenty-four hours a day and noise was kept to a minimum. Normally inmates were not directly assigned to the "quiet dorm." A guy I met at Chino was a clerk in the main office. He saw my name on the list and redirected my assignment. It would turn out to be a blessing. God had gone before me to prepare the way and was looking out for me.

Soledad would be my home for nearly two years. I quickly settled into prison life, filling the time with work, volunteer activities, and school. The axiom, "Do your own time," directed my activities and behavior. The application of this wisdom is to make your own place in the system and mind your own business. Prison is at best a challenging place to live; at times it's outright brutal. It's prudent to be careful. An inmate with a sexual offense needs to be extra careful. A prison society has its own standards for right and wrong and its own way of executing justice. I was very concerned about people finding out the actual circumstances of my crime. My plan was to blend in and keep to myself. I told no one the truth about my offense.

My faith stagnated at Soledad. I didn't attend chapel and rarely talked about Jesus, except with Keith. There was no unity among the guys who professed to be believers. The chaplain didn't reach out to the inmates. If you wanted to see him, you had to go to his office. The chaplain in Chino walked the yard; he'd come into the dorms, sit on the bunk, and start a conversation. He had a heart for the inmates. He had been an inmate. He did time for murder, was eventually pardoned, and became a Calvary Chapel pastor.

Soledad was a great distance from family and friends. My mother, sister, and brother-in-law came to visit me a couple of times. The rest of my family, including my children, didn't know where I was. My mother was the master at family secrets. She told family and friends that I was at college. When I first went to prison, as many as twenty people from Encinitas Calvary Chapel wrote me. Within six to eight months no one wrote. Of course I quit writing them first.

For a while I worked as a clerk in the laundry. It turned out to be a profitable position. Many guys were willing to pay a monthly fee to insure they got the best clothing issue. Later I took a position as the head cook for the officers' cafeteria. I even catered the annual Christmas party for the officers and their families. Working in the officers' cafeteria, I was the highest paid inmate in the prison at ninety dollars a month. So to pad my meager pay, I made extra money selling food I smuggled back to the yard. Anything for an extra buck, I even cut hair for members of the Hell's Angels. What did I do with the extra money? Bought drugs, of course.

I smoked pot regularly in prison. My smoking buddy was Keith. Marijuana was expensive but readily available. Additionally, Keith's wife brought him pot when she came to visit. Drugs were smuggled packed in balloons hidden in body cavities. We smoked on a secluded bench or walking the yard. I smoked by myself in the shower where the steam cleared the smoke and smell. Sometimes we'd smoke in the dorm with someone looking out for the guards. There was very little drug testing at Soledad; personally I was never tested. It seemed as though the guards didn't care, although anyone caught was punished.

To occupy my time I joined the Volunteers of Soledad, a project where inmates read books onto tapes distributed to libraries. To be accepted I had to pass a reading test and have a clean prison record. It was a small group, no more than a dozen guys. The benefits were great! We had our own recreation area, television room, and private shower. We were also allowed to be out past curfew. By the end of my stay, I was the inmate coordinator for the project. I took the position reluctantly; I didn't want the responsibility; it was too high profile. I wanted to stay under the radar, do my own time. Furthermore I wasn't very good at it. I didn't have the backbone to direct the guys and maintain the integrity of the program. By the time I left, the project was in disrepair. I wouldn't be surprised if they ended up closing it down.

Soledad was the only prison in the state that offered a bachelor's degree as part of their education program. I took advantage of the opportunity, mostly as another way to occupy my time, anything I could do to stay out of the mainstream prison population. The only major offered was a social science degree through San Jose State University.

Some might wonder about the quality of such a program. What professor would go to a prison to teach? Amazingly, we were honored with some of the best professors San Jose State had. These guys were recognized leaders in their fields. Most of them admitted that their motivation was not just altruistic. They were there to study us; they wanted first-hand experience with the prison system to expand their professional knowledge. Classes were tough; we were held to high academic standards. Repeatedly we were told that we maintained an academic excellence that exceeded their regular students.

In 1984 I was one of the first three inmates in the California correctional system to receive a bachelor's degree. The prison put on a show for the media. The warden participated in the ceremonies. A local television station taped the event and aired it that evening. The media interviewed each of us. I decided to try an experiment. My conjecture was that the media deals in sound bites, short quips that make good copy. So I rehearsed a couple of one line statements that I thought they would pick up on. I was right. The media ignored most of the other guys' intelligent but verbose speeches and picked up on my one-liners. In turn, the broadcast was picked up and aired across the country and Canada.

A social science degree has little vocational value. It has even less value for a convicted felon. Improving the inmates' employability was not the goal. The assumption was that an education could rehabilitate, that through education inmates would learn to overcome the behaviors that got them into trouble. They're wrong. Worldly knowledge doesn't hold the answers to overcoming sin.

Don't get me wrong; I'm grateful for the education I received. I gained insight into the unbelieving world; it expanded my vocabulary and enhanced my communication skills. Later in life God would use my education to open doors. Writing this book would be much more difficult without it. But education did nothing to help me overcome sin in my life. I was still a drunk, a liar, and a pervert. Only now I was an educated and articulate drunk, liar, and pervert.

Isolated and alone in the midst of a thousand inmates, I longed for a connection with the outside world. Prior to my offense, I had been involved with a woman for several years. Our relationship went all the way back to when I lived in Visalia. We had lived together for a couple of years and had a child together. She had moved to Illinois to live with her parents shortly before I committed the offense that landed me in prison. While I was going through the court process we talked on the phone and she came out to see me. Now in prison we talked and corresponded regularly. On April 26, 1984, in a prison visiting room, we were married. She subsequently moved into my mother's house in Oceanside California to await my release.

The last few months of my sentence were spent in a halfway house in San Diego California. The concept of a halfway house was to integrate felons back into society. Participants were expected to secure employment. Prior to my offense, I had worked part time as a bookkeeper for my mother's tax accounting business. She was now operating the business out of her home. So for employment I was allowed to work at my mother's house where my wife and two children lived. After a short probationary period, I was allowed to spend weekends with my family. Weekdays I was with them during the day and slept at the halfway house at night, then I'd spend the entire weekend at home. It was a nice arrangement.

As soon as possible we began searching for a church. Looking in the phone book I discovered Oceanside Calvary Chapel. After notifying the halfway house of my plans, we packed the kids in the car and headed for church. Walking in the door that first time we were greeted by a tall, muscular ex-marine named Matthew "Chik" Chikeles. Chik had only been a believer for a couple of years and was serving in the ushering ministry. It was by no means a chance meeting; it was ordained by God. At that time I had no idea how important Chik would be. No other man has had as great an influence on me (although I haven't always felt that way).

From the time I was first approved to go to the halfway house to the end of my sentence, I was very careful not to get into trouble. I quit smoking pot altogether. In the halfway house drug testing was required; consequently many guys were sent back to prison for drug use. I had a good thing going and didn't want to screw it up. I stayed sober and followed the rules to the letter. As a consequence I was pressured into being the resident spokesperson: facilitating house meetings and representing the residents' issues. I tried to refuse. When I was at the house, which was as little as possible, I stayed in my room. I didn't want anything to do with house politics or the other guys. I knew there were drugs all around me and didn't want to take any chances. The position was thrust on me, so I only did the bare minimum performing my duties as resident spokesperson.

Motivated by self-interests, I discovered that I could stay sober and behave myself. For six months I didn't use any drugs. You'd think that I'd continue to be motivated upon my release, but I wasn't. I started smoking pot immediately. Within the first few weeks after my release, I was charged twice with drunk driving. You see, the sin hadn't been dealt with; I had merely put a cap on it. Now, upon release, I let loose.

Unfortunately the consequences were minimal. One of the drunk-driving offenses was on a military base, so it was handled by the military. They didn't look at my civilian record or report the incident to the civil authorities. This was also a time before the courts began getting tough on drunk drivers. I got off easy on both charges.

My parole officer didn't seem to care about any of it. The penal system in California was in trouble. Get tough on crime laws were overloading the system. To deal with the overcrowding, prisons were releasing felons as soon as they were eligible. Parole officers were faced with ridiculous caseloads, so supervision was reserved for only the worst criminals. Parole officers had discretion when to release a felon from parole. Consequently I met with my parole officer only a couple of times and was released from parole within six months.

chapter II

The voice of God

. . . the sheep hear his [the shepherd's] voice; and he calls his own sheep by name and leads them out. And when he brings out his own sheep, he goes before them; and the sheep follow him, for they know his voice. Yet they will by no means follow a stranger, but will flee from him, for they do not know the voice of strangers.

—John 10:3–5

There are many voices in our lives. Parents, teachers, friends, the media, society, religion all have an influence on how we think and behave. Add to these the voice of God and the influences of Satan and it's easy to see why our private world is so chaotic. Yes, I said "the voice of God and the influences of Satan." I readily admit that I hear the voice of God and recognize the influences of Satan in my life. If that makes me schizophrenic, then so be it. I understand that unbelievers are ignorant of these influences. However, I am more concerned for believers who don't recognize the voice of God. His sheep know His voice. If you can't recognize or hear the voice of God you are in a very dangerous place.

God has something to say. He is not silent or distant. Some question, "Why doesn't God just show Himself and speak to us directly?" One answer is that He did; He sent His Son and we killed Him.[1] Another answer is that no man can see God face-to-face and live.[2] Actually God has shown Himself in a myriad of ways yet most of

---

[1] Matthew 21:31–46
[2] Exodus 33:19, 20

humanity has chosen to ignore Him. But that doesn't stop God; He continues to convey His message. To the unbeliever the message is the Good News of salvation. To carnal believers it's a warning, a call to return to their first love.[3] For the believer it's the voice of a loving Father.

> For since the creation of the world His invisible attributes are clearly seen, being understood by the things that are made . . .
>   —Romans 1:20

One way God speaks is through creation. It is difficult to look at the wonders of the physical world and not see God. Scientific analysis consistently uncovers evidence of design in the physical universe. Where there is design there is a designer. Think about it. We've all seen things blown up; yet have you ever seen the flying pieces of debris come together and form anything useful? Whenever I've been tempted to question the existence of God, all I've had to do is look at creation and all doubt disappears.

> . . . the work of the law written in their hearts, their conscience also bearing witness, and between themselves their thoughts accusing or else excusing them . . .
>   —Romans 2:15

God has written His law on our conscience. All people have an instinctive knowledge of right and wrong. This creates inner conflict. Many people try to minimize this conflict through personal accomplishment, good deeds, and religion. It doesn't work. Others sear their conscience with drugs, alcohol, and wickedness. That's the story of my life. It, too, doesn't work. God's voice may be muffled, but it's still there. No matter how far I threw myself into sin, the voice of God was still loud and clear. But the message was always the same, "Remember, Repent, Return."

---

[3] Revelation 2:4,5

Him we preach, warning every man and teaching every man in all wisdom, that we may present every man perfect in Christ Jesus.
—Colossians 1:28

God speaks through His children. The teacher instructs and equips. The preacher extols the deep truths of God. The evangelist proclaims the Good News of salvation. All believers are expected to *"be ready to give a defense to everyone who asks you a reason for the hope that is in you"* (1 Pet. 3:15). Unfortunately most believers and the church as a whole have failed to fulfill this edict. The message has been watered down so as not to offend. After all, the truth isn't always politically correct or polite. We are surrounded by a lost and dying world; eternity apart from God is not friendly. "We should be rude enough to rescue people from hell; they'll thank us later."[4]

Where there is no counsel, the people fall; but in the multitude of counselors there is safety.
—Proverbs 11:14

God speaks to us through the counsel of other believers. We need each other. God never intended for us to go through this life alone. Believers need to seek out the counsel of other believers. But not just any counsel, godly counsel. Too often we look for people to tell us what we want to hear. Good, godly counsel is frequently a hard pill to swallow. The correct path is usually the hard path. So we shop around for people who will agree with our faulty thinking. This is the main reason there is so much shifting of the saints between churches. If people don't like what they hear at one church, they can go to the church across the street.

Now I myself am confident concerning you, my brethren, that you also are full of goodness, filled with all knowledge, able also to admonish one another.
—Romans 15:14

---

[4] Pastor Matthew "Chik" Chikeles

Believers full of goodness (the Holy Spirit) and full of knowledge (God's Word) are qualified to counsel one another. Counseling is the responsibility of the church. We are our brother's keeper! Sadly the church has failed to fulfill this commission. Believers struggling with sin are referred to "professionals." Or worse, they're treated as second-class Christians. It is said that the church is the only army that shoots its own wounded.

God speaks to us directly. He speaks to our heart and mind. God speaks in a *still small voice,"* as He did with Elijah.[5] Yet I've discovered that the volume and tone of God's voice is not limited. He can be as loud as He needs to be when getting my attention. The issue isn't whether God is speaking to us; He is. The question is whether we're listening. Jesus used an unusual phrase when speaking to the crowds, *"He who has ears to hear, let him hear!"* God is speaking; it's up to us to chose to listen to what He has to say.

God uses circumstances in our lives to direct our paths. There are no accidents or chance encounters in the life of a believer. God is orchestrating every aspect of our lives. However, circumstances shouldn't be the primary way we hear from God. Just because a door is open it doesn't mean that it's the path God desires for us to take. He may want us to wait for another door, or He may want us to work at opening a closed door. The great works of God have been met with opposition; God's path is rarely the easy path.

> *The name of the LORD is a strong tower; the righteous run to it and are safe.*
> —Proverbs 18:10

God speaks most clearly to those who call on His name. Try to grasp the significance of calling upon a being who created the universe by speaking it into existence. A being whose presence fills the heavens; the earth is His footstool. The name of the Lord is more than just a title. It implies intimate fellowship with God. God takes His name seriously. His name proclaims His character. To do anything in the name of the Lord is to do His will, His way. The more

---

[5] 1 Kings 19:11–13

you surrender your life to Him, the more you draw near to Him, the clearer His voice will be in your life.

God holds His name in high esteem. Yet, God esteems His Word above His name, *"For You have magnified Your word above all Your name"* (Psalm 138:2). The Bible, not psychology, philosophy or religion, contains the answers to life. Believers need to be students of God's Word. The church needs to teach God's Word. The Bible must be the foundation of counseling. Believers grounded in Scripture are less likely to be deceived by Satan and are better equipped to stand against the schemes of the Enemy. The churches I grew up in didn't teach the *"whole counsel of God"* (Acts 20:27). Teaching lacked practical application. Consequently I suffered from a weak and incomplete knowledge of God's Word.

> *All scripture is given by inspiration of God, and is profitable for doctrine, for reproof, for correction, for instruction in righteousness, that the man of God may be complete, thoroughly equipped for every good work.*
> —2 Timothy 3:16,17

Scripture needs to not just be taught; it needs to be lived. *"But be doers of the word, and not hearers only, deceiving yourselves"* (James 1:22). Young believers need to see older believers applying biblical principals to their lives. Parents need to teach their children by example how to follow Jesus. Let them hear you pray, let them see your effort to draw near to God and live a godly life. I didn't have that, so when the going got rough I had no practical example of godliness that would help me overcome and persevere.

God is not lacking in His effort to communicate with us. But not every voice professing to be God is of God. People claiming to have heard the voice of God have done many hideous things. The church is divided over doctrine. Counsel among believers is contradictory. It is often difficult to distinguish the voices in our head. So then, how do we verify the message?

First and foremost, God never contradicts His written Word. If the message is in conflict with Scripture, it's a lie. If the message adds to or changes the gospel of salvation, it's not of God, *"But even if we, or an angel from heaven, preach any other gospel to you than what we have preached to you, let him be accursed"* (Gal. 1:8). Therefore it is critical that we are thoroughly grounded in God's Word. If we are not willing to seek God through His Word, why should He speak to us at all?

Another consideration in distinguishing God's voice is that He never violates His character, and His character never changes.

> *"The LORD, the LORD God, merciful and gracious, longsuffering, and abounding in goodness and truth, keeping mercy for thousands, forgiving iniquity and transgression and sin, by no means clearing the guilty, visiting the iniquity of the fathers upon the children and the children's children to the third and the fourth generation."*
> —Exod. 34:6–7

The character of God is found throughout the Bible; it's on every page. To learn about God's character, study God's Word. But to know God's character, you have to walk with God. God saves us to have fellowship with Him. The more time you spend with Him, the more you get to know Him personally, the more you will experience His character. The closer you are to God, the clearer you will hear His voice. Know God's Word, know God's character, and know God—that's the secret to hearing God.

chapter 12
Polluted

"For though you wash yourself with lye, and use much soap, yet your iniquity is marked before Me," says the Lord GOD. "How can you say, 'I am not polluted . . .'"

—Jeremiah 2:22,23

Everything was hazy. The light peering through the curtain hurt my eyes. There was a dull throb in my head that turned to screaming pain when I moved. I was hung over again. However, this time I couldn't remember anything that happened the previous night. I had often wished I couldn't remember; there were many times I pretended not to remember; but now the blackouts were real. To frustrate things further, I lost the car and had no idea where it was. It took the better part of the day to locate it at a hotel twenty miles away from home. How it ended up there is a mystery to this day.

The four years after my release from prison were complicated. I attended Oceanside Calvary Chapel, worked, pursued graduate studies, and operated a business in partnership with my wife and mother. I also drank, used drugs, and committed numerous sexual perversions. The battle inside me raged: my old nature, my new nature, Satan, and the Holy Spirit each fighting for control. It was internal chaos—madness. I desperately wanted to be free from the desires of my flesh, but I was held in bondage by my passions.

The night I wrecked my mother's van and was arrested for drunk driving, I had a sexual encounter with a man at a roadside rest area. Throughout my life I have been consumed by an insatiable desire for extreme and perverse behavior. It's as though a dark cloud of depravity engulfs me. It's like I have no choice, as though some mysterious dark force is controlling me. Biblically I would say that this is true. Apart from Jesus we are controlled by the passions of our flesh and the enemy's lies. It is only when we walk close to Jesus, full of the Holy Spirit, do we have power over our sinful nature.

As a dog returns to his own vomit, so a fool repeats his folly.
—Proverbs 26:11

Remorse would always follow acts of perversion. Afterward I would vow to never do it again. Driven by shame, I would behave myself for a while. But in time I'd forget the suffering and return to pursuing lustful desires. This would be the only homosexual encounter I would have for the next ten years. I physically engaged in sexual activity only with my wife. I did frequent local strip clubs and adult movie theaters and fantasized about women other than my wife. The perversion of choice during this period was indecent exposure.

The objective was to sustain the fantasy. The goal was to not make physical contact or to speak to the victim. I had discovered that contact only destroyed the fantasy and broke the spell. Additionally I knew that if I didn't engage in direct contact I was committing a lesser criminal offense. Eventually I'd take it even further by not exposing my genitalia at all. There were numerous scenarios I'd play out. One favorite was to drive around naked or partially naked then position the car where a female victim would get a glimpse of me through the window. Another was to walk the beach and beach communities wearing only a thong. The conclusion was always the same: masturbation, guilt, and remorse.

Drugs and alcohol continued to play a significant role in my life. I drank and smoked pot as usual. But now I found a new drug of choice—crystal meth. Crystal is an insidious drug! It's inexpensive, the effects last a long time, and the high is intense. Besides giving the user an unnatural euphoria, stamina, and energy, crystal significantly increases sexual appetite and prolongs sexual arousal. Just what I needed! Not! Under the influence of crystal I could sustain a sexual fantasy for days.

*For the flesh lusts against the Spirit, and the Spirit against the flesh;
and these are contrary to one another, so that you do not do the things
that you wish . . .*

—Galatians 5:17–18

Now for the paradox—through all this perversion and drug use I
raised a family, worked, started a business, attended school, and attended Oceanside Calvary Chapel. This contrast was more duplicity
than hypocrisy. Hypocrisy is saying one thing then doing something
different. I certainly was a hypocrite. But hypocrite is too simple. I
wasn't just saying one thing and doing another; I was two different
people living in one body. If you're a believer, then there are two of
you as well. Only your sin probably doesn't look as disgusting as does
mine. Yet beware of self-righteous judgment. My sin and yours are
equally offensive to God. Oh, by the way, if you're not a believer, all
you have is a sin nature. Your morality and good works may be com-
mendable to others, but they mean nothing to God.

Sin separates us from God and sin separates us from each other.
My sin was carefully concealed. I told no one. In the midst of people
who loved me I was desperately alone. It affected my relationship
with my wife. I was secretive, withdrawn, and guarded. I was given
to fits of irrational rage and jealousy. It affected my relationship with
my children. I was emotionally detached and frequently harsh. (Except with my youngest son who was born a year after my release from
prison. I was emotionally attached to him the moment he was born.)
All my children suffered because of my sin, but the older two additionally suffered fallout from my first marriage. Because of the pain
I had suffered over the children in my first marriage, I consciously
vowed to not let myself become attached, one of many choices I very
much regret.

Chik continued to show up in my life. While I floundered around
in my sin, Chik went from usher, to deacon, to leading the youth
ministries, to Assisting Pastor. Chik would stop by my business to
talk. He often invited me to participate in ministry opportunities,
and he continually tried to draw me out. I participated as long as
the commitment wasn't too great and I didn't have to get too close to
anyone. I served in the tape ministry, helped clean the sanctuary with

Chik, and participated in outreaches. But my sin kept me isolated. I didn't experience the full joy of ministry and the fellowship of other believers. As Chik would say, I only had $2 of Jesus—just enough to get into the amusement park but not enough to go on the rides.

Chik scared me. I was drawn to him while at the same time I avoided him. So to protect myself I became critical of him and his ministry. It wasn't difficult to find things to complain about. Chik had a strong personality and an unconventional ministry style. So what that he obviously loved Jesus, loved people, and his ministry was fruitful. I know today Chik was not the issue. The issue was my heart and my relationship with Jesus. Chik was living the life I longed for. He had paid the full price of admission and was enjoying the rides, while I stood by and watched.

> *He who loves transgression loves strife, and he who exalts his gate seeks destruction. He who has a deceitful heart finds no good, and he who has a perverse tongue falls into evil.*
> —Proverbs 17:19,20

In the midst of the chaos, I longed to be free. It was painfully clear that I was headed for destruction. I desperately needed help. Unfortunately I wasn't willing to be honest about the full extent of the problem. I was afraid of the consequences if I told the truth. The conflict burned within me. God's Spirit was speaking to me, calling me to Him. I longed for the fellowship I saw among other believers, but was convinced that if they knew the truth I wouldn't be accepted. Meanwhile my flesh continued to control me.

Ralph Wood was the pastor of Oceanside Calvary Chapel. I liked him a lot. Finally I got up the courage to talk to him. My plan was to share just a little of my struggles with him to test the waters. Cautiously I told him that I struggled with sexual thoughts and masturbation. We talked for a while about what the Bible has to say about these issues and then he dropped a bomb on me. Ralph told me I needed to talk to my wife about it. My heart sank within me. I knew he was correct, but there is no way I was going to talk to my wife about these things. The idea was inconceivable. Of course, I hadn't told Ralph even a fraction of the sin in my life.

The way of a fool is right in his own eyes, but he who heeds counsel is wise.

—Proverbs 12:15

Ralph's words scared me so I went the way of the fool. I made the decision to not seek counsel from him again. Instead I sought out an independent counselor who professed to be Christian. Since he wasn't connected with the church I was attending, I didn't fear exposure. Furthermore, I believed that everything I told him would be confidential. I started out slow. For the first several sessions I spoke cautiously, not revealing too much. Finally I began to allude to some of the more serious behaviors. He became panicked; he quickly warned me against sharing anything criminal, stating that he would have to report such activity. Consequently I quit speaking, withdrew, and never went back. My conviction to keep the more serious sin in my life secret was again strengthened.

Amazingly, in the midst of my iniquity, God's Word was taking root in my life. For the first time, I was in a church that taught the Bible, all of it, from Genesis to Revelation. Twice a week I had the incredible privilege of attending Bible studies led by Ralph. Additionally I had access to Bible study tapes through the tape ministry. I listened to hundreds of hours of tapes. I went through the entire Bible with Chuck Smith, the man God used to found the Calvary Chapel movement. The other teacher I listened to was Chuck Missler. Missler is a uniquely gifted teacher. He has a depth of knowledge that I didn't know was possible. He opened my eyes and my heart to the Old Testament and prophecy. He helped me to better understand the divine inspiration of Scripture.

So shall My word be that goes forth from My mouth; it shall not return to Me void, but shall accomplish what I please, and it shall prosper in the thing for which I sent it.

—Isaiah 55:11

While I was growing in knowledge, the Holy Spirit was doing a work in my heart. He created in me a desire to not just know God's Word but to live it. As a teenager I had a simple desire to live out

God's Word in my life. I heard many sermons based on Scripture, but there was little application. I was accused of taking Scripture and my faith too seriously. I was too heavenly minded. Well-meaning people encouraged me to find a balance: "Not everything has to be about God." They were wrong. Everything is about God. He created everything, He sustains life, and by Him all things are held together. Yet people were right about one thing, my faith was out of balance. I wasn't applying the whole counsel of God to my life.

God's voice grew louder and louder. Repeatedly He impressed on my heart that there was much more to life. On the one hand I was convinced that I couldn't overcome drugs, alcohol, and perversion. I had tried to quit sinning so many times I lost count. I tried to adopt the worldview that it was an incurable disease, that it wasn't my fault, that I was the victim. Yet my growing understanding of Scripture and the voice of God told me otherwise. Drunkenness and perversion were sin, not disease, and God's Word is clear about sin.

God's voice in my life continued to warn me that, "If you continue in sin you will lose everything." My thoughts where haunted with this exhortation. As bad as my life had been, I had a sick feeling that it could get worse, much worse. I've never bought into the idea that things can't get any worse, that the worst is over and things can only get better. Sinful behavior left alone doesn't get better. I knew that it was just a matter of time before this warning became a reality. Unfortunately I still wasn't willing to tell anyone. From my perspective it wasn't an option. This would have to be accomplished alone. Well, not totally alone; I had God on my side.

I attended AA meetings to get sober. It didn't help. In fact it was frustrating. AA offered sobriety, but it didn't offer the new life I knew was available through Jesus. The twelve steps of AA are pure religion based on works. Certainly religion can change behavior, but it doesn't offer victory over sin or lasting peace. My observation is that those who achieve sobriety through twelve-step programs increase sin in other areas of their lives. They become prideful, arrogant, and self-indulgent. Whereas those whose victory is through Jesus enjoy the fruit of the spirit: love, joy, peace, and self-control.[1]

---

[1] Galatians 5:22

Behold the proud, his soul is not upright in him; but the just shall live by his faith.

—Habakkuk 2:4

Victory through Jesus is much simpler, just one step—faith. Some may argue that faith in Jesus only changes behavior as long as the person continues in his faith. This is true. We must abide or continue in our faith if we are to enjoy continued victory over sin. But this is also true of twelve-step programs. One of the first things taught in AA is "once an alcoholic always an alcoholic." For AA to be successful, people have to attend meetings and work the steps for the rest of their lives.

A wise man fears and departs from evil . . .

—Proverbs 14:16

Without oath or fanfare I made the decision to quit drugs, alcohol, and perversion. I didn't tell anyone about the decision. Success was uncertain and I didn't want to get their hopes up. Also, I didn't want to answer questions about the extent of my sinful behaviors. My decision wasn't made in response to a specific consequence of sin. I was led by the voice of God and fear over what would happen if I didn't change. I was genuinely repentant.

It was hard. I was terrified. I prayed constantly. Every thought and action was scrutinized. Nothing else mattered, so I took things very slowly. Nightmares, cold sweats, trembling, and tears filled my nights. I'd wake in the morning weeping and disoriented. It would take awhile to convince myself I was all right, that the dreams weren't real, that I hadn't done anything hideous the night before. The days were only a little better. All I could do was cling to Jesus moment by moment. I was miserable; if I had to live the rest of my life like this I'd sooner die!

Days passed, then weeks. Before long I had been sober for three months. During that time I continued to walk with Jesus. I prayed, read my Bible, attended church services and home fellowship meetings. Yet I still hadn't told anyone about the decision I had made. Eventually my family would begin to notice the change. I remember the day I realized God's work in my life. Waking up that morning I jumped out of bed with a song on my heart. In the bathroom getting ready for work I was singing a worship song. I didn't even realize that a change in my countenance had taken place. God spoke to me, and all at once I realized what had happened.

> *Oh, sing to the LORD a new song! For He has done marvelous things;*
> *His right hand and His holy arm have gained Him the victory.*
>
> —Psalm 98:1

I would tell this story of how God rescued me from drugs and alcohol many times. Of course I'd leave out the part about perversion. The truth is that while I did gain victory over the drugs and alcohol I was still in bondage to perversion. Sexual fantasies dominated my thoughts, and on at least one occasion I committed an act of indecent exposure. These were accompanied by great remorse and a renewed effort to do better. I knew deep in my soul that someday I would have to fully confess my sin. I should have done it then. Yet God was gracious with me. He knew my heart, and He began doing a work in my life in spite of me.

God loves us more than we can imagine. He loves us so much that He will not force us to come to Him. He's the perfect gentleman. He gently, yet firmly draws us to Him. He waits patiently for us to take a step in His direction. Then when we do take that step, even if it's a half step, God takes a big step in our direction. He begins to move mightily in our lives. During the next six months God began to heal my damaged life.

> *Good and upright is the LORD; Therefore He teaches sinners in the*
> *way. The humble He guides in justice, and the humble He teaches His*
> *way. All the paths of the LORD are mercy and truth, to such as keep His*
> *covenant and His testimonies. For Your name's sake, O LORD, pardon*
> *my iniquity, for it is great.*
>
> —Psalm 25:8–11

chapter 13

The world according to self

There is a way that seems right to a man, but its end is the way of death.

—Proverbs 16:25

We like to think humanity has advanced socially. We haven't. Mankind has accumulated vast amounts of information and has developed advanced technologies. We have become sophisticated in our thinking. Yet since the beginning of history there has not been a single advancement in the fundamental nature of mankind. Human nature is wicked and deceitful. If anything, the further away from the Garden of Eden, the more decrepit man has become.

The heart is deceitful above all things, and desperately wicked; who can know it?

—Jeremiah 17:9

Some might complain that this negative worldview destroys self-esteem. They're correct, it does. Nowhere does the Bible suggest that the problem with mankind is that we don't think enough good thoughts about ourselves. Quite the opposite, *"For I know that in me (that is, in my flesh) nothing good dwells . . ."* (Rom. 7:18). The Bible speaks of esteeming others, esteeming God, but it does not encourage us to esteem ourselves.

A man's steps are of the LORD; how then can a man understand his own way?

—Proverbs 20:24

The world in which we live is obsessed with self. If you don't agree try this simple experiment. Go to the store and stand in front of the magazine rack. Notice the titles of the publications and the feature articles. The overwhelming theme is self. I challenge you to find a single article that is predominately others-centered. Mankind worships at the altar of narcissism. The god of this world is self.

Give us help from trouble, for the help of man is useless.
                                                    —Psalm 60:11

"Self" and "love" are contradictory terms. They don't belong together. Real love involves personal sacrifice. It's completely centered on doing what is best for the other person. So to say that someone's problem is that they don't love themselves is pernicious (causes harm). It's insidious to say that someone can't love others until they first learn to love themselves.

The counterpart to self-love is the presumption that someone can't forgive unless they first forgive themselves. We don't need to forgive ourselves. We need the forgiveness of others. We especially need God's forgiveness. Forgiveness is about not holding someone's sins against them. To recognize my need for forgiveness is to acknowledge that my actions have harmed others. Ultimately God is the one I have offended the most, and He's ready and anxious to forgive. All I have to do is ask. To accept God's forgiveness then say, "I can't forgive myself" is ridiculous. What makes me greater than God? The problem isn't forgiving myself, it's that I'm wallowing in self-pity.

Guard what was committed to your trust, avoiding the profane and idle babblings and contradictions of what is falsely called knowledge . . .
                                                    —1 Timothy 6:20

Evolving from the humanist ooze of the psychobabbler's chair, the worship of self has destroyed countless lives. Tragically these deceptions have infiltrated the church. I challenge you to find any support whatsoever in the Bible for self-esteem, self-love, or for forgiving oneself. If they were why didn't Jesus address these issues in His earthly ministry? Instead He talked about salvation, repentance, hell, denying self, being born again, and forgiving others.

Beware lest anyone cheat you through philosophy and empty deceit, according to the tradition of men, according to the basic principles of the world, and not according to Christ.

—Colossians 2:8

Self-esteem, self-love, and self-image are traditions of men born out of the psychoanalytical movement. In a nutshell, psychoanalysis is an attempt to explain and cope with the sinful nature of man apart from God. It's the equivalent of a self-taught aircraft mechanic ignoring all the technical information available from the manufacturer. "I don't need no stinking technical manuals, I can just figure this out for my self. Let me see . . . let's try this. Oops, that didn't work . . . *crash and burn* . . . Guess I'll try something else." God gave us everything we need to know so we can function as He intended. Why do we insist on looking everywhere else but in His Word for the answers to life?

Again, the kingdom of heaven is like treasure hidden in a field, which a man found and hid; and for joy over it he goes and sells all that he has and buys that field.

Again, the kingdom of heaven is like a merchant seeking beautiful pearls, who, when he had found one pearl of great price, went and sold all that he had and bought it.

—Matthew 13:44–46

The "treasure in the field" and the "pearl of great price" in this passage is God's children, those who have put their faith in Jesus. They speak of the great price God paid for our salvation and how precious we are to Him. Paul in Ephesians 1:18 refers to the believer as *"the glory of His inheritance."* I don't understand it, but we are God's inheritance. We are what He gets out of this deal. We are of great value to God, not because He needs us or we're worthy. We're a treasure to God only because He ascribed value to us. Take a dollar bill out of your wallet. Why does it have value? The paper it's printed on isn't worth a dollar. It's worth a dollar because we ascribed that value to it. Likewise, God has ascribed value to each of us, the value of His one and only Son. Unlike the dollar, God's standard will never change; there is no inflation in God's economy. If you're looking for something to feel good about, there it is.

Among the myriad errors in secular counseling is the notion that good feelings produce good behavior. That's the presumption underlying self-love and self-esteem. The hope is that if people feel good about themselves it will affect a positive change in their behavior. This is totally backward; the opposite is true. Good behavior produces good feelings. Healthy emotions are the product of a moral life, not the other way around.

Consider the example of Cain and Abel in Genesis 4. Abel's sacrifice was acceptable to God and Cain's was rejected. Why? Hebrews 11:4 explains that Abel's sacrifice was an act of faith and Cain's wasn't. And in 1 John 3:12 we learn that Cain's works were evil while Abel's were righteous. Consequently Cain bummed out because God rejected his sacrifice—

> So the LORD said to Cain, "Why are you angry? And why has your countenance fallen [feel bad]? If you do well, will you not be accepted [feel good]? And if you do not do well, sin lies at the door . . ."
> —Genesis 4:6,7

Do well, be accepted by God, feel good. It's that simple. Of course to *"do well"* does not mean trying to earn a relationship with God through good works. It means to walk by faith and live in obedience to God. The alternative is to succumb to the sin that lies at your door and desires to control your life. Cain chose sin and the rest is history—the first recorded murder. As a result, he added to his suffering, *"And Cain said to the Lord, 'My punishment is greater than I can bear!'"* (Gen. 4:13). We have the choice to live by faith and obedience like Abel or be driven by self, as did Cain. Let us heed the warning to not go the way of Cain.[1]

---

[1] Jude 1:11

A wise man will hear and increase learning, and a man of understanding will attain wise counsel . . .

—Proverbs 1:5

SECTION THREE

The Woodshed

Winona reprieve

*. . . You have been a shelter for me, a strong tower from the enemy.
I will abide in Your tabernacle forever; I will trust in the shelter of
Your wings.*

—Psalm 61:2–4

E ntering Nebraska from eastern Arizona the geography changed
abruptly. We went from high desert to plains and rolling hills.
I've never seen so much corn! The plain states have a unique beauty
that grows on you. However it's a beauty that is best appreciated
standing still, not at 70 mph. After three days with two adults and
three children in a small car I was beginning to question the decision
to move to Minnesota. "Please, Lord, don't let Minnesota look like
Nebraska or Kansas."

It really didn't matter what Minnesota looked like. We were more
a family than ever before and we were on an adventure, a venture
of faith. Soon after I began dealing with my sin, God put it on our
hearts to move. Yet this time I wasn't moving to run away; this time I
sensed that God had a plan for us somewhere else. We prayed about
and explored several options, all in the western states. Moving to the
Midwest didn't occur to us . . . until.

"I spoke with my father today. He heard that we're considering
moving." My wife went on, "He said that if we move to Winona he
would help us buy a house." I was immediately intrigued by the offer. Her parents had bought a house in Winona where they planned
to retire. But it was a long way from California and my family, and

I didn't know anything about Minnesota. This would require a trip to the library.

The more I learned, the more I fell in love with the idea. We had a peace about the move; there was no question in my mind that this was God's will. So we quit our jobs, packed our belongings, said goodbye, and headed for Minnesota.

I have fond memories of that trip. I believe it was a joyous time for us all, although I could be wrong. My wife and children may feel differently. We did some sightseeing, visited my wife's sister in Kansas, sang songs, and had fun. We were together as a family; all we had was each other. It was an adventure into the unknown filled with excitement and expectation.

Nothing but cornfields for hundreds of miles was beginning to concern me. My apprehensions were unnecessary; Winona is a quaint town on the Mississippi River, nestled below limestone bluffs in the scenic Hiawatha Valley. It was as though we had stepped back in time into a lost world. Nineteenth and early twentieth-century homes, paddleboats, and barges on the river. Strangers greeted you.

The move to Winona was exhilarating. It was a fresh new world. Places to explore, people to meet, the changing of the seasons, everything was exciting. Even the frigid Minnesota winters offered a welcome change. I had lived in mountain ski resorts in the west, but I had no idea what cold was. My senses almost overloaded the first time I witnessed the wonder of a winter ice storm. The past was behind me. New opportunities lay ahead.

I didn't fully understand or appreciate it at the time, but God had brought us to a sanctuary, a safe place to build a foundation and give me a chance to deal with sinful behavior. It was also an opportunity for God to give me a taste of what my life could be like. The gifts and calling of God blossomed. I gained respectability in the community. Miraculously God provided me with employment beyond my imagination.

Somehow, somewhere I developed a work ethic. My work habits were not all good; I wasn't always honest or dependable. I changed employment frequently. Yet I almost always had a job and had a reputation as a hard worker. Usually I took a great deal of pride in my work, not a healthy pride, a self-centered, self-indulgent pride.

Employers usually found me to be creative, innovative, willing to take on responsibility, and highly motivated . . . at least for the first few months. After the honeymoon, employers would begin to see my lesser qualities. I'd become bored and disenchanted. That's when I'd move on to the next job.

Prior to moving to Minnesota, shortly after my release from prison, I started a business with my wife and mother. Culinary Artists produced handmade marzipan candies and chocolates that we sold wholesale to gourmet candy stores. Every Christmas growing up my family would produce large quantities of the confection for gifts and charitable endeavors. It had long been a dream of mine to make a business of this family tradition. While in prison, I began to develop a business plan and production process. Upon release I presented the idea to my mother who provided the financial backing.

The business was never truly successful, at least not financially. Marzipan is labor intensive and the market is seasonal. At best, one year we broke even. However the business did provide a limited amount of personal accountability: I worked with my wife, and initially the business was located across the street from Calvary Chapel. Chik often came by to torment—I mean visit (with the love of Jesus). Yet I still found ways to pursue sinful behaviors. Much of my job was away from the shop handling sales, deliveries, and procuring raw materials.

Culinary Artists employed around half a dozen seasonal employees. Depending on where my heart was at the time the work environment could be very spiritual. A great deal of ministry went on. I frequently brought in Bible teaching tapes. Everyone listened then we'd engage in a conversation about the material. At other times I drank and did drugs with the employees. No one knew about my perverse behaviors. I kept that part of my life hidden. Around women at work or church I was always respectful.

Culinary Artists was failing financially. After much consideration we made the decision to dissolve the business . . . but God had other plans. We sold Culinary Artists to the Association for Retarded Citizens (ARC). Their interest was to use the business as a training center for developmentally disabled adults. They already had a retail candy store so the addition of Culinary Artists seemed natural for them.

We would all find out that there are big differences in teaching the developmentally disabled to serve retail customers and have them staff a manufacturing process.

Part of the deal with ARC was that I had to stay on to manage the operation. Overnight I went from owner of a food service business to social worker and case manager. "What about your criminal record?" you might ask. Because I wasn't hired through traditional employment channels, it didn't come up. "But didn't you have an obligation to tell them?" No, I didn't. At least that's what I was told upon release from prison. If an employer doesn't ask about my criminal record, I'm under no obligation to tell them.

This may be an outrage to you, someone with my criminal history working with vulnerable adults. Fortunately it wasn't a problem. I cared very much for the clients. I wouldn't have done anything to harm them. It never even crossed my mind. As a business, Culinary Artists didn't operate any better under ARC. Yet it did have a huge impact on the clients. My wife and a former employee worked with me. None of us had any training or related experience. We treated the clients with respect and as adults. The focus was on their abilities, not their disabilities. The results were obvious and dramatic.

> *Trust in the LORD with all your heart, and lean not on your own understanding; in all your ways acknowledge Him, and He shall direct your paths.*
>
> —Proverbs 3:5,6

I'm convinced that if a believer were to only follow this wisdom he would never fail. Trust God. Don't lean on your own understanding. Include God in everything. You can't go wrong! The move to Winona was one of the few times in my life I followed this instruction. I was totally open to whatever God had for us and lived in great expectation that He would do miraculous things. I was correct.

We came to Winona without jobs and very little money. My father-in-law had bought a house for us so we had a place to live. I immediately began looking for work. The economy wasn't in good shape. There was high unemployment because of several recent plant closings. That didn't matter because my trust was in God and I was willing to take whatever employment was available. I knew God was going to direct my paths.

The first job I took was picking up trash for a recycling company. Not very prestigious or profitable, but it put food on the table. A fire at the warehouse where the recyclables were stored ended that job within a few weeks. Continuing to trust the Lord, I took a job as a manager trainee for a coffee shop chain called Happy Chef. Not much of a step up from the recycling center. It was humbling. I had spent many years in the food industry, mostly working for trendy restaurants and five-star resorts. But who cared; my trust was in Jesus and He was directing my path.

In California I'd have never gone to a government employment service for help. Government offices conjured all the typical stereotypes: rude civil servants, long lines, and creepy people. In my experience a government employment service might be a place to score drugs, not a place to find work. The first time I went to the Job Service in Winona I thought it was a private business. Initially I asked about fees. When I found out it was a government agency a knot formed in my stomach and I immediately wanted to leave. Yet it didn't look like any government office I'd ever seen and the people were friendly, so I stayed.

By now I knew the routine. I handed the list of prospective jobs to the receptionist, sat down and waited for my name to be called. Because of my military experience, I met with the veteran's counselor. We had met many times over the past couple of months; he saw my motivation and knew my qualifications. On paper I looked pretty good: supervisor and case manager for ARC, accounting degree, bachelor's degree in social science, and graduate studies in business.

This day the counselor set aside the jobs I had pulled off the computer. We engaged in conversation for a few minutes. It was obvious that he had something on his mind. His countenance, the wiry smile, the conversation all implied he was about to reveal something. Cautiously, with an air of secretiveness, he pulled a piece of paper out of his drawer and slid it face down across the desk. "I believe you should be considered for this job," he said in a tone so as not to draw attention.

Reading the announcement I was in a state of disbelief. The job was for an employment counselor to manage a one-year project assisting dislocated workers affected by the recent plant closings. He went on, "Because this is a temporary position it is not being announced to the general public. Six candidates for the job are being hand selected by staff. You would be a good candidate. Can I schedule you for an interview?"

For a long time I had desired to get out of the food service industry. This seemed like the perfect opportunity. I could master new skills and abilities, and it would be a different work environment. Additionally I would be working with employers, community agencies, and the public. What better way for me to get established in the community? It didn't matter that it was only a one-year project with no potential for permanent employment (that's what I was told). There would have to be something seriously wrong if I couldn't secure new employment at the end of the project.

The interview was unlike any I had ever experienced. It was a formal process with two interviewers, the office manager and the project manager asking scripted questions—tough, industry-specific questions. Every candidate was asked the same questions and the interviewers scored the responses. The process was designed to be objective, to help select the best candidate for the job. Based on conventional wisdom I was totally unprepared. I knew almost nothing about the job or how to manage a dislocated worker project. However I had something far better than conventional wisdom. I had spent the morning in prayer and worship. I was packing a secret weapon—the Holy Spirit. They didn't stand a chance.

It started with the very first question. Before I could formulate a thoughtful response words came out of mouth. It's as though it wasn't me talking; it wasn't. I became an observer of the event, listening to my own words thinking, "Wow! That's really good!" Then all of a sudden I would hear the word *Stop!* God knew that I have a tendency to babble on even after I've made my point. So I'd finish the sentence and force myself to stop. The interviewers glanced at each other with a look of disbelief. If I wasn't paying attention I might have missed it. They seemed to be asking each other the unspoken question, "What just happened?" This same process was repeated for nearly and hour and over a dozen questions. I'd speak without knowing what was going to come out of my mouth. The Holy Spirit would say, *Stop!* The interviewers would look at each other in disbelief. All anxiety and stress disappeared; there was total peace; I was resting in Jesus. By the end of the interview it was though I had just sat through a spiritually-charged after-glow or worship service.

The first day on the job the manager called me into her office and shut the door. "I want to talk to you about your interview," she began. "I've been doing this for over twenty years. In that time I've never experienced an interview like yours. The other candidates weren't even close." Her tone was serious and she seemed a little concerned. She went on, "I have to ask you. Who in this office gave you the interview questions and coached you on how to respond?" A wave of relief came over me. The subject of a criminal background hadn't come up. I thought this was it, my career as an employment counselor would end as soon as it had begun. "Uh, no one gave me the questions," I replied. Then I added (a bit timidly I'm ashamed to say), "It was God's will for me to be here."

It was the perfect job and I was the perfect person for the job. I was like a duck in water. You would have thought I had been doing this kind of work all my life. This is not merely my assessment; it was obvious to everyone who worked with me as well. I loved going to work. I was passionate about the job. I developed a job-search curriculum and taught employment seminars, provided employment and career counseling, helped people go back to school, coordinated with other community agencies, and worked with employers. For the next four years it would be the job of my dreams.

That's right "the next four years," so much for being a temporary one-year project with no chance of permanent employment. I wasn't there six months when the office manager began hatching a plan to get me on as a permanent employee. It wasn't easy. First she had the project extended for a year. Then she intentionally created an emergency situation whereby she could appoint me as a provisional employee. Finally after six months in provisional status I became permanent.

While making my position permanent, I was asked for the first time to fill out an application. An application wasn't required for temporary positions. Now after two years, I faced the dreaded question about my criminal record. My heart sank within me. I seriously considered not answering or even worse lying. I prayed a lot. Finally I resigned that God miraculously provided this job therefore whatever would happen was up to Him. I answered the question honestly and wrote a long explanation on a separate page as requested. I didn't sleep very well that night. The next morning I went into the office ready for the worst.

Finally I got up the courage to approach the manager. I walked into her office and shut the door. "I have the application you asked for." As I handed it to her I turned it over and said, "We need to talk about this question." There was a quick glance from the application to the paper with my explanation still in my hand. Without hesitation she looked me in the eye and simply said, "No we don't." Not satisfied that she understood I gestured to give her the paper and started to say more. She cut me off. "I don't want to know and I don't need to know." She went on to give me a short lecture on my virtues then sent me on my way with the explanation still in my hand. I quickly found a quiet place so others wouldn't see the tears.

> *. . . let all those rejoice who put their trust in You; let them ever shout for joy, because You defend them; let those also who love Your name be joyful in You. For You, O LORD, will bless the righteous; with favor You will surround him as with a shield.*
> —Psalm 5:11,12

Upon our arrival, the first order of business, even before I began my job search, was to find a church. I knew before the move that there wasn't a Calvary Chapel in the area. Yet I was certain God was alive and well in Winona and that He would not leave us without a church. It would be difficult to find a church to replace Calvary Chapel. I had high expectations. At Calvary Chapel I was not the most active congregant, but I loved the church and Pastor Ralph. Admittedly I was, and still am, biased when it comes to Calvary Chapel. But I'm not deceived into thinking that Calvary Chapel is the only game in town.

Our criteria was simple, we were looking for an evangelical church that taught the Bible. I'm surprised how difficult it is to find such a church. Many churches believe the Bible and teach *from* the Bible, but they don't teach the whole Bible. Additionally we were looking for a church that worshiped and where there was genuine fellowship among the believers. After visiting almost every church in town, sometimes two churches on a single Sunday, God led us to our new home.

I knew nothing about the Evangelical Free Church. I took it all in. The traditional building, the parking lot filled with cars, the wide range of ages, the mix of casual and formal dress. The people were friendly and there seemed to be a real depth of fellowship. Looking around it was obvious that people weren't just singing songs; they were worshiping God. Although it was different than what I was accustomed to, I felt at home. Then when the pastor got up to speak it all came together. It was obvious that he was teaching through Scripture, picking up where he had left off the previous week. But the clincher was that morning he was teaching from exactly where Ralph was teaching when we left Oceanside. I don't believe in coincidence; it was clear that this was to be our new church home.

Within a couple of weeks I met with the pastor. I shared some of my background with him (but not all of it) and informed him that this was our new church home. Unfortunately I also made it clear that I considered Calvary Chapel to be superior. Thankfully he was gracious and didn't take offense. The EV Free Church in Winona would be an important part of my life for the next four years. I would grow in many ways through that ministry. Not the least of which would be a change in my attitude about churches other than Calvary Chapel.

God equips all believers with at least one spiritual gift for the work of ministry. I have the gift of teaching. I have always had an innate ability to expound on God's Word. Over the years I have had many people recognize this aptitude, so I know this is not speculation or wishful thinking. There also is no boast in making this proclamation. It is God who equips; we have nothing to do with it. Previously this aptitude revealed itself in one on one conversation or in small groups. I hadn't taught in a formal or structured setting.

Listening to Ralph expound on God's Word fueled my desire to teach. Ralph would read the passage, bring understanding to the words and then apply the message to our lives, just like Ezra did for the Israelites after the captivity (Neh. 8). It looked simple. It is, if God has called you to that ministry and equipped you with the gift of teaching. It is certainly a lot simpler than teaching a topical study. Expository teaching is a distinctive of Calvary Chapel. The entire Bible is taught, book-by-book, chapter-by-chapter, and verse-by-verse. This way the people receive all of God's counsel. Teaching all of God's Word serves to minimize the spread of false teachings and divisions over disputable matters.

The announcement in the church bulletin read, "Teacher needed for college-age Sunday school class." My heart leaped; there was no doubt in my mind that I was the man for the job. But I didn't know if they would let me teach the class. We hadn't been coming for very long and we were not official members of the church. Then silly me had told the pastor that I'd never be a member because I didn't believe in a congregational church government. Fortunately they didn't hold it against me and I was allowed to teach the class. Additionally within six months God humbled me and we submitted to the work He was doing by becoming church members.

At home I was already having Bible studies with my family. When we first moved to Winona I talked to the Lord a lot about my desire to teach. His response was that I needed to begin by teaching my family. It was a great time for us. During the first couple of years the kids were so into our family Bible study that they would invite their friends. It's interesting to me that the opportunity to teach the Sunday school class came shortly after we started our home study. I don't believe it was a coincidence. True to God's Word, once I was faithful in the one area, God opened up new opportunities. Although it wasn't my perspective at the time, today I'd say that the greater and more important ministry was teaching my family.

College Sunday school was a tough class. I suspect that may be why it was so easy for me to get the job. Attendance was sporadic. With two universities Winona is not short on college students. Yet there was usually only one or two students and rarely the same people showed up two weeks in a row. Many weeks no one showed up. Yet

I remained faithful to study God's Word and prepare to teach each week. During the year and a half that I taught the class, there wasn't any growth in numbers, however there was evidence of growth in the lives of those who attended.

In addition to teaching at church, I had the privilege of ministering to the guys in the local jail. Over the years I've discovered a lot of believers in jail. Not just temporary jailhouse conversions, but guys who have a personal relationship with Jesus but have not dealt with sin in their lives: guys who have never been taught God's Word or been discipled. I could totally relate. My standard procedure was to first determine if they were saved. Once that issue was settled, we'd spend the time exploring God's Word with an emphasis on application. At the time, I spoke to them with boldness and authority believing I had it together. Looking back I realize that I had little to offer. Whatever fruit came from that ministry was the result of God working in spite of me, not because of me.

The summer Sunday school session was coming and it was time to confirm my continued commitment. I was considering taking the summer off. The college class was nearly non-existent in the summer months and I admit that I was getting discouraged at the poor attendance. I never got the chance. The Sunday school director informed me that the college class was canceled for the summer. He went on to say that they planned to offer two adult classes instead and wanted to know if I would teach one of them. Without hesitation I jumped at the chance. Actually my flesh jumped at the chance. Finally a real opportunity to teach. Maybe I'd finally get the recognition I deserved. How pathetic!

Typically the adult classes were topical studies based on some book other than the Bible. I had been teaching the college class using the expository method I learned from Calvary Chapel. It was very effective. No one, except the students (who were generally not regular church members), knew how I structured my lesson plan. No one asked, and I was left alone to do whatever I thought best. But now I was asked to submit a lesson plan with information on the book I planned to use. I received a quizzical look when I said that I was using only the Bible and my outline was the book of Daniel. At one point I was challenged that teaching directly from the Bible wouldn't work, that people wouldn't be interested. I was convinced that they were wrong.

The first day I arrived overly prepared. Filled with anticipation and high hopes I set up the classroom and waited for the students to arrive. To my dismay only two people came. Careful to conceal my disappointment, I poured everything I had into that class. But it was hard to remain focused over the commotion from the other adult class. There must have been fifty people in that room! To add to my frustration I could recognize the voice of the teacher; it was the pastor of the church! My class didn't stand a chance. As far as I was concerned we should just move my class in with his and forget the whole thing.

One of the two students was an older gentleman, a man of spiritual maturity and good reputation. At the end of the class he stayed back to talk with me. His were words of encouragement. Simply teaching from the Bible was refreshing for him. He told me that it was obvious that I had the gift of teaching. He exhorted me to persist and not become discouraged. He left and then the pastor came in to talk to me. He said that he knew that teaching a class opposite the pastor would be difficult. They had considered that when they made the decision to have two classes. It was also why they asked me to teach the class. They noted my faithfulness in teaching the college class and believed I would be the right person for the task. He also encouraged me to persist and not become discouraged. On top of that, God was speaking to me. It didn't matter how many people came. I was to remain faithful and let Him deal with the outcome.

So what could I do? What else was there to do? I humbled myself, submitted to the Lord, and continued to teach the class. Then to my amazement the class began to grow. A couple of new people each week until by the end of the summer there were over twenty people regularly attending. I went on in the fall to teach another adult class and it grew. For the next two years I would teach an adult Sunday school class. Eventually the class had to be moved into the main sanctuary because there were over eighty people attending.

I struggled with my pride while teaching that class. The Lord often had to remind me that this wasn't about me; it was about Him. Whatever ability I had was a gift from God; I didn't earn it or deserve it. Truthfully there wasn't that much giftedness in my teaching. I simply followed the example of expository teaching I had learned at Calvary Chapel. I wasn't at all original. I listened to teaching tapes and stole from everyone. I'm convinced today that what was really going on was that God's people were hungry for God's Word. In Numbers 22 God spoke to Balaam through a donkey: this time I was the ass He chose to use.

In addition to teaching adult Sunday school, I facilitated a couple of midweek classes. One was a prophecy series using materials from Chuck Missler, and the other was a series using the "Jesus Style" by Gayle Erwin. Additionally I was involved in coordinating a worship night where the worship team from Twin Cities Calvary Chapel led the music. I helped organize men's retreats, participated in evangelistic outreach, taught a Bible study in the public housing facilities, and was on the church counseling team.

Within a short time I became a recognized member of the community. I couldn't leave my house at two o'clock in the morning without running into someone who knew me—far different from my life in California were I could easily live in obscurity. Winona provided me with accountability that made it difficult to pursue sinful behavior. Consequently I didn't drink or use drugs, and I had self-control over my perverse sexual habits as long as I stayed in Winona. However, every time I would leave town, usually a couple of times a year for work, I would fall back into old patterns of sin. I wouldn't drink or use drugs, but I did watch pornography in hotel rooms, frequent strip clubs, and commit acts of indecent exposure. This was always followed by intense remorse and a vow to never do it again. At one point my answer to the problem was simply to never leave Winona: impractical, and as I would find out, not God's will.

I wasn't open about my struggle. The pastor knew a little, but not much. I shared just enough to gain credibility with the guys at the jail. I tried to convince myself that it was between me and God, that no one else needed to know. I knew better. Ralph's words still echoed and I was acutely aware of what the Bible had to say. But I relished the esteem people had for me and didn't want to spoil my reputation. Consequently my life lacked real fellowship, and there was a wall keeping out those who cared for me the most. This cloud of secretiveness cast a dark shadow on all my relationships.

For many people the definition of "friend" is simply someone with whom you are "friendly." In my vocabulary that would be an "acquaintance." For me a friend was much more. A friend would be someone I could trust with my deepest secrets. They would be intensely loyal and dependable. They would never knowingly hurt me. Their love would be unconditional. Sounds like I was looking for a dog, not a person. Consequently throughout my life I have had many acquaintances but few friends. Painfully, my egotism destroyed the few friendships I did have. It seems I wasn't willing to be the friend that I wanted others to be.

Throughout my life I have had a strong desire for this depth of relationship. Today I know that person should have been my wife. In Winona I began looking for someone to fill this role, and I mean only one. It hadn't occurred to me that it was possible to develop fellowship with more than one person at a time. In reflection, I feel sorry for the unsuspecting soul chosen to fill this void. They better not have any other friendships, because meeting my needs would be a full-time job.

It took three years in Winona before I was willing to trust someone. It was a brother in the church I met shortly after we arrived. We hit it off immediately and our friendship began to blossom. It's difficult to say why; we were very different people with totally different backgrounds. Yet from the beginning I trusted him. He was one of only three people in the church who knew I had been to prison (of course none of them knew the true circumstances of why I went to prison). Our families spent time together; we ministered together; he even attended a couple of Calvary Chapel conferences with me. When I became overbearing with my constant patter of "That's not how we did it at Calvary Chapel" he was the guy who said to me, "You're not at Calvary Chapel anymore." He could rebuke me without my becoming defensive. Amazing!

We were both involved in the church's counseling ministry. The ministry was Bible based using material developed by Dr. Neil Anderson ("The Bondage Breaker," "Victory Over Darkness"). Dr. Anderson promoted confession as a tool in breaking the bondage of sin. The counseling format was for the person to write a personal life inventory that he then shared with another mature believer. I had sat through a couple of these sessions providing prayer support. Seeing the benefit firsthand and believing in its biblical soundness I began to write my own inventory. My inventory was over sixty handwritten pages that took over six hours for me to share. This brother was patient and gracious. When finished, I was drained but had a sense of accomplishment. However, something was still missing. I wouldn't discover what it was until much later. It's one thing to come into the light; it's quite another thing to walk in the light. Furthermore, there was someone else who needed to hear my account, someone who should have heard it first—my wife.

chapter 15

Foxes in the vineyard

Catch us the foxes, the little foxes that spoil the vines . . .
—Song of Songs 2:15

"Little foxes," fox cubs, spoil the vines by eating the fruit, the new growth and the tender roots. The damage isn't usually enough to destroy the plant, just enough to stunt its growth and ruin the produce. Fox cubs may seem cute and innocent. But an experienced vinedresser knows just how destructive they can be and will take precautions to keep them out of the vineyard.

This passage is not about horticulture; it's a metaphor. The vines are the life of the believer; the foxes are those things that threaten that life. "Little foxes that spoil the vines" are everyday things that challenge the spiritual life and vitality of the believer. Little foxes are often guised in innocence; they hide behind good intentions. Gross persecutions and trials usually strengthen a person's faith. It's the little compromises and distractions that eat away gradually at the fruit, the new growth, and the tender roots of a believer's life.

The big, the bad, and the ugly—gross sin that caused great damage characterized my life. The persecutions and trials were self-induced. I'm ashamed that I find myself under the conviction of Peter's words, *"It is better . . . to suffer for doing good than for doing evil"* (1 Pet. 3:17). My suffering came from doing evil. Yet, to God's credit I'm still here. He has been faithful to preserve me in spite of my foolishness. But not without consequences; a lifetime of turmoil has left its mark.

Picture an old and weathered grapevine, gnarled and scarred from years of abuse. The trunk is twisted and misshapen; the years of heavy pruning are evident. While it's not considered one of the prize vines in the vineyard, this vine is precious to the vinedresser, so He gives it the extra care it needs. He is determined to keep it alive and see that it bears fruit. Consequently the root has grown deep; every year there is new growth and the fruit, while not always abundant, is good. Yet this vine is especially susceptible to the damage caused by the little foxes. Their mischief won't utterly destroy this plant, but the damage to the new growth and fruit is especially devastating.

There have been many little foxes in my life, distractions that keep me from following God wholeheartedly, compromises that draw me away and limit my ability to bear fruit. The cares of this world, the pursuit of recreation and leisure, the desire for personal accomplishment and recognition, selfish ambition, and the love of money, all things that the Bible warns against, things that hinder the lives of all believers. Given my capacity for sin, the last thing I needed were "little foxes" further hindering my relationship with God.

The phone rang; it was Mike, pastor of Twin Cities Calvary Chapel. I knew Mike from Oceanside. Mike had moved to the Twin Cities prior to our coming to Winona. I contacted him shortly after our arrival. Upon answering the phone, Mike said he had a surprise. Before I could respond someone else was on the line. The voice was unmistakable; it was Chik. Chik had moved to Minnesota to assist Mike, but the Lord had plans for two Calvary Chapels in the Twin Cities. Ultimately Mike would pastor Twin Cities Calvary Chapel while Chik would pastor St. Paul Calvary Chapel.

By the end of the conversation Chik was coming to Winona. I had more than a little apprehension about the visit. Chik is a nut, a total nut for Jesus. In Oceanside I admit I was critical of Chik, yet at the same time I held him in high regard. I cautiously looked forward to his arrival. Later I would learn that Chik was even more apprehensive. The last he knew of me I didn't have a very good reputation. To be prepared for the worst, Chik and his wife armed themselves with a secret signal that communicated it was time to leave. They didn't use it.

We had a great time. We discussed what God was doing in each of our lives; he shared the vision for Calvary Chapel in the Midwest. It was a time of fellowship and getting to know each other better. Chik and his family spent the night and came to church with us in the morning. He saw the work that God was doing through the EV Free Church and how God was using me.

Over the next couple of years we would get together often. At his invitation I attended the Midwest Pastor's Conferences in Indiana and the Upper Midwest Leadership conferences in Wisconsin. Eventually I began to open up. I shared many things about my life that were previously kept hidden. I had no idea at the time the extent of what God would do through this friendship. I certainly didn't know that Chik was praying for God to move me up to the cities to be a part of the work God was doing through Calvary Chapel. Personally, I think it should be a lesson to Chik to be careful what you pray for; things don't always turn out the way you want.

The job as an employment counselor was still going strong even after three years. It showed no sign of slowing down. After I was hired on a permanent basis, a less enthusiastic colleague challenged me, "You've got the job, you can slow down now." She missed the point. I loved what I was doing. Slowing down didn't cross my mind. Actually, it surprised me a little that not everyone shared my enthusiasm.

In spite of my passion for the job, I was becoming restless. The problem? I had mastered most everything there was to learn. My duties had become rote; there were few new challenges. It wasn't in my character to settle into a routine for the next twenty years just to collect a retirement check. I began looking for new opportunities.

When first hired, I was walking in simple faith in God, trusting Jesus to direct my path. I was respectfully vocal about my faith with colleagues and clients. Four years later, I had become comfortable and secure. My trust was less in God and more in my achievements. I had tasted the fruit of worldly success and hungered for more. No longer was I in awe of how God had supernaturally provided. I had told the story of the miraculous interview so many times it had become routine, just another tale. The little foxes were in the vineyard.

Hiding in Winona was not truly dealing with my sin. I wasn't drinking or using drugs, and perverse sexual behaviors were much less frequent and extreme. However, this victory came from the external sanctuary God had provided. Sinful habits reemerged whenever I was away from the safety of community, church, and family. God desired for me to have victory over sin. It was time to move.

For a while I had been looking at other opportunities in state employment. Faithfully I checked the announcements for open positions, promotional opportunities, and short-term projects. Nothing I came across was significant enough to uproot my family and leave the security of Winona. It was going to take something big, really big. It would have to be an irresistible opportunity of a lifetime: something challenging that would spur my passion and hold my attention. Additionally there would have to be significant financial incentives, and all my relocation costs would have to be covered. Not likely!

I must have read the announcement a dozen times and I still sat there staring at the bulletin in disbelief. This was it, the ultimate opportunity. There couldn't have been a more perfect position if I had designed it myself. It was as though they had created the job with just me in mind. To some extent they had; my manager was on the team that created the position.

Government employment services had changed little since their inception in the nineteen thirties: labor-intensive, archaic, bureaucratic, it was time for a change. In their defense, not all government employees fit the common stereotypes. Most are competent and highly motivated. There is a real commitment to quality. They are passionate about their work and believe they are contributing to the greater good. However, it was time for a significant change in process and business philosophy. Consequently, the Redesign Project was conceived.

The Redesign Project was an effort to bring needed change into government employment services in Minnesota. The project team would recommend statewide changes in specific areas such as employer services, applicant services, marketing, and technology. Recommendations would be based on research from focus groups and surveys with employers, applicants, and staff. The team would be comprised of five staff under the supervision of a director. To provide credibility and a monetary incentive, the staff positions would be classified as Management Analysts. For me it was a very large jump in pay. Additionally, all my moving expenses were paid including all closing costs to sell our house and purchase a new home.

The mission of the project was to recommend changes to management. Once the recommendations were complete the project would be dissolved and the staff would either go back to their previous positions or move on to other opportunities. There were no guarantees. However, there was inference that staff from the project might be retained to implement the recommended changes. It never made it that far; six months into the effort the project was shut down.

The director notified the team on a Friday that the project was being disbanded. She painted a bleak and despairing picture for our futures. She was openly critical of the powers to be and made no effort to hide her own frustration. Needless to say, we all left that day feeling abused and abandoned. Each of us went home to contemplate our futures. For my part I vented my frustration working arduously in the yard while praying. I wanted to rest in God and trust that He had a plan. But the more I prayed and thought about my situation, the harder I worked at pulling weeds and the angrier I became.

Work that next week was difficult; a dark gloom seemed to fill the room. Everyone was solemn, a far cry from the highly optimistic and enthusiastic work environment of the past six months. We were all waiting for the axe to drop. Other than that one conversation with the director, there was nothing official. In fact, everything was quiet, too quiet. The silence only made it worse. The team was falling apart. The anger and the tension continued to increase. Someone had the foresight to notify the assistant commissioner and an emergency meeting was immediately scheduled.

The project director began the meeting with an apology. She had been instructed not to release information concerning the future of the project to the team. When all plans were finalized the assistant commissioner intended to meet with us personally. The project director also had no business venting her frustrations with us. The assistant commissioner went on to tell us that although the project was being shut down, the redesign effort would continue. Short-term, the project had limited potential to affect change. Therefore redesign of employment services would be integrated into the ongoing operations.

I was reassigned to a permanent position as a management analyst reporting directly to the assistant commissioner. Eventually the position reported to a director of operations. Additionally my job duties were expanded to include implementation of new business processes and services. The work was innovative, creative, and challenging. My involvement was so extensive and varied that I was introduced at a conference as the department's own Renaissance man.

- Facilitated work teams
- Conference speaker at state and national conferences
- Developed and implemented statewide job search curriculum
- Taught technical classes and workshops
- Total quality management facilitator
- Evaluated ISO9000 standards for use in government services
- Facilitated strategic planning sessions with management
- Represented the agency at interagency meetings and before government officials
- Evaluated and implemented computer software
- Member of agency's Internet Standards & Practices oversight team
- Developed one of the first on-line applications for unemployment benefits in the country

I was involved in many projects and initiatives; the previous list summarizes only some of them. If I weren't asked to participate in a project in which I had an interest, I would volunteer. Within a short time I had established a good reputation among employment service providers throughout the state, and had an excellent reputation with management.

On two occasions I was offered management positions in a field office. I declined. I liked working at the state level; managing a local office would be boring in comparison. Furthermore they couldn't offer any financial incentive since I already made as much or more than an office manager. I'd hold out for something at the state office. My supervisor on a couple of occasions spoke to me about my future; in time I would become a director. He even told me once that he could see me as a future assistant commissioner. My future was secure. I had weathered two major lay-offs (management found ways to keep my position protected). I was assured that I was the last person they wanted to see leave. So it was a huge shock when I gave notice that I was quitting. But I'm getting ahead of myself.

Surely men of low degree are a vapor [empty], men of high degree are a lie [fail]; if they are weighed on the scales, they are altogether lighter than vapor [vain].

—Psalm 62:9

Men at their worst and at their best live vain empty lives apart from God. I have been that man of low degree, empty and alone. I have also tasted of what it's like to be a man of high degree, at least by the standards of this world. This, too, is vain.

Throughout my life I longed for worldly success. Academic and psychological reports always contained a statement that I was not living up to my potential. The world around me conveyed happiness and success as synonymous, the prime measures of success being the esteem of others and the accumulation of wealth. I bought into the idea that fulfillment comes from professional accomplishment. This helps to explain why for so much of my life I was dissatisfied and discontent. While living a life of low degree I was longing for a life of high degree. Eventually I would discover that both are meaningless.

Do you see a man wise in his own eyes? There is more hope for a fool than for him.

—Proverbs 26:12

My employment with the state of Minnesota began in simple faith, trusting in God's wisdom to guide me. I sought God's counsel and applied biblical wisdom in my duties. I would pray before speaking in meeting, counseling clients, or presenting workshops. But most important, I was content and happy to simply be one of

His children. By the end of my employment nine years later, I had become wise in my own eyes. What had started as a work of faith was now being sustained through my own effort. I put myself back under the curse and my labor became toilsome.

> *For the love of money is a root of all kinds of evil, for which some have strayed from the faith in their greediness, and pierced themselves through with many sorrows.*
> —1 Timothy 6:10

Money is not evil. The love of money is the problem, a problem that plagues the rich and the poor alike. As long as I can remember I've loved money. It didn't matter if I had little or much. In my youth I envied the lives of my wealthy friends. I coveted the lifestyle and affluence that accompanies wealth. So through my employment God allowed me to learn first hand that money doesn't satisfy. Our combined income went from just above poverty prior to moving to Minnesota to a healthy middle-class income. Instead of bringing security and fulfillment to our lives, it was the root of all kinds of evil and contributed to my straying from the faith.

Money became one of the little foxes in my life. It wasn't enough by itself to destroy my faith. Instead it brought compromise and complacency. No longer did I have to trust God to provide for our needs. I stopped praying over the finances. There was always money to buy things. Abundance encouraged the pursuit of recreation and leisure. The accumulation of more became an obsession. I tithed faithfully and gave generously, but it wasn't a sacrifice. It came from our excess or abundance. It was a larger amount of money, but it required much less faith to give.

> *He who trusts in his riches will fall, but the righteous will flourish like foliage.*
> —Proverbs 11:28

"So, how was work today?"

"Biblical. It was everything God promised it would be."

*"Cursed is the ground for your sake; in toil you shall eat of it all the
days of your life . . ."*

—Genesis 3:17

Most of my life has been characterized by a desperate need for recognition. This compulsion has motivated my work and play. Consequently, fulfillment in my labor has been elusive; I'm rarely content. My labor has been toilsome (employment, academic, ministry). Not just a physical burden by the sweat of my brow, but emotionally and spiritually toilsome.

When Adam and Eve fell, they brought down a curse on mankind. Overnight everything changed. Paradise was gone, replaced by toil and suffering. They became slaves to the very creation that they once ruled. No longer could they live content in intimate fellowship with God. Now they had to struggle to survive. Their relationship with God was strained.

Many people believe that work is the curse. Work is not the curse; the curse was that our labor would become toilsome. There is a perception that before the fall Adam and Eve did nothing but hang out in the garden. Actually, as soon as God created Adam He gave him something meaningful to do—name the animals.[1]

It's God's nature to labor. Just look around. God is an architect, engineer, and artist. He holds all things together, directs celestial bodies, and presides over His creation. Since Jesus' ascension into heaven, God has been preparing an entirely new dwelling place.[2] It took God six days to create the wondrous world in which we currently live. He's been working on a new heaven and earth for over two thousand years. Do the math! Just try and imagine what heaven will be like (for a glimpse check out Revelation 21).

Many believe that heaven is an eternal retirement plan where we will sit around with nothing to do. I don't agree. I'm convinced that there will be meaningful things to do in heaven; yet I admit I have no idea what they are; but I am certain they will not be toilsome. Some might complain, "Heaven is supposed to be a place of rest." That's

---

[1] Genesis 2:19,20
[2] John 14:2; Revelation 21:1

true. But in God's economy what is rest? Certainly there is a rest that implies the absence of labor. God rested on the seventh day (from His creative efforts, not from His administrative duties). Jesus and His disciples rested. Yet is rest only a state of physical inactivity? Or, is there a different kind of rest? A rest for our souls that is available to us in the midst of our labors.

> *Come to Me, all you who labor and are heavy laden, and I will give you rest. Take My yoke upon you and learn from Me, for I am gentle and lowly in heart, and you will find rest for your souls. For My yoke is easy and My burden is light.*
> —Matthew 11:29–30

To "rest in Jesus" doesn't mean the absence of labor. Rest in Jesus produces an absence of toil and strife. When Jesus died and was resurrected, He redeemed more than we can imagine. The fall brought a curse on our labor, but Jesus has overcome the curse. When our labor is done to glorify God, it is no longer toilsome. In Jesus our labor becomes meaningful worship to God. But when we labor to glorify self, we place ourselves back under the curse. We then share in Solomon's lamentation—

> *Then I looked on all the works that my hands had done and on the labor in which I had toiled; and indeed all was vanity and grasping for the wind.*
> —Ecclesiastes 2:11

When I speak of labor, I refer to both our vocation and our avocation. I'm not just talking about what we do to earn a living or our domestic responsibilities. I'm including our service to God, our hobbies and interests. Any place we employ our time, talent and energy is our labor. Everything we do is done best when it's done unto the Lord. Jesus wants to be a part of our whole life. There should be no separation between secular and spiritual in the life of the believer.

> *For we are His workmanship, created in Christ Jesus for good works, which God prepared beforehand that we should walk in them*
> —Ephesians 2:10

Jesus came as a man, lived, died, and was resurrected so that we could have a personal relationship with Him; period. God didn't save us because He needs our help. We are "His workmanship," literally His poem, His creative expression. God has prepared "good works" for His children to do because He loves spending time with us and knows that it's healthy for us to keep busy.

Envision a very young child helping his father. The child will slow the progress and ultimately create more work. Yet the father loves spending time with the child so much that he doesn't mind the inconvenience. Furthermore, when children get bored they tend to whine and complain; they're more likely to fight with their siblings and get into trouble. Children are happier and healthier when they have something to do.

If you want to grow in your relationship with Jesus, participate with Him in the work that He has prepared for you. However don't become a Martha who was distracted by her labor and missed out on fellowship with Jesus.[3] Learn to know when to sit at His feet and when to serve by His side. Never let your labor take you away from your relationship with Him. Be aware that your self-centered sinful nature will resist and Satan will come against you. The last thing Satan wants is for you to enjoy being a productive member of the body of Christ.

God doesn't ask us to accomplish a good work without also giving us the necessary tools. Every believer has at least one spiritual gift and numerous talents and abilities. God intends these to be used for His purpose.

Are all apostles? Are all prophets? Are all teachers? Are all workers of miracles? Do all have gifts of healings? Do all speak with tongues? Do all interpret? But earnestly desire the best gifts.
—1 Corinthians 12:29,30

We are not all called to do the same ministry in the same way. Ministries may be similar, share the same vision, and have the same philosophy, yet God works uniquely through the individual. The

---

[3] Luke 10:40

prophets of the Old Testament had many things in common. They were a uniform and consistent voice proclaiming God's truth. Yet their ministries were very different. Compare the lives of the Major Prophets: Isaiah, Jeremiah, Ezekiel, and Daniel. They were very different individuals with unique backgrounds and ministries, yet all prophets. Likewise no two believers are gifted in exactly the same way. It's up to each one of us to seek (desire) the best gifts. "What are the best gifts?" you might ask. The answer is, the gifts that God wants you to have; those gifts that will equip you for the work of the ministry to which you were called.

God equips the called, He doesn't call the equipped. God isn't looking for people with specific skills and abilities. He isn't screening applicants to fill a job description. Your great intellect and natural ability are not important to God. He's looking for people who share His heart for a lost and dying world. Our great potential means nothing. People with seemingly the greatest potential are often the least productive. All that matters in God's economy is the condition of our heart. God can use a donkey to speak for Him,[4] or he can have the stones proclaim His glory.[5] If you have a heart for the things of God and desire to be used by Him, you have met the qualifications for ministry.

> *Let this mind be in you which was also in Christ Jesus, who, being in the form of God, did not consider it robbery to be equal with God, but made Himself of no reputation, taking the form of a bondservant, and coming in the likeness of men.*
> —Philippians 2:5–7

Jesus went before us and set the standard for us to follow. Jesus didn't take advantage of who He is, God in the flesh, *"In the beginning was the Word, and the Word was with God, and the Word was God"* (John 1:1). He also didn't exercise His power and authority but *"made Himself of no reputation."* Ponder this: *"He [Jesus] was in the beginning with God. All things were made through Him, and*

---

4 Number 21:22–36
5 Luke 19:40

without Him nothing was made that was made" (John 1:2,3). God, the Creator of the universe, humbled Himself and became a man of no reputation. But that's not all. He also became a bondservant (slave). The idea of willingly becoming a slave is difficult for us to comprehend. Slavery was common in the days of Jesus and the early church. In the Roman Empire one-third of all persons were slaves. People became slaves through conquest, indebtedness, and birth. Slaves were bought, sold, and traded. Some entered into slavery for a specific period of time. Others were able to purchase their freedom.

The bondservant was a unique class of slave. The bondservant willingly and willfully entered into slavery for life. This is the picture given us of what Jesus did when He came as a man, submitted to the Father, and gave His life for us. Jesus came to serve, not to be served. He was others-centered, not self-centered. Instead of building His reputation, He humbled Himself and became of no reputation. This is the mind-set and attitude we need to have. We need to learn to become bondservants.

> *As each one has received a gift, minister it to one another, as good stewards of the manifold grace of God.*
> —1 Peter 4:10

As we grow in our faith God expects us to become good stewards of the resources with which we have been entrusted. Again, we do this not because He needs anything from us, but because it is to our benefit to submit to God. These resources include our time, our talents, and our treasure. We are responsible to God for all three; one out of three or even two out of three isn't enough. We can't do more with one to compensate for the others. For example, we can't justify not tithing because we are faithful to serve, or conversely we can't buy back our time by tithing more.

Unfortunately too many believers do not seek out the good works God has prepared for them. There are many excuses, but the end result is the same. Believers who do not get adequate spiritual exercise become fat and lazy. They lack discipline. They whine and complain and frequently need their diapers changed. When you have a whole church full of immature believers, you have a smelly mess.

Encourage others to get out of themselves and serve Jesus. Persuading other believers to exercise their fat spiritual butts is one of the most loving things you can do for them. Be aware, they will resist and misunderstand your motives. Don't let their resistance stop your discipleship. You may have to back off for a time, but don't quit. They will thank you later . . . or not. It shouldn't matter as long as you're being faithful to God's call in your life.

If you're a church leader, find something for everyone to do. Keep the sheep moving. There will be much less backbiting and complaining, and little time for gossip. But don't forget to stop and let the flock enjoy the green pastures and still waters.[6] There is strength and unity in an active, serving church. Those who participate in the work of ministry share in the vision; they grow in their faith and enjoy a greater depth of fellowship with other believers. Those who do not are stagnant in their faith and detached from fellowship. Typically they complain about the church being cold and uncaring. In a vibrant church they almost never last very long.

---

[6] Psalm 23

chapter 16

Chik

D o you know what to do if something happens to us in Israel?"
Chik said as he handed me the keys. "I know how to lock the
doors and call Ralph." It was funny at the time. Chik wasn't really
concerned about it; he knew everything was in God's control. He
also knew that I was anxious about being left in charge while much
of the church went on a tour to Israel. But, as the only elder not going, I was the obvious choice.

It was 1997 and I had been in St. Paul for three years. The church
was small. It was small when we came and wasn't much larger three
years later. But Calvary Chapel St. Paul has never acted like a small
church.

There seems to be no limit to the vision that God has given Chik.
There is also seemingly no limit to his motivation and energy. For
many years Chik worked part-time jobs to support his family, attended college classes, and home-schooled his children while he
worked the ministry full-time. Frequently I've heard him challenge
interns and assisting pastors, "If you can catch up to me in ministry,
then you can be the pastor." Good luck! It's not likely to happen.
Anyway those who've come close now pastor other churches that
God has used Chik to plant in Minnesota.

While the church was small in numbers, it was large in heart. It's
a serving church boasting over sixty percent of its members actively participating in the ministry (compared to ten percent in most
churches). Other Calvary Chapel pastors have said to Chik they wish
God would send them people like his. That's funny. People don't

generally arrive at Calvary Chapel St. Paul with a heart for ministry and ready to serve. It's a direct result of Chik's discipleship.

Chik started the Intern program when there were maybe only thirty people in the church. The program teaches the vision and philosophy of ministry while strengthening a person's faith and increasing their knowledge of Scripture. Anyone destined for ministry, therefore everyone, is encouraged to participate. Later on he would add the Joshua Group for training future pastors and assisting pastors.

Chik has the heart of a pastor; he's a shepherd who will lay his life down for the sheep. He fiercely protects those whom God has entrusted to his care. Woe to anyone who tries to deceive, manipulate, or harm his flock. Yet he's quick to forgive and full of grace for those who are repentant. He's the guy you can call to jump start your car at two o'clock in the morning, and he'll do it joyfully as though it's a privilege. Chik is the most selfless man I've ever known. A virtue lost on many people because they misinterpret his confidence, boldness, and gregariousness. This world is full of uncertainties, but one thing I am absolutely certain of is that Chik loves me and there is nothing I can do about it.

Chik has the gift of badgering and he's not afraid to use it. While respectful, he's not a respecter of persons; he's not afraid to lovingly hurt your feelings. "Open rebuke is better than love carefully concealed. Faithful are the wounds of a friend . . ." (Prov. 27:5,6) exemplifies Chik. He believes that we are to be our brothers' keepers and isn't afraid to get his hands dirty. I've heard him say on several occasions that the church would have a larger attendance if he would just stay out of people's business. However, the ministry would not be nearly as successful.

In the early days of Calvary Chapel St. Paul there was a family in distress. They were homeless with two young children living in a car. The father had brought this plight on his family as a result of his sinful behaviors. Chik and others in the church had been counseling the man, but he was rebellious and unrepentant. So when they lost their home and were on the streets Chik addressed the congregation. "Do not help them. God is using this situation to do a work in their lives. If you help them, the sin that got them there won't be dealt with. You will only prolong their suffering." I was horrified. I had become friends with the guy and I had the means to help. But I chose to respect Chik's counsel and waited to see what would happen.

To everyone's delight the man repented. As soon as he did, Chik and the church raced in to help them get back on their feet. Years later they are still walking strongly with the Lord. The right thing to do is not often the easiest. God uses the consequences of our sin to get our attention. Easing those consequences is not usually the loving thing to do. Chik loves people enough to do the right thing, even if it seems harsh. "They'll thank me later," would be his response. As for me, I've learned to trust Chik's wisdom.

"The church is here for the people, the people aren't here for the church." Churches have a bad reputation for taking rather than giving. The focus is on what the people can to do for the church and how the ministry desperately needs their support. Calvary Chapel St. Paul is about the people and Chik goes to the extreme to break the stereotypes. We don't collect tithes and offerings as part of our services. Those who are part of the fellowship know how to give, and Chik is faithful to teach what the Bible says on the subject. The only time the congregation is called upon publicly to give money is when it's to support an outreach event or missionary family; even then it's made clear that only those who consider this their church are asked to give. There are no fund-raising activities such as bake sales or rummage sales. Instead, the church hosts massive community events proclaiming "God's Not Broke," where everything, including those precious bake goods and unwanted household items are given away for free.

"No one in this church will go with an unmet need!" Key words in this Chikism are "in this church" and "unmet need." Usually a person's wants and desires are better left unmet. God established local church bodies to provide for His people and accomplish His work. A believer has to be a part of the fellowship to enjoy this benefit. People not part of the fellowship who call asking for help are referred back to their own church. "Your church won't help? Why not? What's your pastor's name? I'll call him and see what's going on . . . Oh I see, you're not part of a church? Bummer! In this church people's needs are met."

This is not as cold hearted as it might sound. Instead of simply putting a band-aid on the problem this provides a discipleship opportunity. If the person is merely scamming churches, the conversation will go no further. Then they will be on to the next listing in the phone book. However, if receptive, this is an opportunity for them to get plugged into a church where more than just their physical needs can be met.

This isn't to say that Calvary Chapel doesn't minister to people outside the fellowship. Over the years many people outside the church have been helped. Imagine the impact on a single mom or elderly lady (who is not a believer) when a dozen guys with trucks show up to help her move. Or, when brothers and sisters from the church spent two weekends helping a couple (also unbelievers) with repairs on their house. These activities are not rare. This kind of ministry goes on all the time. Calvary Chapel St. Paul is all about reaching the community with the love of Jesus, only meeting the needs (not wants and desires) of those in the fellowship comes first.

"The church is here for the people, the people aren't here for the church" carries a double edge. The church is the people. The church is not an organization or building. The people are the church, so we are to be there for each other. Unfortunately too many believers think they have the bird dog ministry. They're always pointing out needs and making suggestions, but they don't lift a finger to help. Chik would say, "If it's broken fix it; if it's dirty clean it; if there's a need meet it."

Chik defies convention; he doesn't fit the stereotypes of a pastor. Even among Calvary Chapel pastors he's unique. Chik is completely true to the distinctives of Calvary Chapel. At the same time, he's not bound by tradition. He's a man who seeks God's direction and is obedient to His will. Because of early life experience and training, Chik has a unique wisdom and perspective on ministry. He has a gregarious personality and is zealous in his faith. Following are some other common Chikisms:

> ➤ "Those who sweat in training bleed less in battle."
> ➤ "Suck it up! People are dying and going to hell!"
> ➤ "So how does that make you more like Jesus?"
> ➤ "Obedience is the believer's safety net."
> ➤ "What in hell are you looking for?"

- ➢ "Vomitus, carnal, flesh bag of pus."
- ➢ "Always a chance to accept or reject Jesus."
- ➢ B-I-B-L-E, Basic Instructions Before Leaving Earth.
- ➢ "What you do with this information is solely, wholly, totally dependent upon you."
- ➢ "May you leave here more on fire, more committed, more in love with Jesus than when you came."
- ➢ "You're here now."
- ➢ "Not convenient! Ministry isn't supposed to be convenient."
- ➢ "I'd rather be rude enough to get someone into heaven than polite enough to see them go to hell."
- ➢ "I love you and there's nothing you can do about it."
- ➢ "When you come upon something you don't know, fall back on what you do know."

Chik is a unique piece of work. He's one of those guys who leaves a lasting impression. If you've met him you will remember him. When visiting other Calvary Chapels or at church conferences someone might ask, "Who's your pastor? Maybe I know him." If they hesitate at all when you say "Chik," then they've never met him. In the early days other Calvary Chapel pastors would jokingly respond upon hearing that Chik was your pastor with, "I'm sorry, we'll be praying for you." Sadly I would respond by hanging my head saying, "I know, I know." Not anymore. Today without hesitation I quip, "Don't pray for me; my pastor rocks!" Anyway I've noticed that others don't cap on Chik the way they once did. The fruit of his ministry is obvious and his wisdom is undeniable.

> *Then Jesus said to them, "A little while longer the light is with you. Walk while you have the light, lest darkness overtake you; he who walks in darkness does not know where he is going. While you have the light, believe in the light, that you may become sons of light."*
> —John 12:35,36

Since the early days of my faith I've read passages referring to light. They were mysterious to me, even confusing. In sermons these verses

were generally spiritualized ideals without practical application. I
can't recall having witnessed anyone living out these passages; certainly not in the way I see them lived out today. Yet I knew that these
verses were not just theoretical, they were suppose to be lived out in
my life. That scared me! To live these passages meant being open,
honest, and transparent with those around me.

Chik wasn't the first pastor I'd heard teach the practical application
of these verses. Every Calvary Chapel pastor has taught on "walking
in the light." Chik is however the first person I'd known who mod-
eled this behavior.

What you see is what you get with Chik. He is the same in private
as he is in public. He intentionally lives his life in a fish bowl for
everyone to see. Even from the pulpit he will share very personal
struggles and intimate details of his life. The church has lost more
than a few members due to his candor. But that doesn't stop him. He
knows he will lose some. He will even predict it at the beginning of
a message. "Some of you will leave us after tonight; we can't minister
to everyone. If you want a nice polite church where you won't be
confronted with real life issues, see me after the service. I can refer
you to several churches where your faith won't be challenged. As for
this church, we get our hands dirty."

*There are those who rebel against the light; they do not know its ways
nor abide in its paths.*
—Job 24:13

I've believed in Jesus since I was eleven years old; yet I continued
to "abide in darkness." I rebelled against the light because I didn't
understand its ways. It scared me. I worked hard at keeping my sin
hidden. Being open, honest, and transparent was inconceivable. At
the same time I was drawn to the light. Instinctively I knew it would
be the source of healing and victory. God's Word and His Spirit were
loud and clear; there would be no victory over sin, no rest in my life
until I learned to abide in the light. So the conflict within me raged
and my life was isolated from those around me.

A man who isolates himself seeks his own desire; he rages against all wise judgment.

—Proverbs 18:1

The word "isolates" in this passage means to separate or to be out of joint. Isolation is not simply a matter of being alone. On several occasions, Jesus sought solitude. He wasn't isolating himself. God has wired us each a little differently. Some people thrive on social interaction while others prefer solitude: I'm not talking about the party animal or the recluse. Extroverts and introverts can both be driven by selfish sinful motivations. Both personalities usually result from the people thinking of themselves not others. It's just as easy to isolate oneself in a group as it is in solitude. Isolation in the life of the believer is to separate oneself or be out of joint from honest fellowship with other believers. It's to rebel against the light and abide in darkness.

"He who believes in Him is not condemned; but he who does not believe is condemned already . . . And this is the condemnation, that the light has come into the world, and men loved darkness rather than light, because their deeds were evil. For everyone practicing evil hates the light and does not come to the light, lest his deeds should be exposed."

—John 3:18–20

Upon moving to St. Paul, the sanctuary of Winona ended and perverse behaviors resumed. I didn't totally abandon my faith and throw myself headlong into sin; there was an effort on my part to overcome my flesh. Yet my attempts at self-control failed because I was trying to do it alone. While I had taken steps to come into the light, I hadn't learned what it meant to "abide in the light." Furthermore I hadn't taken my struggle to the most important person—my wife.

For the first months of my new job I stayed with Chik during the week and went home to Winona on the weekends. My job would have paid for me to stay in a hotel, but I decided that would be too much temptation. Staying with Chik didn't keep me from sin, but I believe it did minimize it. I can only imagine what I might have done if I had stayed in a hotel. As it is I committed acts of indecent exposure and frequented strip clubs while staying at Chik's. After each offense I would ask God for forgiveness and vow to try harder. I didn't tell anyone about the struggle. Furthermore, I isolated myself to avoid discovery, embarrassment, and confrontation.

Once my family was moved to St. Paul, my perverse behaviors were less frequent (but not absent), at least for a while. I was busy with work and active in the church. One of the areas in which I was involved was in leading the men's ministry. By this time I knew that walking in the light was a missing piece in my life. The emphasis in the men's ministry was small groups. Three to four guys who would meet regularly to pray for each other and be open and honest about their lives. It was immediately apparent that I wasn't the only guy who struggled with living an open and transparent life.

I met with a small group of guys for over two years. These weekly meetings produced good fruit in our lives. I developed friendships that continue today. However, I was guarded in my conversation. I avoided talking candidly about what I was struggling with at the time. Instead I'd talk about past struggles, and even then it was heavily censored. I knew which things I could talk about without losing respect; consequently I never used phrases like indecent exposure, homosexual acts, or attempted rape. (I was still telling people that I went to prison for burglary.) When I did talk about current struggles my words were obscure. I'd talk about "struggling with sexual sin" but not describe specifically the behavior. Struggling with sexual sin means something different to each person. For one person it's a struggle with their thought life, another may be into pornography or strip clubs, while someone else is having an affair.

Amazingly, even with the censorship, I was more open about my life than the other guys (except Chik). I've been told many times how courageous it was for me to be so open and honest. My openness scared many of the guys. Most everyone is hiding something about themselves; it makes people nervous when someone is seemingly being honest. They didn't know that the things I didn't tell them were the big-ticket items. All this did was to increase my lockjaw. If this was too much for the guys to handle there is no way I'd be able to tell the whole story.

I was closer to the light than ever before. For the first time I tasted real fellowship and friendship. There were a few guys that I had begun to open up to on a deeper level. Gradually I confided in them more and more. Yet I couldn't bring myself to tell them my darker sins. I was afraid of what they would think. All guys struggle with sexual sin. For me to talk about it in general terms or talk about socially acceptable sins was deemed honorable, even noble. But if I confessed my depravity, I would risk losing their respect. Never mind that this respect was founded on an abridged and carefully-censored biography. This served only to keep me at arms length from the fellowship I desired and desperately needed.

> He [Jesus] humbled Himself and became obedient to the point of death, even the death of the cross.
>   —Philippians 2:8

The Creator of the universe humbled Himself so that I could have a personal relationship with Him. I couldn't humble myself enough to come into the light and deal with sin. That's pathetic! I was totally hung up on trust. Some people simply don't know how to keep a secret. What if they told someone or held it against me in some way? I still had a prison mentality about not "fronting someone off." It means to not draw attention to another inmate's activities. It's subtler than blatantly ratting (telling) on someone.

An example occurred one night after a men's meeting. With my wife standing next to me, one of the guys said, "I'll be praying for you about that struggle with sexual sin." That was awkward. It immediately threw me into a panic. I couldn't believe he said that in front of my wife. She was the last person with whom I planned to have this discussion. Consequently it strengthened my resolve to keep the truth hidden. He may have done it intentionally to force me to confess to my wife, but I doubt it. It was as though he was oblivious to what he said. Whatever the motive, it served to strengthen my resolve to be careful about whom I trust.

Chik's relationship with his wife terrified me. Chik tells his wife everything, and I mean everything. They both purposed from the beginning of their marriage to be completely open and honest with each other. They admit that it wasn't always easy, but the fruit it produced is phenomenal. I have never witnessed a stronger or godlier marriage than theirs. Chik encouraged the guys to be open and honest with their wives. I knew in my heart he was right. Ralph had told me the same thing back in Oceanside. It was time to give it a try.

"We need to talk," I said mustering up all my courage. Later I'd discover that my wife lived in fear of those four words. Working from the outline I had used with the brother in Winona, I gave the account with the same exclusions. In conclusion I asked her for help in overcoming sexual sin. Instead she withdrew from me more and more over the next months and years. Unfortunately there were several pieces missing from my understanding of marriage. I had no idea what it meant to be a husband. The effort produced no fruit in either of our lives or our marriage.

Chik is not easily deceived. He reads people very well. For some reason Chik has always seen something in me. He knew about my past better than anyone else. He knew I struggled with sexual sin. I don't know if he knew what form it took or how perverse it was. In retrospect he couldn't have known. If he'd known there is no way he would have asked me to become an elder or talked to me about pastoring a church. I remember when he asked me to be an elder I said something about not being qualified because I struggled with [sexual] sin. He replied that the key word in my statement is "struggle." We should be struggling with sin; it's when we cease to struggle there's a problem. I really wanted to be an elder, so I accepted.

The decision to be an elder was fraught with conflict. The irony wasn't lost on me; I was acutely aware of the contradictions. From all outward appearances I looked like I had it together. I was prospering in a good job and was a leader in my church. Outwardly I appeared respectable while a battle raged within. My flesh screamed for fulfillment while Satan toyed with my thoughts. At the same time, God's Spirit continued to speak to my heart while my pastor challenged me to walk in the light. "The water's warm. Don't just get your feet wet. Come all the way into the pool." It was torment. Abandoning my faith wasn't an option, yet sin had a stronghold on my life. Laying it on the line and confessing everything was the obvious next step in the battle.

"Israel will change your life. You will never look at the Bible the same. Scripture will go from black and white to living color." Chik had been promoting the trip to Israel for a long time. I wanted to go. I knew that it would be a life-changing experience. I'm certain that it was God's will. I didn't go . . .

The reasons I stayed behind aren't important. The consequence is what matters. It may be wishful thinking or regret, but today I'm convinced that things would have turned out much differently if I had gone to Israel. It was a difficult time. The duties overseeing the church weren't a problem. From a ministry perspective it was an uneventful two weeks. However, Satan and my flesh worked overtime. The voices in my head screamed, "You're here under false pretense. If people knew the truth, you wouldn't even be allowed to attend this church. Women and children would run from the room screaming." My life was lived in the shadows; on the fringe were light and dark converge. I was headed for one more trip into outer darkness.

chapter 17

Broken cistern

For My people have committed two evils: they have forsaken Me, the fountain of living waters, and hewn themselves cisterns—broken cisterns that can hold no water.

—Jeremiah 2:13

"Two evils." It continues to amaze me how God can cut through the muck and get straight to the point. I'd have said that God's people had committed many more than two evils. Yet it appears that although sin may take various forms, it all boils down to two issues—forsaking God, the source of life, then attempting to fill the void through our own efforts. The best we can hope for apart from God are *"broken cisterns that can hold no water."*

Nevertheless I have this against you, that you have left your first love.
—Revelation 2:4

Just like no one falls in or out of love, no one stumbles into then out of a relationship with God. Believers don't "fall away" from their faith. They walk away. I didn't lose my first love in Jesus; I left Him. By all outward appearances I had it together—good job, family, church leader, respected by those who knew me (or who thought they knew me). The façade I had carefully woven was as Jesus described the religious elite, *"white washed tombs full of dead men's bones"* (Matt. 23:27–28). I looked good on the outside while inside I was rotting away.

For my life is spent with grief, and my years with sighing; my strength fails because of my iniquity, and my bones waste away.
—Psalm 31:10

I had been leading the men's ministries ever since we had arrived in Saint Paul. My heart was for guys struggling with sin (which is all guys at some time or another). The goal was to create a safe place for men to deal openly and honestly with sinful issues in their life. Small group accountability and discussion was the format. Establishing and maintaining trust was paramount.

As incredible as it sounds, I was perceived as one of the most open and honest participants in the group. That's not saying much. I was very careful about what I'd share. It's only that my life is so foul that even a small whiff is offensive. I'd share just enough to stay ahead of the group, usually focusing on carefully-edited past accounts: prostitutes, adultery, drugs, prison (but not the truth about why I was there). When I talked about current struggles, I would speak in generalizations such as, "I'm struggling with sexual sin." I was careful not to define what I meant by sexual sin.

What was the truth? What was I doing at the same time that I was working a great job, raising a family and participating as a leader in my church? What did I mean by "sexual sin?"

All right then, here it is:

I took part in perverse talk on telephone chat lines, frequented strip clubs, and spent countless hours viewing Internet pornography. I engaged in nefarious dialogue on Internet forums role-playing perverse fantasies. I continued to commit acts of indecent exposure. I engaged in sexual activity with prostitutes, and there were several homosexual encounters.

I can't find the words that accurately capture the drama and turmoil. Either you get it or you don't. I can't explain the contradictions, I can't articulate the emotions. The conflict was intense. My appetite for extreme lust was insatiable. It didn't matter that I desperately desired to be free. As long as I was trying to overcome on my own, in my own strength, I remained in bondage to my perverse passions.

Writing this book has caused me great anguish. It took me two months to write the previous paragraphs. Every time I tried, I found myself in tears. I became frustrated and angry. Reliving my life has been exhausting. The thought of someone reading this is horrifying. Like Jonah, I desperately wanted to flee from God's call. During this tumultuous period I wrote the introduction to this book (now might be a good time to review what I said).

My life was a broken cistern. I desperately tried to cover up the cracks, but they were beyond repair. A lifetime of sinful behavior had taken its toll. I was fighting a losing battle. I didn't know it at the time, but it was a battle I needed to lose. You see, the battle wasn't about patching the cracks in my life. I was fighting against God. I had committed the two evils: forsaking God and trying to do it myself.

> *"Because they have ceased obeying the LORD. Harlotry, wine, and new wine enslave the heart . . ."*
> —Hosea 4:10

"I'll come with you." Chik's offer was generous. He was willing to disrupt his schedule and leave his family to go to a conference with me so I wouldn't fall into sin. It caught me off guard. The idea that someone would inconvenience himself for my sake was inconceivable. I turned him down. Ten years later he still laments, "I should have gone to that conference with you." Then he'll say, "You were going to do what you wanted to do. It was just hard to watch you trash your life."

The conference was being held in Chicago. In my work I would attend several conferences of various sizes throughout the year. This was the big one, the National Workforce Center Conference. I was scheduled to speak at one of the breakout sessions, so there was no getting out of going. Brothers from church knew that conferences were a problem for me. They just didn't know how big a problem they were. In their mind the greatest danger was watching the wrong movies in my room. I wish it were that simple.

Chik coming with me to the conference would have most definitely hindered me from pursuing my perverse appetites. God's voice was clearly telling me that it was the right thing to do. Yet my flesh recoiled from the idea. I wanted to pursue my lust. Furthermore I was embarrassed about having my colleagues meet Chik. I had a nicely packaged image to maintain that wouldn't fit with Chik's persona. Furthermore how could I explain why he was there? I wasn't going to tell people that I'm a pervert and need my pastor with me so I don't do something stupid.

From the moment I arrived I began my pursuit of sexual pleasure, and it continued until I went home. I attended very little of the conference. I spent hours in my room looking for pornography on the Internet and watching adult movies. At night I walked the streets looking for strip clubs and prostitutes. The whole time God's voice was strong; He was calling me back to Him. It was horrible. At every turn, my efforts were thwarted. I couldn't find any prostitutes or open strip clubs in Chicago! The pornography didn't satisfy. I knew what was going on. Someone was praying for me. God was giving me one more chance to deal with my sin before turning me over to my passions.

> "Therefore the LORD will give you meat, and you shall eat. You shall eat, not one day, nor two days, nor five days, nor ten days, nor twenty days, but for a whole month, until it comes out of your nostrils and becomes loathsome to you"
> —Numbers 11:19–20

Throughout the Bible there are examples of God giving His children what they wanted or allowing them to run headlong into their own folly to teach them a lesson. He holds people back from their passions for only so long until He lets go. God is a gentleman. He never forces us to walk with Him. If we are hell bent, then a taste of hell is what we will get. Yet He loves His children and won't forsake them. God is determined that His children will be conformed into the image of His Son.[1] This is not always a smooth or pleasant process.

---

[1] Romans 8:29

Matthew Chikeles
Calvary Chapel St. Paul
June 14, 1998
   At the June Board Meeting for Calvary Chapel St. Paul
leadership options were presented. Those options were El-
der/Board of Directors, Board of Directors, or the Joshua
Group (Assisting Pastor). After praying about and considering my continued leadership role, I have decided effective
immediately to resign as an elder of Calvary Chapel St. Paul.
I will not be pursuing any of these options at this time. My
intent is to focus on my walk with Jesus, resolve long-term
habitual sin, and a return to the basics of prayer, fellowship,
and Scripture. This decision in no way represents any dissatisfaction on my part with the ministry of Calvary Chapel
St. Paul. It is my desire to increase participation with the
fellowship. I hope that at some time in the future I will again
have the opportunity to participate in leadership.
   Thank you for the opportunity to serve as an elder of Calvary Chapel St. Paul. It has been a learning experience and
a blessing.

   Reflecting on my resignation as an elder, I have to wonder if any of
this was true. I may have honestly intended to "resolve long-term habitual sin," but I was not planning to come clean about my activities.
As far as I can tell, the rest of this letter is garbage. The truth is that
I was intensely dissatisfied with Calvary Chapel and frustrated with
Chik. I know today that this had everything to do with my sin and
nothing to do with Chik or the church. The realities are that I did
not increase my participation with the fellowship or dedicate myself
to prayer and Scripture. Instead I gave myself over even further to the
pursuit of my passions.
   Following my standard routine, I scoped out the self-service laundry to see who was there. The only person in the place was one woman. The perfect set up. I grabbed the bag of clothes from the car and
went inside. The plan was to look like I was innocently doing a load
and needed to wash the clothes I was wearing. I would strip down

to a pair of shorts (not underwear, a real pair of shorts). That was it; that was the extent of the exposure I had planned. By this time I had become very cautious about overexposing myself. There had been too many close calls. I had been questioned a few times by the police for my behavior. I thought that there was no way to get into trouble if I stuck to the plan.

As soon as the woman saw what I was doing (assuming I was planning to fully expose myself) she ran to the front of the store where, unknown to me, were two guys. They headed my way so I ran. Driving away I frantically prayed for God's forgiveness and made my customary promise to never do it again. At the time, I dismissed the possibility of any criminal consequences. I knew the guys got my license number, but in my mind I hadn't done anything illegal. So it was a bit of a surprise when I got a summons in the mail that I was being charged with indecent exposure. It was an even bigger surprise when they made the charges stick. It was obvious they weren't going to let me off the hook. No doubt they took into account my previous suspicious activities.

The event shook me. It was the final motivator for me to resign as a church elder. I desperately wanted to be free from this bondage. Not because it was wrong, or it hurt those who love me, or it broke the heart of God, but because I hated the consequences. Knowing that confession was a part of God's restoration, not simply confessing to God but to another believer, I went to a brother in the church whom I trusted and told him what had happened. To his credit he stuck to one counsel—I needed to go to Chik. As far as I was concerned, that wasn't going to happen. To his discredit he didn't force me to take it to Chik and as far as I know he didn't go to Chik himself.

I hadn't used alcohol or drugs for nine years, since before we moved to Minnesota. The chaos in my heart and mind was unbearable. I desperately wanted to drown out the noise. After I confessed to the brother, I went to a park and drank a six-pack of beer. It did its job. Of course it didn't stop there. I was immediately thrown back to before I quit. Within a short time I was drinking hard alcohol every day, and it didn't take me long to find a source for pot. I guess the adage "once a drunk always a drunk" is true.

As you might expect, things didn't get better, they got much worse. It wasn't long before I wasn't attending church at all. My wife had already begun distancing herself from the church and me. She focused on her work and spent much of her time with her family in Winona. As for me, I became even more consumed with erotic fulfillment. No more indecent exposure. Instead I frequented strip clubs, browsed the Internet for pornography and perverse dialogue, engaged in sex with prostitutes, and had several homosexual encounters. I'm not going to elaborate any further on these activities. I see no reason to say more. It would be offense to the reader (at least it should be). If it's not offensive, then I run the risk of helping create another pervert.

I hate this book! Have I made that clear? If you ever meet me, please don't start a conversation about my life. Once this book is finished, I'll have said all I plan to say on the subject of me. I'll talk about the biblical principles, or better yet we can talk about you. Only I expect you to be as honest as I've been. Whatever you do, don't ask me to sign a copy of this book or try to ascribe any glory to me for this writing. If you do, expect a verbal thrashing that you won't soon forget. Some of the brothers in my life have already asked me for a signed copy, or they assume I'll be doing book signings when this is finished. This tells me that they don't get it. Anyone who has read this book should be able to understand why I don't want that kind of attention.

Enough of my ranting, I'll get back to the story now.

The last year in my employment had been spent leading an innovative technology project. We successfully created an on-line application for unemployment benefits. It may not sound like much today, but at that time no state in the union had a functional on-line application. All the states were under a directive to develop an application and there was a race to be first. Attending the technology conference in Washington D.C., I was stunned to hear the progress reports from what were considered to be the more progressive states on this initiative. They weren't even close to a functional application. It shook the entire conference when I politely announced that our application went live that very morning. Upon my return from the conference I submitted my resignation.

Everyone was in shock. I was a golden child of the department. I could have easily ridden the wave of my success and reputation for a long time. Yet I had grown intensely dissatisfied with my employment. The idea of working a job to simply support a family and eventually retire was appalling to me. Don't get me wrong, I admire men who can remain content with their employment, motivated by their duty to provide for the needs of others. I'm too self-centered and easily bored. I've always looked for what might be my next great adventure.

Perverse behavior and alcohol use were beginning to affect my work. I knew it was just a matter of time before I did something that would destroy my employment. There had been too many close calls. I was almost arrested for drunk driving while driving a state vehicle. My use of sick leave had increased. I was drinking at work. I was becoming increasingly perverse while traveling. At a technology conference in Vancouver, Canada, I binged on high-class prostitutes and expensive scotch until I was so sick from alcohol poisoning that I couldn't get out of bed. Since it was obvious to me that I wasn't going to quit in the near future, it seemed better to leave my employment with my reputation intact.

My new plan to prosperity was to become a real estate investor. That's right, a real estate investor. Influenced by late night infomercials and a genuine interest in real estate, I started a business buying houses to remodel and resell. I began this new endeavor prior to leaving my employment. Contrary to the infomercials, I wasn't deceived into thinking this would be easy. I thoroughly studied the subject, secured a source for funding, obtained a contractor's license, and incorporated. It was all very businesslike. Upon reflection, it should have succeeded. Yet I failed miserably. There was no way that God was going to let me prosper in my sin. He loves me too much. However, like everything else, He has managed to use it to accomplish His purposes.

I honestly thought that the remodeling business would help me get control over my personal life. I'd be at home. I wouldn't have to travel so much. On the other hand, I wouldn't be accountable to anyone but myself. That was dangerous.

With her enticing speech she caused him to yield, with her flattering lips she seduced him. Immediately he went after her, as an ox goes to the slaughter, or as a fool to the correction of the stocks, till an arrow struck his liver.

As a bird hastens to the snare, he did not know it would cost his life.

—Proverbs 7:21–23

I fully understand that the Internet is amoral; like any other technology it's not good or evil. It's what man chooses to do with it that matters. However, the Internet was a seductress enticing me into new realms of wickedness. As far as I'm concerned the Internet is under the control of the demonic. The wickedness is beyond most people's comprehension. Don't get me wrong; there are good things on the Internet. God certainly is using the Internet to accomplish His work, but He is not dependent upon it.

Satan used the Internet in my life as a hook. Believers cannot be possessed, but they can be deceived and manipulated through their sinful nature. Surrounded by demonic chaos, I spiraled out of control. It started out seemingly very innocently. My travels to the depths of Internet darkness were gradual. It was private and safe. When on the Internet I wasn't out in public being stupid. It seemed a safe alternative to other perverse behavior. But soft-core pornography gradually turned to hard core. Sexual banter in chat rooms increasingly became more and more perverse. The Internet took me into a dark world beyond my imagination.

Today I can regretfully say that I've been exposed to every sexual perversion imaginable: sadism, masochism, torture, rape, bestiality, scatology, necrophilia, and pedophilia. (If you don't know what these are don't look them up. You are better off not knowing.) While initially I found each of these repulsive, the perversion captured my imagination. I'd find myself going back for more and more until I was in total bondage. In the end it would cost me everything—everything except my salvation.

For what profit is it to a man if he gains the whole world, and loses his own soul?

—Matthew 16:26

chapter 18

Hit him again, Gabriel

*"The stone which the builders rejected has become the chief cornerstone."
Whoever falls on that stone will be broken; but on whomever it falls, it
will grind him to powder.*

—Luke 20:17,18

T his is not merely the consequence of your sin. God is doing this. He is crushing you. You had the chance to willingly throw yourself on the stone and be broken. Now God is going to grind you to powder." Chik's words startled me. I never considered this aspect of God before. I assumed that the trouble I was in was simply the result of my sin.

"But this is a good thing." Chik went on. "God loves you enough to crush you. He will never leave you, He'll go through this with you." Emboldened by his words I proclaimed, "Then bring it on. If this is what it takes to be free, then let God do whatever He needs to do." "All right then," Chik shot back jokingly. "If there's even a twitch of life left in the old Kevin, I can hear God saying, *'Hit him again, Gabriel!'"* We both laughed, although I admit that for my part it was a nervous laugh.

> *Come, and let us return to the LORD; for He has torn, but He will heal
> us; He has stricken, but He will bind us up.*
>
> —Hosea 6:1

It had only been a couple of months since I'd come to Chik and confessed everything. My life was a mess. My marriage was failing.

My wife had found the child pornography on the computer. Then to complicate things further, I made a complete fool of myself at her family reunion. Her father had to ask me to leave. My son agreed to drive me back to Minnesota. The ride home was miserable. It took all my energy to not end my life by jumping out of the van going 70 mph. I can't begin to describe the emotional pain and turmoil. Upon my return I immediately called Chik.

Sitting at Sojourner's Café (a ministry of Calvary Chapel St. Paul) I confessed my deepest secrets. Each time I'd reveal another depravity Chik would say, "That's forgivable. Nothing I haven't heard before. Is that all?" He told me I might as well get it all out in the open. So we kept going until there was no more. "Now that you've come into the light you might as well continue to walk in the light," was Chik's final encouragement.

My wife rightfully insisted that I move out of the house. After my confession to Chik, I made the same confessions to her. I could have stayed in a house that I was remodeling, but was afraid of being alone. Chik promptly offered for me to stay in a house the church rented from Pastor Mike Fernandez. It had been a "Brother's House" ministry, but was being remodeled with plans to rent it to sisters in the church. It was a safe place to stay for a short while. Of course while I was there, I'd help out with the remodeling efforts.

I immediately began attending church services and enrolled in the Intern Program, a ministry where believers discover their gifts and calling and learn about the ministry of Calvary Chapel. At Chik's encouragement, I began walking in the light. I was honest about my circumstances. It was difficult, but it was the only way I'd be free. I didn't dump my life story on everyone I met. That would be a bit much. But I didn't try to hide or minimize the truth about my circumstances, and whenever appropriate I began sharing my real testimony. Simple things like instead of saying, "I went to prison for burglary." I'd say, "I went to prison for attempted rape." I was openly confronting my life of sin and taking responsibility for my actions.

I came back to church broken and in need of intensive healing. The years of abuse had taken their toll. I needed spiritual life support. I was in poor health: overweight, suffering from hypertension and liver disease. Emotionally I was a basket case. My thoughts were chaotic and I'd cry easily. At one of the first services I attended after my return, a brother whom I had known for years began to welcome me back. I immediately burst into tears. I was in desperate need of a church family.

Fasting is a biblical concept that until this time I didn't fully understand. Most fasting (done for spiritual versus dietary reasons) is an act of religion. It's an act of self-righteousness or penance. It's done to get God's attention or obligate God in some way, or worse, it's done to impress others and has nothing to do with God. While fasting can be a voluntary act of our will, I'm convinced that more often meaningful fasting is involuntary. It's in response to God, not a way to get God to respond to us. When Nehemiah learned of Jerusalem's state of disrepair, he was so upset that he fasted.[1] When the Ninevites became aware of their sin and the imminent judgment of God, they fasted.[2] When we become acutely aware of our sin, the sinful condition of others, or the holiness of God, fasting is a natural response.

I fasted. Call it whatever you want. Regardless, I didn't eat for weeks. It wasn't an act of my will. I didn't say to myself, "Self, maybe if I quit eating God will accept me." No, I was so overwhelmed with the sin in my life that I couldn't eat. It wasn't a conscious effort on my part. I was so consumed with my wretched life that I didn't think of eating. It was over a week before it occurred to me that I hadn't eaten. Yet I still had no desire for food. Eventually I had to force myself to start eating again.

When I came back to church, I had no expectations. If I was just allowed to sit in the back row and keep my mouth shut, I'd be happy. I really thought there was no church that would have me if they knew the truth. In many churches I wouldn't be welcome. Some would be self-righteous and judgmental. Most would be well meaning but wouldn't know what to do with me. The church as a whole is ill equipped for ministry in today's perverse world. This is really sad considering the church has been entrusted with all the answers to life and godliness—God's Word. While my life is one of extremes, you'd have to be deaf, dumb, and blind to not realize that the world

---

[1] Nehemiah 1:4
[2] Jonah 3:5

in which we live is full of perversion. I'm not the only pervert attending church.

To my amazement, I found myself being integrated back into the ministry. Chik enlisted my service to help with building maintenance on the church properties. I'd been back a very short time when he told me there was going to be a staff meeting and he expected me to be there. That was confusing. "I'm not staff." I explained. "Just be there." To my astonishment I wasn't being treated as a second-class member of the church. It was expected that I would use my gifts and calling in the work of ministry. One of the philosophies of Calvary Chapel St. Paul (Chik) is "Give everyone something to do. An active sheep is a healthy sheep."

However Chik also gave me stiff counsel about how I had limited my access to ministry because of my sin. There are things in the church that I would never be able to do. I don't remember the entire list but I do remember, "You will never be an elder and you will never serve in the children's ministry." Nearly everything else was still possible. Fair enough.

"Dad, let's do a Bible study at Sojourners on Friday nights. You and me." A Bible study with my son certainly seemed like a good idea, simple, and innocent. I assumed he meant just the two of us. As far as I was concerned my days of teaching were over. Chik didn't include it in his list of things I'd never do again, but I had. Yet a study with my son certainly seemed appropriate.

When on the first night my son rounded up half a dozen other guys to join us, I was a little dismayed. I tried not to lead and not to expound on the Scriptures. But it just isn't in my nature to hold back. For the most part all these guys were young believers ready to receive God's Word. Of course it didn't help that my son kept pitching me soft balls. When some simple question would be unanswered, or guys would be confused about the basic tenets of the faith, or there would be a pregnant pause, my son would draw me out with a look or a word.

Within a couple of weeks, the Friday night Bible study was in full swing. Ten or more guys were regularly participating with my son and me. Although still concerned about teaching, I had given up on holding back. If I had something to say (not just wanted to say something) I'd say it. This particular night with Bible open, speaking to half a dozen guys who were listening attentively, I looked up to see Chik watching me through the window. Uneasiness came over me. I had no idea how he'd react. Part of me expected him to shut us down or at least question me on what was going on. Instead he sent his daughter with a note. She quietly set it on my Bible as I was speaking. All that was on it was a smiley face with a Scripture reference. As soon as I had a chance I looked up the passage.

> *For the gifts and the calling of God are irrevocable.*
> —Romans 11:29

This verse was a healing salve. I have since wrestled with this passage and its application in my life. Reconciling it with the flip side that I have limited my access to ministry has been a challenge. But at that time it was a great encouragement. At a time when I could see nothing in me but a life of darkness, it brought a beacon of light. There was still the possibility that I could be a functioning member of the church. It was certainly clear that at least two people, my son and my pastor, were not ready to give up on me.

> *"My son, do not despise the chastening of the LORD, nor be discouraged when you are rebuked by Him; for whom the LORD loves He chastens, and scourges every son whom He receives."*
> —Hebrews 12:5

When I arrived at my wife's house, the police were waiting for me. "Are you Kevin?" they asked. "We would like to ask you some questions." In the house they went on to explain that I was under investigation for possession of child pornography. My name showed up in an ongoing investigation of a pornography site that had been shut down by authorities. With my heart in my throat and a conviction to walk in the light, I admitted to their accusations. I also explained all I had done in the past weeks to correct my behavior: confessing to my pastor and my wife, deleting images off my computer, and installing blocking software so I couldn't further access pornography sites. Willingly I let them examine my computer. Unfortunately they found pictures I failed to delete that were questionable. She could have been eighteen, but probably wasn't.

It was all very surreal. Although hesitant, I tried to be honest. From their response and the police report, I believe they could see my candor. Honesty is not something to which the authorities are accustomed. Most people lie and hide. At a minimum they simply refuse to cooperate. That's what I normally would have done. I didn't have to let them in the house or look at my computer. They didn't have a warrant. In the past, deception may have minimized the short-term consequences, but it never helped in the long run. This was uncharted territory. All the while I could hear Chik's words, "What you've done in the past hasn't worked. From now on do the opposite."

As the police were leaving, they commended me on my efforts and assured me that this would be the end of it. They said they saw no reason for it to go any further. They even told me that I didn't need to tell my wife about their coming to question me. I assured them this was not an option. I would tell her. So you can imagine the shock I had two weeks later when I turned the corner and saw half a dozen police cars in front of the house. I panicked and kept on driving. When they were gone I called my sons, who were put through an ordeal I wish they never had to experience. This time they had a warrant to confiscate all computers and data storage devices. When I called the detective who left his card, he simply told me that they would be in touch.

Every day I waited in anticipation for what would happen next. The fear was paralyzing. Chik encouraged me to simply trust God. "He knows the future. God hasn't abandoned you. He's crushing you. . . . Anyway, why worry about what might happen. We might not even be here. Jesus could come back at any moment." It was a difficult time. The emotional turmoil was terrible. I was scared. On top of waiting for what the police were going to do, my marriage was failing and my finances were a mess.

I was depressed—that's right, depressed. I believe in depression. What I don't agree with is the world's view that depression is a medical condition to be treated with drugs. While physical ailments can cause emotional reactions including depression, depression is not a medical condition. It's a spiritual condition. Depression is the result of a broken relationship with God because of sin. The Bible is full of depression. I can't think of a single character in the Bible who didn't at one time or another display symptoms of depression. In every case it was because of sin, either their own sin or the sin of others.

I was distraught over my wasted life. In my despair I modified popular worship songs. For example:

> *Jesus draw me close, closer Lord to You, let the world around me fade away.*

Became—

> *Jesus kill me now, take me home to you. Make this world I live in go away. For my desire is to die now and go home.*

The children's song *"Jesus Loves Me"* became—

> *Jesus loves me this I know because He crushed me so. God disciplines those He loves. He must love me an awful lot. Yes Jesus loves me, because He crushed me. Yes Jesus loves me, the Bible tells me so.*

I hated my life. It took everything I had just to get out of bed. Many days I didn't. I was afraid to go outside. I was afraid to drive. I was afraid to be out in public. It seemed as everyone was watching me, everyone knew. I lay awake at night wishing I could die, praying, begging God to take me home. I obsessed over suicide, how I could do it so it was painless yet looked like an accident, how ending my life had to be the best thing for everyone. My wife would certainly be better off. Most of my children wouldn't miss me. In fact I am certain that at some time or another they've all wished me dead . . . all but one.

In all of my wretched life I've never came as close to committing suicide as I did during that period. Whatever your theological view is on the subject, I had reconciled my own beliefs. I had a plan that I was ready to implement if things got bad enough. The bottom line was that I was not going to prison . . . I would die first. The one thing I couldn't reconcile was my youngest son. We were close. He saw me through a different set of eyes than his siblings. I couldn't imagine what my suicide would do to him. That is probably the one thing that kept me from following through.

My cell phone rang. Looking at the caller ID I knew who it was before I answered. It was the police detective. "I'd like you to come down to the station to answer some more questions." I was walking in the light, and I was trusting God, but I wasn't stupid. I knew that I was going to be arrested.

Investigators had been able to find everything I'd ever had on my computer even though it had been erased. I had heard they could do that, but somehow I thought it was a myth. They even found the outline I made for my confession to my wife. Chik told me not to do it on the computer, but I didn't listen. It was a full confession. But what did it matter. I had already confessed. I had been honest with the police when they came to the house.

Sitting in his office he asked me the same questions I was asked before. I gave the same honest answers. But this officer didn't seem satisfied. I suppose it was his view that everyone lies so I had to be hiding something. I finally said, "I've been completely honest with you. I think it's time I got an attorney." "That's too bad because now we're going to have to arrest you for possession of child pornography." "Be honest, you were going to arrest me anyway." "We'll, yes we were."

I was in county jail for a few days before the arraignment. It was hard for me, not because it was a hard place. It was comfortable compared to the jails I had been in before. It was the sense of desperation, isolation, and uncertainty that terrorized me. I called Chik and my wife constantly. At the arraignment the judge set bail for $20,000 thinking it would keep me in jail for a while. To my amazement and gratitude, my wife posted bail and I was released within an hour. I called Chik to let him know I was released.

Although being out of jail was good, it was not a good day. My life was miserable. There was an ominous dread of what else could happen.

Sitting (hiding) that same afternoon at the house where I was staying, my phone rang. This time I didn't recognize the number. It was a reporter from a major Twin Cities newspaper. She was doing an article on my arrest and wanted to know if I had any comments. Shocked I said, "Absolutely not." Panicked, I called Chik, then my wife to warn her that this may become public. When the article was released, it turned out to be not much of anything. But for the next few days my imagination ran wild with the possibilities.

Later that same afternoon my wife came over. We talked for a long time. In the end she made it clear that we were over. She couldn't do this anymore. She planned to file for divorce. I called Chik once again. (As a side note, it's been over five years since this day and we are still married . . . separated . . . but still married. What the future holds is in God's hands. I'll say no more on the subject of my marriage. It's my conviction in writing this book that I will do what I can to keep my wife out of this story. She's suffered enough.)

That night, alone in the house, I decided it was time to call my sister. We talked for a long time, an hour or more. By now it was late, almost midnight. Before trying to sleep I went to the bathroom. When I opened the door I noticed a light on in the living room. To my surprise, there was Chik sitting in a chair reading. "What are you doing here?" "Making sure you're all right." "If I hadn't got up I wouldn't have known you were here." "Then I guess you were all right and I'd have gone home."

We sat and talked for a long time. Most of the conversation is lost. However, at one point, after a long silence, Chik got a knowing smile on his face.

"What?" I knew he had something to say.

"You can't see it now, but one day God is going to use all this to do a great work."

"Huh?" Genuinely puzzled by his words.

Chik went on, "You're going to be able to minister to a lot of guys through all this."

Ministry was the furthest thing from my mind. He talked of the great opportunities that lay ahead, how we would reach guys struggling with sin. I listened attentively, trying to grasp his vision of light at the end of this dark tunnel. Then he became very serious, his voice trembled, it seemed as though he fought back tears.

"Kevin, some of those guys are going to rip-your-heart-out!" he said, accentuating each word. "You know how I know?" Waiting just long enough to be sure he had my full attention, "Because, Kevin . . . you ripped-my-heart-out!"

I was stunned. His words hit me hard. I didn't know what to say. Then in an instant change of countenance he was back to his usual self, "But you're here now."

I will never forget that night. A common Chikism is "I love you and there's nothing you can do about it." Until that night they were just words. Now they hit home with full impact. This was a man who really loved me. I would never look at Chik the same.

chapter 19

Real men repent

Because He loved me, God crushed me. God is not the initiator of evil; it wasn't His will for me to pursue wickedness. God crushed me by turning me over to Satan for the destruction of my flesh.

> *It is actually reported that there is sexual immorality among you, and such sexual immorality as is not even named among the Gentiles . . . deliver such a one to Satan for the destruction of the flesh, that his spirit may be saved in the day of the Lord Jesus.*
> —1 Corinthians 5:1,5

God simply removed His covering and protection in my life and allowed me to run headlong into my sin. It worked. It brought me to my knees and I repented. When I confessed to Chik, I had no idea that I was under investigation for possession of child pornography. I just couldn't go on living in my sin any longer. When the police first approached me, the fruit of repentance was already evident. I wasn't putting on a show in an attempt to minimize the consequences. Quite the opposite, by the world's wisdom I did everything wrong. I was too honest and cooperative. I literally handed them their case against me.

Some might think (for a moment I did) how unfair it was of God to have me charged and jailed for my sin when I had clearly repented. This is what I was complaining about when Chik lit into me with "God is crushing you." Oh, by the way, there is absolutely nothing man can do to me as a child of God without God's permission, so God was the initiator of these consequences in my life. And yes I know the verses about how you reap what you sow. I see no conflict; it's all part of God's economy. Even though these were difficult times, that would not get easier in the months to come, I recognize today that these consequences were an act of mercy. If I was ever to be free from this bondage, I absolutely had to be crushed.

> *Now I rejoice, not that you were made sorry, but that your sorrow led to repentance. For you were made sorry in a godly manner, that you might suffer loss from us in nothing. For godly sorrow produces repentance leading to salvation, not to be regretted; but the sorrow of the world produces death.*
> —2 Corinthians 7:9, 10

Genuine repentance is frequently misunderstood. Repentance is often accompanied by great emotion. When we realize how far we have strayed from the feet of Jesus and wounded the heart of God, it produces sorrow. However, it's a mistake to judge remorse, sorrow, and regret to be the fruit of repentance. Many people under the weight of their sin express intense emotion, but never repent. Conversely when we see a lack of emotion, we presume the person is unrepentant. The reality is we don't always get to see what the person is really going through. Most people have learned to conceal their emotions, or they could simply be cried out.

Repentance is not an emotion. Repentance is an act of the will; it's a choice to change direction. Biblical repentance is a decision to turn away from sin and turn toward God. Sometimes it's accompanied by emotions; sometimes it's not. It's not the emotions we should be looking for. We should be looking for evidence that the person has changed direction. That is the fruit of repentance. Frequently in my life true repentance is accompanied by a quiet determination. No fanfare. No empty promises. Action.

John the Baptist called people to *"Repent, for the kingdom of heaven is at hand!"* (Matt. 3:2). His was a ministry preparing the way for the Messiah. John expected repentance to be accompanied by actions, *"Therefore bear fruits worthy of repentance . . ."* (Matt. 3:8). An apple tree produces apples, orange tree oranges; a tree is known by its fruit. When people repent, when they turn away from sin and turn toward God, they will bear *"fruits of repentance."*

Repentance is at the heart of salvation. Unbelievers are on a path headed away from God. When people embrace the gospel, they change their mind about the path they are on. They accept the truth of God's Word, ask for forgiveness, and invite Jesus to come into their lives. At that moment they have passed from death into life;[1] they are born again.[2] This radical transformation will be evident in a person's actions and attitudes; it will produce fruit of repentance.

It is an error to believe that all someone has to do to be saved is say the sinner's prayer, or go forward at an evangelistic invitation, or be baptized. Salvation is a free gift of God, but it has to be received. Let's say someone with a life-threatening disease is offered a pill that will cure him. This pill has cured thousands of other people with the same disease. The person with the disease can hold the pill in his hand and proclaim its virtue. But until he takes the pill for himself, he will not be cured.

The Israelites complained a lot when they were in the wilderness. God was very patient with them, but He wasn't slack in showing them their error. At one point God got their attention by sending poisonous snakes into the camp.[3] Many died as a result. The people repented. They came to Moses and asked him to pray that God would take away the snakes, a seemingly legitimate request. God had another plan.

> Then the LORD said to Moses, "Make a fiery serpent, and set it on a pole; and it shall be that everyone who is bitten, when he looks at it, shall live."
>
> —Numbers 21:8

God didn't take away the serpents; he provided a cure. The people had to participate, they had to take action, they had to look upon the bronze serpent to be healed. That simple. Yet I suspect that there were those who chose to ignore God's provision. Maybe it seemed too simple. No doubt there where those who looked for another

---

[1] John 5:24
[2] John 3:3–7
[3] Number 21

cure. There wasn't one; they died. This account becomes even more intriguing in view of Jesus' proclamation:

> *And as Moses lifted up the serpent in the wilderness, even so must the Son of Man be lifted up, that whoever believes in Him should not perish but have eternal life.*
>
> —John 3:14,15

Every person is born with a terminal disease—sin. The serpent has bitten each of us. God has provided His Son as the cure. We have to simply believe in him to be saved. Simple? Unfortunately it's too simple for most people. The word "believe" means to "put faith in." It means more than just acknowledging the truth. It requires action. It requires repentance.

Accepting Jesus into your heart is a life-changing event. If there is no change in a person's life, it casts doubt on his salvation. Salvation is in the hands of God; we cannot judge another person's salvation. However we can and should look for the fruit of salvation, not so we can condemn people, but so we can know how to best minister to them. If it appears that they do not have a personal relationship with Jesus, then we share the Gospel with them. It's futile to try to disciple those who aren't God's children. On the other hand, if they are believers, then we enjoy the fellowship and encourage them in their relationship with God.

A couple of years ago God brought a guy into my life. He liked hanging out with the brothers. He could see the close fellowship we had. But by my best judgment and the judgment of others, he was not a believer in Jesus. Privately he'd make questionable comments about women. He'd ogle women walking down the street. His personal philosophies and convictions were all over the map. So I kept trying to encourage him to make a decision for Jesus. One day sitting in my truck after a service I was once again giving him the Gospel. This time he adamantly insisted that he was a believer. So I asked him, "Can I talk to you like a believer?" He responded, "Yes." So I lit into him, rebuking his inappropriate behavior. We didn't see much of him after that.

The point of this story is that there was no fruit of repentance or salvation in his life. So my job was to give him the Gospel. To some extent, I needed to be patient with his behavior because he wasn't a believer. He couldn't be expected to know any better. Don't get me wrong; the brothers were keeping close watch on him and more than once I had to tell him that his behavior was inappropriate. And I never left him alone with a sister; there was no telling what he might say. But when he insisted on being treated like a believer I spoke to him as I would a brother in the Lord.

> *If we confess [repent] our sins, He is faithful and just to forgive us our sins and to cleanse us from all unrighteousness. If we say that we have not sinned, we make Him a liar, and His word is not in us.*
> —1 John 1:9,10

Repentance is fundamental to the ongoing life of a healthy believer. Sin doesn't cease when people ask Jesus into their lives.[4] Only the penalty for sin has been eliminated—eternal separation from God (death). In fact the battle against sin has just begun. Believers struggle with sin, or I should say believers *should* struggle with sin. The keyword is *struggle*. A person who is struggling with sin is making an effort to cease from sin. The struggle itself is evidence that the person is repentant; there is an effort to turn away from sin and turn toward God. Too often, however, there is no real struggle with sin, only words and emotions. Repentance requires action. It begs the question, "What will you do to cease from sin?"

Cut off your hand?[5]

Pluck out your eye?[6]

Put a millstone around your neck?[7]

David was God's choice to be king over Israel. He was described as a man after God's own heart.[8] What made David so special? What

---

[4] 1 John 1:8
[5] Matthew 5:30
[6] Matthew 5:29
[7] Matthew 18:6,7
[8] 1 Samuel 13:14

makes a person great in God's eyes? David is the original Renaissance man. He was a great warrior; they sang songs about the tens of thousands David had slain. David played the harp, danced, and wrote music and poetry (psalms). David was a great statesman, strategist, builder, and leader. In contrast to these virtues, David was also an adulterer, a polygamist, a lousy father, and a man of blood who murdered innocent people. So what made David a man after God's own heart? David was a man of repentance.

In 2 Samuel 11, David committed a series of hideous crimes. He stayed home when he should have been leading his armies in battle. Spotting an attractive married woman, Bathsheba, David abused his power by engaging in sexual relations with her. His sin had consequences; Bathsheba became pregnant. To cover it up David devised a plan to make it look like her husband, Uriah, was the father. It didn't work. Uriah was too much a man of honor and integrity. So David arranged to have Uriah killed in battle. David probably thought that was the end of it. It wasn't. God sent Nathan the prophet to confront David about his sin.[9] David repented.

Have mercy upon me, O God, according to Your lovingkindness; according to the multitude of Your tender mercies, blot out my transgressions.

Wash me thoroughly from my iniquity, and cleanse me from my sin. For I acknowledge my transgressions, and my sin is always before me.
                                                            —Psalm 51:1,2

For the believer, unconfessed sin is like a cancer. It causes great emotional distress, physical illness, and mental instability. David was miserable before his sin was exposed. Psalm 51:8 makes reference to this suffering: *"Make me hear joy and gladness, that the bones You have broken may rejoice."*

Create in me a clean heart, O God, and renew a steadfast spirit within me . . . Restore to me the joy of Your salvation, and uphold me by Your generous Spirit.
                                                            —Psalm 51:10,12

---

[9] 2 Samuel 12

Sin separates us from God. That was David's greatest suffering. He longed to have his relationship with God restored. Even though his sin had damaged many lives David knew that ultimately it was his sin against God that mattered. Thus David confessed in verse 4, *"Against You, You only, have I sinned . . ."* Maybe David was a man after God's own heart not because he was like-minded with God, but because he sought the heart of God. Literally, David was a man who desired to be close to the heart of God.

David let his own sinful desires lead him away from the heart of God. Yet David was a man who knew what it took to restore that relationship. Not good works, religious ceremony, or penance—repentance. *"The sacrifices of God are a broken spirit, a broken and a contrite heart—These, O God, You will not despise"* (Psalm 51:17). Repentance is humbling. It means saying you're wrong or that you screwed up—again. Repentance is accompanied by brokenness and surrender along with changes in behavior.

In contrast to David is Saul, the first king of Israel.[10] Saul knew God. I'm convinced that Saul had a personal relationship with God and that he is in heaven right now (although I could be wrong). But Saul was not a man after God's own heart. Saul was the people's choice for king: tall, handsome, and a great warrior. Saul was the model of the modern politician: get in power, increase your power, stay in power. Consumed by his own self-interests, he lived in rebellion toward God. He wanted what God could do for him; he wasn't grateful for what God had already done. More important, he didn't cherish the incredible privilege of having a personal relationship with the Creator of the universe.

Saul suffered greatly because of his self-centered life. He lived in fear that David would take his position away from him, even though David did everything possible to prove his loyalty. Saul's unwillingness to repent caused him great turmoil. He suffered from depression. He became irrational, unstable, and violent. His foolishness destroyed his witness and the reputation of the nation. Ultimately his unwillingness to repent cost him his ministry, his life, and the life of his son Jonathan.

---

[10] 1 Samuel

As many as I love, I rebuke and chasten. Therefore be zealous and repent.

—Revelation 3:19

Sin destroys lives, separates us from God and from each other. Because He loves us God takes sin seriously. He disciplines us as a loving father disciplines his children. It is prudent to be zealous for God, to repent and surrender our lives to Him. When we refuse to repent, we find ourselves stuck in the cycle of sin and despair described in Romans 7. But when we repent and seek the heart of God, we move on to the victory found in Romans 8.

There is therefore now no condemnation to those who are in Christ Jesus, who do not walk according to the flesh, but according to the Spirit. For the law of the Spirit of life in Christ Jesus has made me free from the law of sin and death.

—Romans 8:1,2

My unwillingness to repent has cost me nearly everything. What my life could have been had I repented and surrendered to God at an early age is beyond my comprehension. Yet God is gracious. I'm still here. There's enough life left in me to give it another try. Since I'm one of God's children and He will never give up on me, I'm confident I can't fail. No more Romans 7 for me. It's time to live Romans 8 and beyond.

. . . If God is for us, who can be against us? He who did not spare His own Son, but delivered Him up for us all, how shall He not with Him also freely give us all things? Who shall bring a charge against God's elect? It is God who justifies. Who is he who condemns? It is Christ who died, and furthermore is also risen, who is even at the right hand of God, who also makes intercession for us. Who shall separate us from the love of Christ? Shall tribulation, or distress, or persecution, or famine, or nakedness, or peril, or sword? As it is written:

"For Your sake we are killed all day long; we are accounted as sheep for the slaughter."

Yet in all these things we are more than conquerors through Him who loved us. For I am persuaded that neither death nor life, nor angels nor principalities nor powers, nor things present nor things to come, nor height nor depth, nor any other created thing, shall be able to separate us from the love of God which is in Christ Jesus our Lord.

—Romans 8:31–39

SECTION FOUR

Samson Of a Man

chapter 20

Saved soul, wasted life?

The essential story of the Bible is who God is and what He has done. God Himself is the only hero. However, the Bible also tells the stories of men and women throughout history. It tells of their victories and failings, their strengths and weaknesses, their struggles and sufferings. There is wisdom to be gleaned from studying their lives. When you look past the cultural differences and recognize that all that is miraculous is of God, you'll discover that these men and women are no different than you and me.

Meditating on the lives of biblical characters is a good use of time and energy. It's a healthy way to occupy the playground of our minds. The parallels between my life and that of David or Saul are obvious. Like them, my sin has caused great damage. Yet I'd like to think I'm more of a David than a Saul. At least David had a heart for God and was willing to repent (even though it took Nathan the prophet confronting his sin to motivate him). Saul seemed to have no redeeming qualities. On the other hand, I'm definitely not a Job, Joseph, or Daniel: all men of great integrity.

But then again I could be a Samson.

Disregard any traditional Sunday school image you may have of Samson. He is not a great man of valor. As for his gift of great strength (which was from God and had nothing to do with him or his hair), he spent it on his own interests. Don't be deceived by passages that refer to how God used Samson or "came upon Samson" to accomplish His purposes. It had nothing to do with Samson. God used him in spite of himself: as God frequently does in all our lives.

Again the children of Israel did evil in the sight of the Lord, and the Lord delivered them into the hand of the Philistines for forty years.
—Judges 13:1

It was during the time of the judges and the nation of Israel was as usual suffering from their rebellion. Samson was a man with great potential. The hand of the Lord was clearly on his life even before he was born. God intended to use Samson to *". . . deliver Israel out of the hand of the Philistines"* (Judges 13:5). So God equipped him with great strength to accomplish the work to which he was called. Samson was aware that he was special. But instead of willingly pursuing God's call and rescuing his people from their bondage, he spent his abilities on his own passions.

Sound familiar? I see strong parallels between my life and the life of Samson. I've never had supernatural physical strength. But God's hand was clearly on my life from a young age. It was obvious that God gifted and called me to accomplish His purpose. And like Samson, I spent what I had on my own passions. I, too, wasted my potential.

Potential: a latent excellence or ability that *may or may not* be developed. *Webster's College Dictionary*

I hate the word potential. My entire life has been plagued with people telling me how I've wasted my potential, or how I'm not living up to my potential. Potential is overused and abused, especially among Christians. It's the measure used to weigh our expectations of each other. "What can this person contribute?" What resources do they bring?" Sadly our motivation too often has to do with exploiting a person to accomplish our goals. One consequence is that we focus too much attention on those people we believe have the most potential at the expense of others.

When I first met Chik, he was rough. Superlatives that come to mind are crass, caustic, coarse, crude, boisterous, boorish, raw, rude, and uncouth. I don't feel this way anymore and I don't believe today that this was a fair assessment of him even then. Yet it was a common opinion of him among many people in the church. My opinion of Chik today is that he is one of the great spiritual men of our time.

The point is that in those early days Chik was a man in whom few people saw great potential. When Ralph came to pastor Calvary Chapel Oceanside he saw something in Chik that most people didn't see. Ralph saw a man who loved Jesus and had a heart for people. Ralph took Chik under his wing and raised him up in the ministry. At the time, I thought Ralph had lost his mind. Today I'm grateful for Ralph's foresight (no doubt inspired by the Holy Spirit) and willingness to invest himself in Chik.

Our preoccupation with potential isn't always driven by selfish ambition. Frequently it's motivated by an honest desire to see the person live a happy and fulfilled life. The assumption is that people are happiest when they are fully utilizing their personal resources. The more resources (potential) people have, the greater their contribution, the greater their contribution the higher their self-esteem. The higher people's self-esteem, the happier they are. You should already know where I stand on the subject of self-esteem and real happiness.

This isn't to imply that we're not accountable for our time, talent, and treasure. God expects us to use our resources for His purposes. *"For everyone to whom much is given, from him much will be required . . ."* (Luke 12:48). The parable of the talents makes it perfectly clear that we are to be good stewards of our talents and abilities.[1] Yet the point of the parable isn't how many talents (potential) did people have, but how they used their resources.

Being available for God to use you is far more important than having great potential. God can speak through a donkey or a rock. He doesn't need our talents and abilities to accomplish His work. He doesn't need anything from us. Our potential means nothing to God. On the other hand, what God wants is to have a loving relationship with us as His children. As part of that relationship, He wants us to participate with Him in His work. He loves having us near Him. He knows that it's healthy for us as his children to keep busy by His side.

---

[1] Matthew 25:14–30

If you are a person considered to have great potential, you have above average intelligence and abilities, get over yourself and start using your talents to serve your heavenly Father. And if you're not a person with great potential, then simply make yourself available for His use. As strange as it seems, God uses broken vessels. The only way to realize your potential is to be submitted and surrendered to Him. Therefore throw yourself on the stone and be broken. Take my word; it's far better than being crushed.

Samson would find out what it's like to have the stone fall on him and be ground to powder. But not until his passions had thoroughly destroyed his life. I strongly recommend you stop here and read the story of Samson. It can be found in Judges chapters 13 to 16. It won't take long. I'll wait.

OK, now that you've read the story and are with me I'll go on. If you didn't stop and read it, which is what I expected, then so be it.

We all know how Delilah tricked Samson into giving away the supposed secret to his great strength—his hair. It was never about his hair. Samson's great strength came from his relationship with God. In spite of all the foolishness in his life, Samson had a relationship with God. He had been set aside from birth to be a tool for God to use. The hair was merely an outward symbol of this relationship. The hair being cut is symbolic of Samson's broken relationship with God.

In spite of Samson's rebellion, God never abandoned him. God used Samson to accomplish the work of defeating the Philistines in spite of himself. Yet because of his rebellion, victory came at great personal cost. Had he submitted to God in his youth, his victory over the Philistines may have come with great honor. But instead, God had to break him and bring him to a point of despair.

> *Then the Philistines took him and put out his eyes, and brought him down to Gaza. They bound him with bronze fetters, and he became a grinder in the prison.*
>
> —Judges 16:21

When I picture Samson, I don't see a man of strength and virility. I see a man aged before his time, a man weakened by his chains and hard labor—beaten, scarred, and blind. It's not a pretty picture, but it's what a life lived for worldly pleasure does to a person. Samson made the mistake of presuming that God's blessing would continue in spite of his bad behavior. It didn't occur to him that God would remove His protection and allow him to be crushed by his own sin.

However, the hair of his head began to grow again after it had been shaven.

—Judges 16:22

Blinded and serving a life sentence of hard labor, I'm sure Samson had time to think about his wasted life. I picture him reflecting on every twist and turn that led him to this dark place: the glory days of his youth, his parents' commitment to God, and the vow they made to raise him as a Nazarite. In his mind he was taken back to a day when his relationship with God was at its best. Maybe for the first time he realized that his great strength had nothing to do with his hair.

To further humiliate Samson, the Philistines put him on display. It was a huge celebration. Everyone was there. The Philistines mistakenly believed that their god Dagon had delivered Samson into their hands. They didn't realize that the one and only true God was still in control. God is the one who delivered Samson into the hands of the Philistines. He wasn't finished using him to accomplish His purpose. As far as the Philistines were concerned, Samson was no threat to them. They were correct. Samson never was the threat. Samson was just a tool in the hands of God.

Then Samson called to the LORD, saying, "O Lord GOD, remember me, I pray! Strengthen me, I pray, just this once, O God, that I may with one blow take vengeance on the Philistines for my two eyes!"

—Judges 16:28

"Samson called to the Lord." Sadly this is the only place this statement is made about Samson, and at that he wasn't truly repentant

. . . not like David. Samson's motivation was to *take vengeance on the Philistines for my two eyes!*" When David repented, his motivation was the restoration of his relationship with God. Samson wasn't a man who called on the Lord. It took losing everything to bring him to a place where he had to trust in God. Samson knew better than to simply trust in the fact that his hair was growing back. Finally Samson would become a man of faith.

> *And Samson took hold of the two middle pillars which supported the temple, and he braced himself against them, one on his right and the other on his left. Then Samson said, "Let me die with the Philistines!" And he pushed with all his might, and the temple fell on the lords and all the people who were in it. So the dead that he killed at his death were more than he had killed in his life.*
>
> —Judges 16:28–30

Samson is the model of a man with a saved soul and a wasted life. Yes, God used Samson to accomplish His purposes. That has to do with God, not Samson. Samson squandered his life on his own passions. He took God for granted. In the end, it cost him everything.

It had been over three years since I had repented and God had first crushed me. A lot had transpired. My life had changed radically. The writing of this book was underway. Out to dinner with Chik one night he began to tell me a story. I've learned that Chik rarely says anything without a purpose unless he's obviously jesting (which is frequently). Chik doesn't make small talk. So having no idea where this story was going, I listened attentively.

Chik told of a man, a brother in the Lord who had recently died. This brother was an icon of the early days of the Calvary Chapel movement. God had used him in mighty ways. Yet this brother's life was plagued by unresolved sin. He was given over to perverse passions. His sexual appetites led him into bondage. Over the course of his life he caused considerable damage, leading others astray and causing divisions among believers. Ultimately he died of AIDS.

Chuck Smith was asked to speak at his funeral. What could Chuck say about this man? He cared about him. Yet Chuck chose to speak the truth. Chuck eulogized him as "A Samson of a Man," then went on to talk about having a saved soul and a wasted life.

As soon as he finished the story, Chik was on to some other subject. I don't know if he had a specific purpose or if the Lord was simply directing the conversation. Either way, "Samson of a man, saved soul and a wasted life" haunted me. Am I a Samson of a man? So far, my life has been mostly wasted. What will be said at my funeral? I couldn't get it out of my head. It was so bad that I expressed my concern with brothers at a home fellowship. The next day I got a call from Chik, "Kevin, you're not a Samson of a man. Had the Lord taken you home three years ago, then you would have been a Samson of man. Not anymore." It was good to hear. Yet I know that what I do with the rest of my life will ultimately determine whether or not I am a Samson of a man.

Amazingly Samson is recognized as a man of faith in Hebrews 11. That's a tribute to God's habit of seeing only the best in His children. It gives me hope knowing that God is on my side, not holding my sins against me, counting even my smallest acts of faith as righteousness. Jokingly I've said that when I arrive at heaven's gate there will be no warm welcome. I'll be quietly escorted to a back entrance so as not to embarrass the legitimate guests. But amazingly, I may actually be welcomed as a man of faith like Samson, or the apple of God's eye like David.

Ultimately my status in heaven is up to God. What I know for sure is that I'll be there. Meanwhile the question is, "What will I do with what's left of my life here?" It's a question that every believer must answer. You don't have to be steeped in gross sin to have a wasted life. Wasted lives take many forms. Doing nothing, as did the man in the parable of the talents, results in a wasted life. We all should ask the question, "What will be said at our funeral? Will we be eulogized as a Samson of a man? Will ours be a saved soul but a wasted life?"

chapter 21

You're here now

". . . hold fast what you have till I come."

—Revelation 2:25

Or said another way, "guard what is left."

Sitting in the common area at the government center, I was anxious. I couldn't get hold of Chik and I had to make a decision. Accept the offer from the prosecutors or take the case to trial. I prayed and considered the correct action. My attorney said we had a solid but uncertain defense. I don't even begin to understand the logic. The entire defense was based on the fact that I had ceased from the behavior and had taken action to correct my life prior to knowing that I was under investigation. I had one of the best criminal defense attorneys in the state. He admitted that it was an uncommon defense, but he had been successful with it in the past.

The offer, on the other hand, was reasonable. After all I wasn't trying to get out of the consequences. The primary goal was to stay out of jail and out of the state-sponsored sex offender program. The horror stories I heard about the state program from Chik, my attorney, and a therapist were unimaginable. The state-sponsored program would have been unbearable and counterproductive.

I took the offer. It was the right choice. I just wanted to hear it from Chik. Anyway if I'd had gone to trial they would have required my wife and children to testify. The jury would have viewed all the images they had pulled off my computer. I just couldn't put them or myself through it. The offer was for no jail time, five years supervised probation, regular drug testing, annual polygraphs, no Internet, no contact with girls under the age of 18, continued treatment with a private therapist, and register as a sex offender for ten years.

"This is great! Check out how a pastor signs his letters, 'In His Grip.' I like that. I think that's how I should sign my letters. What do you all think?" The prosecutor, court reporter and bailiff all nodded. My attorney smiled. This was no ordinary judge. I found out later his nickname is "Judge Happy." While I was waiting for my case to be called, I watched him handle other cases; he reminded me of the judge on the old TV series Night Court. (Your loss if you don't know what I'm talking about.)

As I stood in front of the judge, he began extolling all the positive things I had been doing through my church. He went on about Calvary Chapel St. Paul and Chik repeatedly referring back to Chik's letter.[1] Of course it helps that Chik is a St. Paul Police Chaplain. In conclusion he said, "I want you to keep doing what you've been doing with your church. Oh, and do all this other stuff," referring for the first time to the sentencing guidelines from the prosecutor. In essence I was sentenced to Calvary Chapel St. Paul.

A year and a half had passed from when I first repented and the day I was sentenced. It wasn't easy. My wasted life overwhelmed me. My finances were a mess. My marriage was broken. There were court appointments, therapy sessions, psychological testing. But with the support of my church family and a commitment to persevere, I not only survived, but also grew. God continued to work in my life, molding, shaping, and preparing me for what would come.

Not a day went by that I didn't struggle with the "would have, could have, should haves." So many failures, so much garbage, it was unbearable. The common Chikism, "You're here now," was a soothing salve to my troubled heart and mind. The past is past; I can't change what has happened. I wish I could. I wish I could start over. But I doubt I'd do any better the second time around.

---

[1] See Appendix "Chik's Letter"

Therefore do not worry about tomorrow, for tomorrow will worry about its own things. Sufficient for the day is its own trouble.
—Matthew 6:34

Or as a friend of mine would say, "Kevin, quit trying to beat yourself around the corner." I was anxious about what would happen next. There was always something coming up in my immediate future that consumed my thoughts. Simply trusting that God was in control went against my frail human nature. Chik frequently had to remind me that God knew the future even if I didn't. Nothing was going to happen that God didn't ordain. I could trust Him. Chik further warned that obsessing might lead me to self-fulfill the very thing I feared. He always finished with, "God could come back at any time. We might not even be here. All this energy spent on what might happen is a waste. You're here now."

Today, this moment is all we really have. This is true for the believer and unbeliever alike. We can learn from our past, we may need to correct something (confess, ask for forgiveness, make restitution or face consequences), but we can't change the past. It's over. We can plan and prepare for tomorrow, next week, or next year; yet we have no control over the future. In a very literal sense we are all limited to the here and now. It's all we have. For the person apart from God this can be hopeless and depressing. We are not in control of our own destinies. But for the believer, it should be liberating. God has forgiven our past and is able to redeem our failings. God knows the future and is in control of our circumstances. We can trust His love for us.

Ask, and it will be given to you; seek, and you will find; knock, and it will be opened to you. For everyone who asks receives, and he who seeks finds, and to him who knocks it will be opened.
—Matthew 7:7,8

The house where I'd been staying was only a short-term option so I had been praying about where I would live. God answered. Around the same time I was arrested, God miraculously led me to purchase the house two doors from my wife's house. It was my wife's house now. I gave her all our possessions. Holding on to material things seemed pointless.

The small "For Sale by Owner" sign in the yard caught my eye. Initially I ignored it, but God's voice encouraged me to call. So I conducted my usual market research to come up with a price; however, a much lower price kept coming into my mind. A price that seemed too low. It seemed an insult to approach the owners with such a low offer. Yet I knew it was God's voice. To my amazement the owners readily accepted my offer. They had moved out of state and were just glad to have found a buyer.

With a sense of awe at God's handiwork, I moved into the house. It was perfect. I had a place to stay and was near my family. To complete the picture, God provided a brother in the church to live with me. I would live in that house for eight months, when I was able to sell it for a profit. Then through another series of divine interventions I would buy another house one block away where I would live for nearly another year. God is good!

> *So why do you worry about clothing? Consider the lilies of the field, how they grow: they neither toil nor spin; and yet I say to you that even Solomon in all his glory was not arrayed like one of these. Now if God so clothes the grass of the field, which today is, and tomorrow is thrown into the oven, will He not much more clothe you, O you of little faith?*
>
> —Matthew 6:28–30

Getting out of bed that morning was especially difficult. The paranoia and depression weighed heavily over me. God had not abandoned me. The house, big and empty as it was, was obviously a miracle. But now what? I had a house but no money to fix it up for resale. My credit cards were nearly all at their limits, and I was falling behind in my payments. The attorney fees were going to cost $10,000. I was broke. I had created an excellent opportunity for God to do more miraculous things. As I prayed that morning a peace came over me. God is in control. I can't fix this. Anyway, what's the worst that can happen? No one can take away my salvation. Does anything else really matter?

In the midst of these thoughts my phone rang. It was a brother from the church I'd known for many years. "My parents need some work done on their house, doors and windows replaced, is that something you can do?" I had been doing most of the work on my own houses. To make it easier to work with the city, I even had a contractor's license. I hadn't been doing work for others, but why not? "Sure, I can do that. When do you want me to come over?" So a new era in my employment history had begun.

My primary source of income ever since has been residential remodeling and handyman services. For the past five years it has been one miracle after another in how God has provided me with work. I have done some advertising, but most of my work comes through word of mouth. I can't count how many times when I've needed more work all I did was pray, and within a short time the phone would ring. It so amazing that its almost comical, like someone standing at a light switch amazed that every time they flip the switch the light goes on or off. Every time I have a need that involves housing, food, or clothing, I pray and God answers.

That's not to say that I always get what I want or that it's been comfortable. Frequently it's been humbling. God has used these circumstances to direct and shape my life. I've had to learn to ask for help when needed. That's not easy for me. James 4:2 ". . . *you do not have because you do not ask.*" has been a tough lesson for me. I've had to learn to lean on my church family.

Everything seemed to be pressing down on me. I needed to get the house finished and on the market, but it was too much. I finally got the courage to ask a brother for help. "I'd be happy to help. Who else have you asked?" Sheepishly I admitted that he was the only one. Sensing how difficult this was for me he said, "Come on, I'll show you how it's done." In less than ten minutes we went around the church and announced to over twenty brothers and sisters that I needed help and gave them a day and a time to be at my house. Relieved to be past that embarrassment, I went home and prepared for maybe two or three people to show up. To my amazement fifteen brothers and sisters showed up to work. Many of them worked through the night to finish. I was so touched that at one point I had to find an empty room where I could sit and cry without being disturbed.

My finances were a mess. Everyone knew that. I was constantly looking for how I could reduce my expenses. Frequently I would look for something I could sell to get some extra cash. Chik found out I had a commercial paint sprayer for sale. He asked me what I wanted for it. I told him and he said the church would buy it from me. The next Sunday he handed me an envelope with a check. When I opened the envelope to my surprise the check was for twice the amount. On the way home, alone in the car, again I cried.

Most of the maintenance I did for the church was strictly ministry. I received no compensation. Yet occasionally Chik would give me paid work. On one occasion, during an especially difficult financial time, I was handed an envelope with a check by one of the elders. Shoving it into my pocket without looking he stopped me. "You better look at it," he said. I opened the envelope expecting to see a check for a couple of hundred dollars. Instead it was for *much* more. "We prayed about it and believe God wants you to have this. Kevin, we love you." Then he walked away.

I had contracted for a job replacing a small rubber flat roof. Recently we had replaced the roof at the church's coffee shop and there was a large piece of rubber left over. Thinking it would be a blessing to all, I coordinated with the brother in charge of maintenance and the administrative assisting pastor to purchase a piece of the rubber. When the job was complete I wrote a check to the church for the agreed-upon amount with a note as to what it was for. Sitting in the coffee shop with a group of brothers Chik marched up to me holding out his closed hand and said, "Don't ever do that again. If you need it, it's yours." He opened his hand and dropped my check torn into little pieces into my hand.

After the second house sold, I purchased another house farther away. Being concerned about living alone and not being close, I moved in with a single brother. I lived with him for nearly a year, paying whatever I could afford. It was here that I began work on this book. It was a great blessing for both of us. Eventually God led him to marry, and to my surprise he asked me to be the best man. A month later, another brother with whom I'd become close also asked me to be the best man at his wedding. In all my life no one had ever asked me to be their best man. Amazingly both of these brothers knew a great deal about my pathetic life and they still wanted me to be their best man. I took it as a testimony to just how much my life had changed.

Since the brother I was living with was getting married, it was time to find another place to live. So I prayed and God answered. There was a house behind the church coffee shop that was being rented by brothers. Formerly it had been a ministry of the church. Having served its purpose, the ministry was closed and a couple of the brothers who had been living there decided to take over the lease. I moved in and have lived there for over two years. It's where I'm living today. There are anywhere from four to seven brothers living in the house at any one time. It has been an incredible blessing and a challenge. I have fellowship and accountability. Brothers are involved in my life on a daily basis. A big part of me would like my own place (one day I expect to have one), but this has been good for me, if not always comfortable.

Believers miss out on so much because they are afraid of being uncomfortable. I've been there; I understand. Unfortunately, we place too high a value on personal comfort. Living with three brothers can be uncomfortable. We get in each other's way. But we also bless each other. There is a depth of fellowship among us. For me there is safety in being surrounded by my church family.

When I repented and came back to church, I knew I needed to get plugged in fast. I didn't have months and years to develop friendships and fellowship. I couldn't wait for just the right guys to come into my life. Trust was irrelevant. What did it matter if someone violated my trust? Everyone knew about my circumstances. There were no secrets that someone could hold against me. What were they going to do? Tell my wife? Tell my pastor? So I put time and energy into developing fellowship. I made it a practice to connect with a brother in the church every day, even if it was just a phone call. It wasn't one-sided, either. I didn't just dump my burden on others. I was genuinely interested in their lives as well. Consequently God gave me ample opportunities to minister to their needs. In a short time I had developed fellowship with over thirty brothers.

Calvary Chapel St. Paul is a church family. Church is not something we do or a place we go; it's not a social club. We are involved in each other's lives on a daily basis. We care for each other, we disciple and counsel each other, we correct each other as necessary. If brothers or sisters are in trouble, we drop everything and come to their rescue.

I've heard people who are not plugged into a church say, "I don't need to go to church to be a Christian. My church is_____" you fill in the blank. I've heard all the complaints about what's wrong with the church and how the people are hypocrites. It's true. The church has problems. That's because you and I insist on showing up. There would be no problems in the church if no one showed up. The people are the church; therefore problems in the church are because of the people. That's why we come together—to biblically work out our relationship with God and each other.

Church is not a man-made invention. God established the church. It's the body of Christ.[2] It's His bride.[3] After Peter's great revelation in Matthew 16, Jesus proclaimed, *"On this rock I will build My church, and the gates of Hades shall not prevail against it."* If you take issue with the church, your problem isn't with man but with God. It's His church, warts and all. Satan has you deceived if you believe you don't need to function as part of the church. You are living in disobedience to God. You and God don't have an understanding or agreement otherwise. God created us to need each other to live complete and fulfilled lives. No one is exempt.

There is a big difference in going to church and functioning in a church as part of the body of Christ. You have to let yourself be vulnerable. You're going to have to open up and let people into your life. Let them get to know you, warts and all. It will be humbling. You will have to learn how to submit to those in authority and to other believers.[4] You may have to learn to ask for help. I guarantee you will be forced out of your comfort zone. And yes, you will get hurt. But it's worth it. The blessings and security of a biblical church family far outweigh the disappointments.

---

[2] Colossians 1:24
[3] 2 Corinthians 11:2; Ephesians 5:22–33
[4] 1 Peter 5:5

chapter 22

Revelations

The fear of the LORD is clean, enduring forever.

—Psalm 19:9

*G*od used a brother I'd known for a long time to confront me about a critical flaw in my relationship with Him. I had ministered to this brother in my earlier days of Calvary Chapel St. Paul. God continued to bring him in and out of my life through the dark years when he had to endure seeing me at my worst. Now that I had repented and was back in fellowship, we met on a regular basis. One day over lunch he began to say something, then stopped. I encouraged him to go on. "You might not like it," he warned. "Go ahead. What?" I wasn't expecting him to say something profound. "I've known you for a long time." He had my attention. "Kevin, you don't fear God."

That was it. I don't remember there being any more discussion. Today he doesn't even remember the conversation. Yet his words hit me hard. They stuck with me for days. I don't fear God. It was an epiphany; God's Spirit within me confirmed the truth of this simple statement. I don't fear God. Yet I still found myself fighting against it. My mind began to debate this truth. Questions began to surface. What about 1 John 4:18, "Perfect love casts out fear?" Or how about 2 Timothy 1:7, *"For God has not given us a spirit of fear, but of power and of love and of a sound mind."* Yet I knew there was truth in his words, "Kevin, you don't fear God."

For the next weeks, months, and even years I studied the subject. What did the Bible say about fear? I knew *"The fear of the Lord is the beginning of wisdom."* (Prov. 9:10) But what else did the Bible say? Why was it that no one talked about fearing God? I can't remember ever hearing anyone teach on the subject. Yet to my surprise I found that the Bible was full of exhortations encouraging and warning us to fear God. In fact, I found 124 direct references to fearing God.

Following is a small sampling of verses. I'll add very little commentary. God's Word can speak for itself.

EXHORTATIONS

Honor all people. Love the brotherhood. Fear God. Honor the king.
—1 Peter 2:17

And now, Israel, what does the Lord your God require of you, but to fear the Lord . . .
—Deuteronomy 10:12

Fear God and keep His commandments, for this is man's all.
—Ecclesiastes 12:13

Do not let your heart envy sinners, but be zealous for the fear of the Lord . . .
—Proverbs 23:17

PERFECTING HOLINESS

Therefore, having these promises, beloved, let us cleanse ourselves from all filthiness of the flesh and spirit, perfecting holiness in the fear of God.
—2 Corinthians 7:1

EFFECTIVE PRAYER LIFE

He will fulfill the desire of those who fear Him; He also will hear their cry and save them.
—Psalm 145:19

GOD'S COMPASSION

As a father pities [has compassion on] his children, so the Lord pities [has compassion on] those who fear Him.

—Psalm 103:13

LIFE ENRICHING

The fear of the Lord prolongs days . . .

—Proverbs 10:27

The fear of the Lord is a fountain of life . . .

—Proverbs 14:27

The fear of the Lord leads to life, and he who has it will abide in satisfaction; he will not be visited with evil.

—Proverbs 19:23

By humility and the fear of the Lord are riches and honor and life.

—Proverbs 22:4

GOD'S MERCY

For as the heavens are high above the earth, so great is His mercy toward those who fear Him.

—Psalm 103:11 (Luke 1:50)

PLEASING TO GOD

The Lord takes pleasure in those who fear Him, in those who hope in His mercy.

—Psalm 147:11

GOD'S PROTECTION

The angel of the Lord encamps all around those who fear Him, and delivers them.

—Psalm 34:7

GOD'S PROVISION

Oh, fear the Lord, you His saints! There is no want to those who fear Him.

—Psalm 34:9

SALVATION NEAR

Surely His salvation is near to those who fear Him . . .

—Psalm 85:9

WISDOM

The fear of the Lord is the instruction [beginning] of wisdom . . .
—Proverbs 15:33; Proverbs 9:10; Psalm 111:10

REQUIREMENT FOR LEADERS

He who rules over men must be just, ruling in the fear of God.
—2 Samuel 23:3

The more frequently a topic is addressed in God's Word, the more important it is. This is a basic principle when studying Scripture. (This explains why there are four books dedicated to the life of Jesus.) Fearing God can be found throughout the Bible, Old and New Testaments. That tells me that it's a very important subject. Besides the 124 direct references, every biblical character can be evaluated by the fear of the Lord. Whenever you read about a man or woman walking in obedience, you can assume that the fear of the Lord is present. Likewise whenever a biblical character fails, the fear of God is absent.

When Nehemiah was appointed governor over Israel, he didn't place any extra burden on the people, as did his predecessors, *"because of the fear of God"* (Neh. 5:15).

When David sinned with Bathsheba, he obviously didn't fear God. But he did fear the Lord later when he repented. David vacillated throughout his life between fearing God and not fearing God. Additionally, David failed to teach his children the fear of the Lord.[1] As a result, his children's lives were out of control.

Abraham was also inconsistent in his fear of the Lord. Sometimes he feared man more, as when he traveled to Egypt and had his wife lie and say she was his sister.[2] On the other hand, when he was obedient to offer his son Isaac, God stopped him at the last moment and said, *"Do not lay your hand on the lad, or do anything to him; for now I know that you fear God, since you have not withheld your son, your only son, from Me"* (Gen. 22:12). This incredible act of obedience is extolled throughout Scripture as a great act of faith. Therefore I conclude that faith in God and the fear of God are interconnected.

In the book of Acts, *"Ananias, with Sapphira his wife, sold a possession, and he kept back part of the proceeds."* When they conspired to lie about it God dealt with them harshly; they both died. The result was *"great fear came upon all those who heard these things"* (Acts 5:5). It should be noted that this fear didn't scare people away from God. Instead, the result was that believers took the things of God seriously. The fear of the Lord produced holiness in their lives.

> *An oracle within my heart concerning the transgression of the wicked: There is no fear of God before his eyes.*
> —Psalm 36:1 (Romans 3:18)

It would be easy to go on and on. Joseph, Daniel, Rahab, Ruth, Joshua, Moses, Esther all demonstrated the fear of the Lord. Ananias and Sapphira, Balaam, Korah, Cain, Ahab, Jezebel, and Judas did not. Samson, while a man of faith and certainly one of God's children, didn't seem to fear God, at least not until he was thoroughly broken.

---

[1] Psalm 34:11
[2] Genesis 20

Now that we've established the importance of fearing God, what does it mean? What should it look like in a person's life? First let's deal with what fearing God is not.

"For God has not given us a spirit of fear, but of power and of love and of a sound mind" (2 Tim. 1:7). The Greek word used for fear in this passage means timid. We are not to be timid.

In 1 John 4:18 we read *"perfect love casts out fear?"* The word here is the word for terror or paranoia. There is such a thing as the "terror of the Lord." But that's not what's being talked about in this passage.

Verses dealing with the terror of the Lord are primarily directed to the unbeliever. Hopefully such terror brings the person into a saving relationship with God. Unfortunately the terror of the Lord usually causes unbelievers to run from God, not ask the question "What must I do to be saved?" Yet many believers have the testimony that it was the fear of hell that initially brought them to Jesus. That's fine, whatever it takes to get a person's attention. However, terror is an insufficient emotion to sustain a person's relationship with God. Remember, *"The goodness of God leads you to repentance . . ."*[3] It's God's love for us that draws us to Him and sustains us.

Terror is not for God's children, unless that child is in rebellion. Then he should be in terror. It's healthy for backslidden believers to be in terror of God's discipline or even question their salvation. It should bring them to repentance and a restored relationship with their Father. Then there is no more need for terror. When I first came to Chik, I told him I was afraid (in terror) that I wasn't saved. His response was "Good! You should be afraid. Now we can fix it."

Let all the earth fear the Lord; let all the inhabitants of the world stand in awe of Him.
—Psalm 33:8

Only fear the Lord, and serve Him in truth with all your heart; for consider what great things He has done for you.
—1 Samuel 12:24

---

[3] Romans 2:4

If it's not timidity, paranoia, or terror, then what does it mean to fear God? An overwhelming sense of awe is an excellent definition. When you consider who God is and *"what great things He has done,"* it's easy to *"stand in awe of Him."* His presence fills the universe, He created everything with a word and His power exceeds the imagination. Then consider what He has done. He loves us so much that He sacrificed His only son to restore a relationship with us. If we begin to comprehend even a small part of this our natural response will be to "stand in awe of Him."

A healthy fear of God draws us to Him; it doesn't drive us away. It produces fruit in the life of the believer. The fear of God produces obedience, holiness, and love. I'm convinced that fearing God and loving God are inseparable. You can't have one without the other. You don't love someone without showing respect.

> *The fear of the Lord is to hate evil . . .*
>
> —Proverbs 8:13

God hates sin. Not because He's the cosmic killjoy, but because He loves us. Sin may be fun for a season, but in the end it brings pain and suffering. God doesn't want His children to suffer. I admit that I don't hate sin. Oh I hate the consequences of sin and I hate some sin, but I don't hate sin the way God hates sin. This was my next revelation after I was confronted with my failure to fear God. God spoke directly to my heart, "Kevin, you don't fear me and you don't hate sin."

> *Do not be wise in your own eyes; fear the Lord and depart from evil.*
> —Proverbs 3:7 (Proverbs 8:13; 16:16)

The fear of God causes us to love God, which draws us near to God. As we spend time with Him and study His Word, the more we are conformed into His image. In time we become increasingly like-minded with God. We grow to love as He loves and to hate what He hates. But in order for this metamorphosis to occur, we have to persevere. This brings me to the third revelation.

"Do you know what I hate? I hate quitters!" Chik's message was especially poignant. Four years later, I can't remember what passage he was teaching or any other specifics of the message. Yet I clearly remember Chik's proclamation, "I hate quitters," and God's voice saying, "Kevin, you're a quitter."

> *Abide in Me, and I in you. As the branch cannot bear fruit of itself, unless it abides in the vine, neither can you, unless you abide in Me.*
>
> *I am the vine, you are the branches. He who abides in Me, and I in him, bears much fruit; for without Me you can do nothing.*
> —John 15:4,5

Abide: to remain; stay; continue; last; endure; tolerate; to wait for; to accept without opposition or question; to persevere

I see two aspects to perseverance. First it means you don't give up. You stick to it no matter what. Second it means that you finish what you started; you complete the task. It is possible to not give up, yet also not accomplish the goal. I was guilty of both giving up and not being willing to do what I knew had to be done. Namely confess my sin and walk in the light.

There was no denying it. The three critical flaws in my relationship with God were I don't fear Him; I don't hate sin, and I don't persevere. Throughout my life I've taken God for granted, entertained sin, and quit when the going got tough. This would have to change if I was going to overcome the patterns of sin and failure in my life.

Fear God, hate sin, persevere became my standard. It was always included in my prayer requests along with, "May Jesus come back soon." Realistically if all I did was learn to fear God, the rest would follow naturally. But the three go together. It caught on, and many of the brothers picked up on this revelation. However, I noticed that most wanted to change it to love God, hate sin, and persevere. Whatever. I understand the apprehension over the word "fear." However, when you look at it biblically, it doesn't seem nearly as harsh as one would presume. Anyway as far as I'm concerned, love God and fear God are two sides of the same coin.

> *. . . giving all diligence, add to your faith virtue, to virtue knowledge, to knowledge self-control, to self-control perseverance, to perseverance godliness, to godliness brotherly kindness, and to brotherly kindness love. For if these things are yours and abound, you will be neither barren nor unfruitful in the knowledge of our Lord Jesus Christ.*
> —2 Peter 1:5–8

It was a revelation for me when I realized that I could add to my faith. I had always believed that there is nothing we're suppose to add to our faith. Yet here it is clear as day. We are to add to our faith virtue, knowledge, self-control, perseverance, godliness, kindness, and love. It should be noted that adding to your faith doesn't mean doing these things instead of faith; it means to build up your faith by exercising these virtues.

This passage tells me that adding these to my faith is a secret to living a fruitful life. Later in verse 10, Peter goes on to say, *"If you do these things you will never stumble."* I want to be fruitful and never stumble. I'd hope that you do as well. Therefore it would seem prudent for us to master these virtues. I consider it paramount to working *"out your own salvation with fear and trembling."* Only be aware that our efforts are not to be done apart from a personal relationship with God. Otherwise they become meaningless religious acts. Don't forget that Philippians 2:12 is followed by 2:13, *"For it is God who works in you both to will and to do for His good pleasure."*

Virtue: moral excellence; valor; boldness; determination

Knowledge: awareness of God combined with information about God that produces an intimate relationship with God

Self-control: constraint; temperance; continence; to exercise control over one's appetites

Perseverance: cheerful endurance; tenacity; continued effort in spite of difficulties

Godliness: obedience to God, reverence to God, worship of God, conforming to the image of Jesus

Brotherly kindness: caring friendship and fellowship toward the brethren expressed through acts of charity and good deeds

Love: agape, the ultimate unfailing love as demonstrated by God's love toward us

The problem is that we forget. Peter goes on to warn, *"For he who lacks these things is shortsighted, even to blindness, and has forgotten that he was cleansed from his old sins"* (2 Pet. 2:9). We are easily distracted. The cares of this world and our sinful selfish nature cause us to lose sight of the goal. Every day we need to be reminded of who God is and what He has done for us. We need to cling to the simple gospel of salvation. We have been cleansed from our sins. We are no longer enemies of God; we are His children.

> *Remember therefore from where you have fallen; repent and do the first works . . .*
> —Revelation 2:5

Paul, in his letters, makes frequent reference to being a "bondservant." As previously noted bondservants were willing slaves, those who chose to give up their rights and personal liberties to serve their masters for life. In ancient times bondservants would have their ear pierced to mark this commitment. This symbol was a reminder to themselves and a testimony to others that they belonged to the master. If they ever lost sight of this commitment, the earring was there to remind them. Paul doesn't make reference to marking his body as a reminder, but Paul also doesn't seem to have a problem remembering to whom he belongs. On the other hand, most of the rest of us seem to easily forget.

Remember, repent, return became another standard in my life like fear God; hate sin; persevere. But what could I do to keep it in the forefront of my thoughts? Piercing my ear wouldn't make much of a statement. Over the years I've met many people with tattoos. In the military and in prison I've witnessed tattoo artists at work. Yet at forty-eight I didn't have a single tattoo. Not because I opposed them, but because I was never certain what I would want. After all I would have to live with it for the rest of my life. Yes I know about the Scripture in Leviticus 19:28 that says the Israelites were not to tattoo their bodies. I don't have a problem with this passage. I'm convinced that the application for us is that we are not to mark our bodies as an act of worship to false gods.

In 2005 and age forty-eight, I got my first tattoos. The one on my arm is a bloody crown of thorns with a scroll that reads, "Remember Repent Return." On my leg is a rendering of the bronze serpent with the foreshadowing of the cross. Underneath is "Fear God" in Hebrew. My tattoos are one of the best things I've done. I plan to get more. Maybe I'll become the illustrated Christian. For me my tattoos are equivalent to the piercing of the ear for the bondservant. They mark me as belonging to Jesus. They help me to remember. They also protect me from adventuring too far in the wrong direction. They are a visible testimony to my faith.

chapter 23

Showtime

This is the message which we have heard from Him and declare to you, that God is light and in Him is no darkness at all.

—1 John 1:5

"A re you ready?" Hesitantly I claimed that I was. It was obvious that I was overwhelmed by what was coming. "You better stay with me until the service begins." Chik could see that I was anxious.

Worship was difficult. I couldn't focus. My heart was in my throat. After worship Chik announced, "Everyone gather up your belongings as though you are about to leave." No one responded. "I mean it. Pick up your stuff." I could feel my heart pounding in my chest as people gathered up books and purses. "Over two years we've been planning for tonight. The message is for mature audiences. We will be dealing with a very sensitive subject. You may not want to stay. No one will hold it against you. Now is your chance to leave." I desperately wanted to leave, but that would have been awkward. No one left.

Walking to the platform, all my anxiety disappeared and a peace came over me. For the next forty-five minutes I shared my story with my church family. The Holy Spirit was with me, giving me confidence. While nowhere near as thorough as this writing, it was a painfully honest testimony of my pathetic life. But like this writing it wasn't merely a tale of wickedness and sin; it was a testimony of God's grace and a study in God's Word: the main theme being "walking in the light." When I finished, Chik spoke further on the subject and how this is a church that gets its hands dirty. "If that's too much for you, then I'll help you find another church where you won't be challenged." To my knowledge no one took him up on his offer and no one left the church as a result of my testimony.

Sharing my testimony this way was not a requirement for me to be forgiven by God or restored to fellowship. It had been over two years since that day I repented and confessed to Chik. The fruit of repentance was obvious in my life. I didn't have to do it; I wanted to. My pastor had asked me, and God's Spirit confirmed it. It was an important step in helping others to come into the light. There was definite fruit that came from that night (including this book). While I'm convinced that all believers should live open, honest, and transparent lives, God doesn't ask all of us to share our lives in this way.

> *If we say that we have fellowship with Him, and walk in darkness, we lie and do not practice the truth.*
>
> —1 John 1:6

To *"walk in darkness"* is to live a secret life, to not be open and honest about who we really are and our struggle with sin. Chik would say, "Who you are in private is who you really are." Unfortunately most Christians don't get this. They live double lives. They live as though who they are in public and how others perceive them is who they really are. This duplicity may not be superlative, we're not all Dr. Jekyl and Mr. Hyde, but to varying degrees we've all learned to hide certain aspects of ourselves. The Bible is clear; we cannot walk in darkness and have fellowship with God. To claim that we do makes us liars.

> *But if we walk in the light as He is in the light, we have fellowship with one another, and the blood of Jesus Christ His Son cleanses us from all sin.*
>
> —1 John 1:7

Every one of us is traveling on a journey through life. We are moving forward toward a final destination—God's judgment.[1] No one is

---

[1] Romans 14:11,12

exempt. The question is will we walk through this life in darkness, or will we walk in the light? Our natural tendency is to walk in darkness, because by nature our deeds are evil.[2] Yet if we walk in the light, two marvelous things happen. We have fellowship with one another, and we are cleansed from our sins.

Koinônia is the Greek word for fellowship. It means far more than social interaction. It implies intimacy, partnership, and communion. Real fellowship requires us to participate in each other's lives on a personal level. Just because believers are outgoing and friendly doesn't mean that they are in fellowship with the brethren. It's easy to have social interaction without engaging in real fellowship. Oftentimes the most lonely and isolated place is in the midst of a crowd. Fellowship happens only as we open up our selves to one another.

Church services and events are good places to meet people. Yet, fellowship flourishes best in small groups or as we serve together in the work of ministry. When people new to the church mention needing fellowship, I encourage them to get plugged into ministry. Initially they don't get the connection. They think it's a ploy to solicit more servants. The reality is relationships grow faster and deeper as we serve alongside each other.

Additionally I encourage people to get plugged into a home fellowship. Home fellowships are small groups that meet for prayer, accountability, to minister to each other's needs, and to apply the lessons taught at the Sunday service. No visitors are allowed, so there is opportunity to get to know each other. However, you can't stay in the same home fellowship for more than a year. This way cliques don't form and people have to expand their circle of friends.

Fellowship can't happen through professional counseling. Secular-based counseling, which includes most "Christian" counseling, is conducted in privacy with an emphasis on confidentiality. This encourages isolation and secrecy. Even the most effective counselors aren't involved in their clients' lives throughout the week. The people most qualified to speak influence into my life are those who are alongside me day in and day out. They have the opportunity to affect my behavior in real time, not in the vacuum of a counselor's office.

---

[2] John 3:19, 20

There are times when believers need to find a private place to deal with the issues at hand. The focus is to establish God's Word in each other's lives. But when we exit from behind closed doors, we don't part company. Instead, we move forward together as a family.

Trust is paramount to any healthy relationship. Being able to trust someone to be responsible and dependable is important. I don't hand my car keys to anyone. Fellowship requires a much deeper level of trust. We have to trust each other's love. We have to allow ourselves to be vulnerable. We give people access to the hidden parts of our lives. Sometimes trust is violated. We fail each other. Don't let that stop you. Make the choice to trust the brethren regardless of our failings. It's worth it. Don't harden your heart. The great physician will heal your wounds.[3]

A talebearer [gossiper] reveals secrets, but he who is of a faithful spirit conceals a matter.

—Proverbs 11:13

The Bible has much to say against gossip. Gossip is a terrible sin that at one time or another we are all guilty of. It destroys trust and encourages isolation. Every one of us should be ready and equipped to shut down a gossiper. Simply tell them, "I don't want to hear it. It's wrong and you need to stop." Or send them back to the person they are gossiping about. We use the three-day rule. "It sounds like you have an issue you need to resolve with that person. You have three days to go to them." After three days you ask the person, "Did so-and-so talk to you?" If they didn't, you go get the gossiper and sit them down with the person and make them talk.

There are times when it would be wrong to keep someone's confidence. You should keep nothing from your spouse. I assume that anything I tell a married brother I'm also telling his wife. I know this is true with Chik. He keeps nothing from his wife. Some church leaders may disagree. They might argue that the burden of ministry shouldn't be put upon their wives. There is a difference in being completely honest with your wives and placing an undue burden on her. Keep no secrets. Satan will use them to drive a wedge into your

---

[3] Luke 5:31

marriage. You are supposed to be one flesh.[4] Act like it. She's supposed to be your helper.[5] Let her.

I keep nothing from Chik. As far as I'm concerned, sharing what I know about someone with my pastor is not gossip. He needs to know what's going on. I've seen too many examples of situations that spiraled out of control because people kept their mouths shut. Wolves in sheep's clothing[6] have infiltrated the church with false doctrines. Sinful behavior that could have been easily corrected has gone unchecked. There was even a man in the church who committed repeated acts of sexual abuse. This went on for several years. Some people who knew him were suspicious. But because he was respected, they didn't go to their pastor or confront their suspicions. He's in prison now, but not without causing considerable damage. I keep nothing from my pastor.

Hiding in the shadows while people around you are in the light can be intimidating, especially when those people are trying to draw you out of the darkness. When one person in a group walks in the light it illuminates the lives of those around him. Like cockroaches some will scurry away further into the darkness. Others will be drawn to the light, but fear will cause them to withdraw. No one who leaves the church claims that it was because of their sin. It's always something wrong with the church or the pastor. Only after God brings them back broken and bloody, needing intensive care, do they admit the truth.

Then there are those who will embrace the light. They submit to the truth of God's Word and experience the joy and freedom that comes through obedience. Walking in the light opens the door to real fellowship. It's the missing piece. All my life I've had an idealized notion of friendship. I gave up on the fantasy at a young age. I used the word friend cautiously. People in my life were acquaintances. Still I longed for something more. Today I know what I was really looking for was *koinônia*, true fellowship only found among believers in Jesus who choose to walk in the light.

---

[4] Genesis 2:24
[5] Genesis 2:18
[6] Matthew 7:15

Another benefit of walking in the light is that we are cleansed from our sins. This is not unto salvation. Believers sin, don't let anyone tell you different. *"If we say that we have no sin, we deceive ourselves, and the truth is not in us"* (1 John 1:8). Every day believers are affected by sin, our own, the sins of the brethren, and the wickedness of the world. Although God cleansed us when we accepted Jesus, our feet get dirty as we travel life's journey.

> *Jesus . . . rose from supper and laid aside His garments, took a towel and girded Himself. After that, He poured water into a basin and began to wash the disciples' feet, and to wipe them with the towel with which He was girded.*
>
> —John 13:3–5

In our culture it's difficult to grasp the significance of washing someone's feet. In ancient times people wore sandals and traveled by foot or by animal. Animal waste was everywhere. People's feet became filthy. Then when you went into someone's home you reclined on pillows, not in straight-back chairs with legs. Your feet would be in plain view for all to enjoy. When you dined with them you reclined at a low table with your feet almost directly in the next person's face. Therefore it was customary for a slave or servant to wash your feet when entering someone's house.

At the last supper no one's feet were washed until after dinner. This would have been disconcerting for the disciples. Their feet were supposed to be washed by a servant. Or, if there were no servants, one of them would have to do it. In that culture the disciple of lowest status would have been responsible. None of them was going to volunteer for that position, so their feet went unwashed.

Think of foot washing as being one step from having to wipe someone's butt. A disgusting thought. No wonder no one volunteered, except the most important person—Jesus. Imagine their dismay as their master and teacher humbled himself and washed their feet. But as the consummate teacher, Jesus had a greater lesson in mind. He told them so, *"What I am doing you do not understand now, but you will know after this"* (John 13:7). The foot-washing incident has to do with our need for continued cleansing and our responsibility to participate in each other's lives, even down to the smelly, dirty details. We are to humble ourselves and become servants to one another.

Peter first declined to have his feet washed. The idea was inconceivable. Jesus wasn't going to wipe his butt (so to speak). Yet when told that if he didn't participate he had no part of Jesus, Peter requested to be washed from head to foot. Jesus replied, *"He who is bathed needs only to wash his feet"* (John 13:10). Jesus went on to assure them that they were already clean.[7] The point is that while we have been cleansed by the blood of Jesus unto salvation, sin continues to sully our lives. We need to be cleansed, which comes through walking in the light.

> *If we confess our sins, He is faithful and just to forgive us our sins and to cleanse us from all unrighteousness.*
>
> —1 John 1:9

> *Confess your trespasses [faults] to one another, and pray for one another, that you may be healed.*
>
> —James 5:16

We are to confess our sins to God and our faults to one another. We do not have to confess to one another in order to be forgiven by God. We confess to one another for strength and accountability, which leads to victory over sin. It is not usually appropriate to confess graphic details of our sins. We need to be careful not to cause to stumble someone who may struggle in the same weakness. However we do need to be specific about our failings. Otherwise we're in danger of minimizing the extent of our struggle. Simply saying, "I'm struggling with lust" is not enough. We need to admit to the specific behaviors that lust has produced in our lives.

> *Can two walk together, unless they are agreed?*
>
> —Amos 3:3

---

[7] John 15:3

Admitting to another person just how pathetic we really are is hard, painfully hard. It means we're vulnerable. It means we may lose respect. The person may even react negatively toward us. If they do, we've chosen the wrong person. We should seek out mature believers in our life. It's a mistake to look to someone who's just as much a "vomitus carnal flesh bag of pus"[8] as we are for counsel. Ultimately, what difference does it make what people think? It's God's esteem that we should desire. The opinions of others are irrelevant.

What good is fellowship based on lies? If you're not walking in the light, then you're lying to those around you. I'd rather have people know the truth. Then if they choose to participate in my life, I know it's based on full disclosure. If they choose not to, or they think less of me, so be it. That's between them and God.

Not letting what others think of me direct my life is easier said than done. The reality is that I want people to be involved in my life. I like being respected and cherish the esteem of others. One of my greatest fears is that if people know the truth they will recoil from me in disgust. Women and children will run from the room screaming. Friends will abandon me. Sadly, my fears are not without foundation. The only friendship I had maintained from my youth was with Steve. In 1994, while I was living in Winona, my mother died. Steve came to the funeral. We were both walking with the Lord at the time so there was a fellowship between us. Steve knew a great deal about my life; he was there for much of it. However, he didn't know about the homosexual behaviors. That night after the funeral I decided to confide in him. He hasn't talked to me since. It rips my heart out. I always thought we'd be friends for life.

Confession of past sin is important. If believers have never come clean about their lives, they are in bondage to their past. Coming into the light is the first step in being set free. However, coming into the light is only the first step. It's walking in the light that produces fellowship. Walking in the light has to do with today. You're here now. The past is done; the future is God's business. It's critical that we are open and honest with each other about what is currently going on in our lives, not just what has gone on in the past.

---

[8] Chikism

Being open and honest about our lives encourages and instructs others. We are able to comfort others with the comfort we have received.[9] It amazes me how many people have opened up to me since I began walking in the light. Most churchgoers are deceived into believing that those around them have it together, that they are the only ones struggling or hiding some dark secret. They come to church, smile, shake hands, and make small talk, all the while thinking, "No one really knows me. They don't really care about me. They would think badly of me if they knew the truth." The thing is that the other person is doing the same thing. If the two of them would just let down their defenses, they'd be amazed at what can happen.

Over the past five years I've worked at living without pretension. What you see is what you get. It can be difficult. My natural tendency is to slip back into the shadows. I get tired of confessing the same sins. Yet it is also very freeing. There are no secrets; no one can hold anything against me. It's really hard to gossip about me. Additionally, knowing ahead of time that I'm going to be honest helps to govern my behavior. I'm more likely to walk away from temptation because I know that I'll have to confess. It's easier and less embarrassing to simply deal with it now instead of later.

Two are better than one, because they have a good reward for their labor. For if they fall, one will lift up his companion. But woe to him who is alone when he falls, for he has no one to help him up.
—Ecclesiastes 4:9,10

Confessing sin, then living an open, honest, and transparent life produces fruit. It brings forgiveness of sin, healing, and spiritual maturity. Yet fellowship can't happen alone. We walk in the light together, caring for one another, cleansing each other. We take responsibility for one another. We are our brother's keeper. We hold each other up in prayer, keep each other accountable, and disciple one another. Jesus instructed us to follow His example in washing each other's feet. This can only happen as we live in fellowship with one another.

---

[9] 2 Corinthians 1:3,4

We know that we have passed from death to life, because we love the brethren.

—1 John 3:14

A brother recently shared a vision he had of Chik. Chik is a man who gets his hands dirty. He's involved in people's lives. This is not because he's a pastor. It's because he loves the brethren. The things you do and the choices you make do not determine who you are (although they will influence where you end up[10]). The person you are determines the choices you will make. Chik would love the brethren and serve others whether he was a pastor or not. The vision this brother had is of Chik knee deep in sheep dung. He's covered in excrement and sweat. All the while he has a huge smile on his face. The joy is apparent. He's experiencing the blessing of caring for the sheep. He's washing feet.

Then Jesus spoke to them again, saying, "I am the light of the world. He who follows Me shall not walk in darkness, but have the light of life."

—John 8:12

Have you ever tried to walk in pitch-black darkness? It's not too bad when there are no hazards or when it's a familiar path; when the worst that might happen is you'd stub your toe. But what if the path was unfamiliar and lined with dangerous obstacles, where every step could lead to disaster? That's life: trials and tribulations around every corner, demonic beings setting traps along the path. We need the light to see where we are going. Jesus is that light. When we walk close to Him and in fellowship with the brethren, life's journey becomes much simpler to navigate. Obstacles and traps are easy to avoid. And we have each other to help get us through the difficult terrain and pick us up when we stumble.

Jesus answered, "Are there not twelve hours in the day? If anyone walks in the day, he does not stumble, because he sees the light of this world.

---

[10] Galatians 6:7–9

But if one walks in the night, he stumbles, because the light is not in him."

—John 11:9,10

Park, enter through the double doors, past the security check point, up the elevator to the fifth floor, fill out the monthly report form, and wait. It was that time of month again; time to report to probation.

Reporting was done in a group. Offenders would share what they had been doing since the last meeting. Whenever someone new came to the group, each guy would give an account of his crime and where he was in treatment. The monthly report form solicits very personal information. Questions include: How many times have you had sex and whom with? How many times did you masturbate? Where? What did you think about? How many times did you have sexual thoughts and what were they about? To say the least, it was awkward and very humbling. Talk about walking in the light!

I was most definitely the odd ball of the group. As far as I could tell none of these guys were believers. Oh, some of them attended church and would probably tell you they are Christians, but they were not following Jesus. Guys talked about their homosexual relationships, which were treated as normal. Sexual activity outside of marriage, as long as it was adult and consensual, was not only acceptable, but also encouraged.

The language of the group was psychobabble. I refused to use their jargon. Instead I spoke in biblical terms and concepts. I was a drunk, not an alcoholic. I didn't talk about sin as a disease. The world's philosophies hadn't produced fruit in the past. There was no doubt in my mind that only the Bible contained the answers to life.

Most guys had very few people in their lives who knew about their offenses. I could name over thirty guys who knew and whom I could call upon for support. Imagine the shock when I reported that I shared my offense with the entire church at a midweek service!

Offenders are required by probation to submit a written "Relapse Plan" outlining what they are going to do to keep from reoffending. Psychobabble is the common language used in these plans. I could have easily written a plan that would have looked good. I know the language. But it would have been a lie. It would not have been a plan that I would follow. Instead I wrote a biblically-based plan that I don't mind being held accountable for.[11]

Walking in the light, being open about my faith, and drawing only from the Bible didn't endear me to the world. The police, courts, probation, and secular therapists have very little respect for Christians. This wasn't always true. At one time the courts openly worked together with the church and Christian organizations. Today they are at best indifferent, at worst contemptuous.

It's our own fault. The church has lost its effectiveness. Responsibility to minister to real issues has been relinquished to secular-based counseling. The Bible isn't treated as the authoritative Word of God. People professing to be Christians, including leaders in the church, have been the perpetrators of hideous crimes. The courts have heard thousands of professions of faith that lack true repentance. It's no wonder that the world has lost confidence in the church.

"Your heart may belong to Jesus, but your butt belongs to the courts." "There are no atheists in fox holes." "What makes your faith in Jesus any different than all the conversions to Islam I've seen among prisoners?" The therapist my attorney set me up with was unlike any counselor I'd ever seen—thirty years as a sex therapist working with criminal offenders, nationally recognized expert witness who has worked with local law enforcement, the FBI, and even the KGB. He was not a touchy feely kind of guy. He was direct and confrontational. And my faith meant nothing . . . at least not in the beginning.

I attended therapy sessions for over two years. We went round in circles, he with his humanist philosophies, while I stuck to my faith and my knowledge of truth from God's Word. I was completely honest with him. I didn't hold back or try to minimize my life. There is nothing in this book that would be a surprise to him. Early in treatment I would leave so drained that all I could do was go home and crash. Later the sessions were so predictable it was almost comical. In the end, I came to respect him. He was tough. I needed that. For his part, after two years he finally recognized that my faith was for real.

---

[11] See Appendix

He told me so, along with, "Kevin, at least you're consistent. In two years you haven't wavered from what you believe."

Many believers would have given in to the pressure to conform to the state religion—humanism. All I would have had to do was change my language a little. Add some psychobabble to my vocabulary. I didn't have to deny my faith, just add to it. Things would have been much easier. However, I know beyond a doubt it was the wrong thing for me. If I was to be free, I had to stick to Jesus and Jesus only, no matter what I was being told (even by some well-meaning brothers in the church). In the end, God has used all this in my life for my good and His glory. Regular probation and counseling meetings kept me on my toes. I wasn't able to forget just how depraved my life had become. Therapy forced me to review my life through the lens of Scripture, which helped prepare me for this writing.

chapter 24

Feed my sheep

"Go therefore and make disciples of all the nations, baptizing them in the name of the Father and of the Son and of the Holy Spirit, teaching them to observe all things that I have commanded you; and lo, I am with you always, even to the end of the age." Amen.

—Matthew 28:19,20

The Great Commission: "Make disciples of all the nations." These simple but direct words of Jesus have driven the church for over two thousand years, sometimes for the good, but often for the worse. Many of the atrocities done in the name of Jesus have hidden behind this exhortation. Wars have been fought and people have been enslaved claiming this passage as their charter. But that's not Jesus. These are the selfish acts of man perverting the truth of God's Word. They have twisted this simple instruction to read:

Go therefore and make converts of all the nations, oppressing them in the name of race, religion, and country. Teach them to observe your religious ceremonies and theology; and since I'm not coming back for a long time, if ever, do what you think is best and put my name on it.

We are to make disciples, not converts. We are to teach people to follow Jesus, not our religious ceremonies, doctrinal distinctives, and cultural heritage. We are to encourage people to grow into the image of Jesus, not into our image. All this is to be done in the name of the

Father and the Son and the Holy Spirit. Remember, to do something in the name of someone else is to do what they would do the way they would do it.

We are to teach people *"to observe all things that I [Jesus] have commanded . . ."* I guess that means we better know the things Jesus taught and His commands. That will take you back through the entire Bible. The red letters found in many Bibles are not all that Jesus taught. He is the inspiration and subject for all Scripture.[1] To get you started, here are two of Jesus' teachings: love the brethren and feed His sheep.

The problem with most evangelistic efforts is too much emphasis on making converts and not enough on making followers of Jesus—disciples. When people accept Jesus as their Savior, they have passed from death into life, they are adopted into the family of God and become sheep in need of a shepherd. Sheep and disciples are synonymous. A disciple of Jesus is one of His sheep. Caring for the sheep is paramount to making disciples. Consequently, feeding the sheep is fundamental to fulfilling the Great Commission of making disciples.

Peter boasted that he would never deny Jesus.[2] Then, fearing man more than God, he denied Jesus three times in one night with Jesus standing nearby.[3] "And Peter remembered the word of Jesus who had said to him, *'Before the rooster crows, you will deny Me three times.'* So he went out and wept bitterly" (Matt. 26:75). I know what it's like to weep bitterly. Peter was broken. He had failed miserably. So he gave up and went back to his old life of fishing. But God is in the business of restoring broken lives. After His resurrection, Jesus found Peter, but this time Peter was not so self-confident.

In John 21:15–17 Jesus restored Peter. He restored him back to a relationship with Himself and recommissioned Peter for the work of ministry. It's a fascinating passage. Jesus asked Peter three times, *"Do you love Me?"* The first time He asked Peter if he loved Him *"more than these."* Was Jesus referring to the fish, representing Peter's old

---

[1] John 1:1–3, John 5:39
[2] Matthew 26:35
[3] Matthew 26:69–74

life, or to the other disciples possibly referring to Peter's boast? Either way there are lessons to be learned.

The first two times Jesus asked Peter if he loved Him, He used the Greek word agape referring to the highest form of love. But Peter couldn't bring himself to profess agape, instead Peter used the word *phileô* meaning friendship. *"Peter do you love Me?"* "Jesus, I like you as a friend." Then the third time Jesus came down to Peter's level and used the word *phileô*, *"Peter are you my friend?"* I'm convinced this is what grieved Peter. Not that Jesus asked him three times, but that he couldn't bring himself to say he loved Jesus unconditionally. In any event their relationship was restored, and in time Peter would love (agape) Jesus. The book of Acts and Peter's epistles are a testimony to this love.

> *A new commandment I give to you, that you love one another; as I have loved you, that you also love one another. By this all will know that you are My disciples, if you have love for one another.*
> —John 13:34,35

"Feed My lambs." "Tend My sheep." "Feed My sheep." Peter's commission from Jesus was to care for the brethren. God's Word refers to believers as sheep. All believers. Peter himself was a sheep. Sheep need a shepherd. Domestic sheep are mostly simple-minded and defenseless. Left to themselves, they would starve to death. Unattended, they wander into danger. Without direction, they bite and nip at each other. The charge to care for God's sheep is the responsibility of the church. There is only one shepherd, Jesus. Yet God establishes undershepherds, pastors, and church leaders to help tend His flock.

Moses was called to help shepherd God's people. As the pastor of the largest congregation in all history, Moses discovered first hand just how unruly and rebellious sheep could be. So Moses solicited help shepherding God's people. He divided the duties among elders and hired an assistant to help him. Joshua was the first assisting pastor. It was Joshua's job to be the arms and legs of Moses. Moses couldn't be everywhere and do everything. Joshua filled the gap. Joshua became an extension of Moses, acting and ministering as Moses would if he were present. While the elders held up the hands of Moses in battle, it was Joshua who was on the front line leading the people. As assisting pastor, Joshua was responsible for the mundane and dirty jobs, anything that would free Moses to shepherd God's people.

Joshua Group is a ministry of Calvary Chapel St. Paul that trains assisting pastors and pastors. Joshua Group participants function as intern assisting pastors. Any brother, upon completing the Intern program, who believes he may be called to a pastoring ministry is directed to Joshua Group. There he learns quickly if he has what it takes. Joshua Group is tough; it's not for the fainthearted or weak; but as long as the brother gives it an honest effort, there is no failing. Many drop out after discovering they are not really called to a pastoring ministry. That's OK. Pastoring isn't what many think; not everyone is happy living knee deep in sheep dung.

Upon completing the intern program, I was directed to Joshua Group. Not because I believed that I was called to any kind of pastoring ministry, but because Chik said it's where I needed to be. Personally, I had abandoned any fantasies of being a pastor. I knew that I was called to write this book. Three days into it I called Chik to resign. Not going to happen. Chik made it clear that I was supposed to be in Joshua Group. I trust Chik, so I sucked it up and gave it my best shot. A year later, I was mercifully and graciously fired by the assisting pastor in charge of Joshua Group participants. OK, no one used the word fired. I was "set free to pursue God's call." It was obvious I was headed for a meltdown.

The year I spent in Joshua Group was one of the hardest years of my life (that's saying a lot considering my life). Not just because of Joshua Group. My broken marriage was an emotional roller coaster. My finances were a total disaster (eventually I'd declare bankruptcy). Work sucked. I'd underbid the job; the customer wouldn't pay me; there would be problems with the materials; I fell off a ladder and ended up in the emergency room; it was always something. My heath was a problem—chronic fatigue, irritable bowl, headaches, high blood pressure—and I had no medical insurance. Eventually, I secured veteran's medical benefits and discovered that I had hepatitis. I had to see a psychobabbler and attend probation meetings every month. Add to this the myriad challenges of Joshua Group and a feeble effort to write this book, and you have the makings of a tough year.

I would never want to repeat that year, yet it was a time of extreme growth. I toughened up and persevered through the fire. I made up my mind that I would not quit Joshua Group; they would have to fire me or the Lord would have to take me home. That was the year I grew a spine. I learned to submit, to confront, and to lead. I'm grateful for the wisdom I gained; it has greatly influenced this writing. No doubt once this book is released, I'll need my new spine. God really does use all things for good in our lives.

When the Israelites wandered in the wilderness, God miraculously provided for their physical needs. Their clothes didn't wear out, and He provided them with food and water. With the morning dew, God provided bread-like substance for their nourishment.[4] The Israelites called this bread from heaven "manna" meaning, "What is it?" As usual, God used this simple provision as a lesson. People were to gather manna for themselves only, and only enough for that day. When someone tried to stockpile manna, it would quickly spoil. The exception was the Sabbath. The day before the Sabbath they would gather enough for two days and it wouldn't go bad.

> *I am the bread of life. He who comes to Me shall never hunger, and he who believes in Me shall never thirst.*
>
> —John 6:35

Jesus, in John 6, refers to himself as *"the bread of life"* and connects God's provision for spiritual nourishment to the manna in the wilderness. Living beings must have food and water to survive. That's obvious. Less obvious is that spiritual beings are just as dependent on nourishment for survival. When we accept Jesus as our Savior, we become spiritually alive and in need of nourishment. Without food and water, we may not starve to death but we will become weak and our growth will be stunted. Jesus is our nourishment. We have to partake of Him every day in order to stay healthy.

---

[4] Exodus 16

A healthy sheep is a self-feeding sheep. The shepherd leads the sheep to green pastures and fresh water. You'd think that would be all there is to it. I don't know much about shepherding sheep, but I've heard that sheep can be really stupid. In a field of green pasture, some sheep will invariably find the one brown spot and try to eat. Or they will insist on drinking from a dirty mud hole when there is fresh water just a few feet away. The shepherd has to be diligent to keep each sheep eating healthy.

Exercise aids digestion. While learning to manage digestive problems associated with hepatitis this truth has become very clear to me. It's amazing what even a little exercise can do for your health. Spiritual health is no different. We need exercise. Otherwise we risk becoming spiritually constipated. Constipation makes one irritable and likely to lash out at other sheep. Then there's spiritual flatulence. Sheep that don't eat right and don't get exercise give off noxious odors.

> . . . be of one mind, having compassion for one another; love as brothers, be tenderhearted, be courteous; not returning evil for evil or reviling for reviling . . .
>
> —1 Peter 3:8,9

Jesus is the great shepherd, the only shepherd. Pastors are merely undershepherds assisting Jesus in leading His sheep. The ministry of the pastor is established by God and is to be respected. Every local church body must have a pastor, one who prayerfully sets the vision and direction for the body. There can be only one pastor in a church; you can't have more than one person, or worse, a group of people setting the vision and direction for the flock. It's ineffective and inefficient and not how God intended. Therefore the pastor can't be a hireling under the authority of the body or some board. He has to be able to set direction and make decisions that may not be popular.

There's one great shepherd and one pastor for each church. Yet all of us are called to assist in shepherding God's people, especially us men. Fathers are to train up their children. Husbands are to lead their wives. We are to disciple one another. I don't care how antiquated and chauvinist it sounds; men are supposed to be protectors. We should be the guardians of innocence and defenders of the weak. The ultimate sign of a godly man is one who will lay his life down protecting others. Unfortunately, in my lifetime I've seen these virtues of godliness disappear. Men have relinquished their responsibilities. They have become weak and spineless.

> *Now we exhort you, brethren, warn those who are unruly, comfort the faithhearted, uphold the weak, be patient with all.*
> —1 Thessalonians 5:14

We live in a wicked and perverse world. More than ever, believers need to be strong and courageous. We need to stand for God's truth and protect the innocent. Sometimes that means we have to get tough. We have to call sin sin. We have to confront and discipline one another. Most churches fail to administer biblical discipline. It's as though Matthew 18 doesn't exist.

> *Moreover if your brother sins against you, go and tell him his fault between you and him alone. If he hears you, you have gained your brother. But if he will not hear, take with you one or two more, that "by the mouth of two or three witnesses every word may be established." And if he refuses to hear them, tell it to the church. But if he refuses even to hear the church, let him be to you like a heathen and a tax collector.*
> —Matthew 18:15–17

Calvary Chapel St. Paul is a church that gets its hands dirty. We're involved in each other's lives. It's a church were people with real problems can come and grow in their relationship with God and fellowship with the brethren. But we're not stupid. We protect each other. My first loyalty is to my church family. If I see someone paying undue attention to the sisters, I confront him about it. When a guy came for a while that I knew had a criminal history for child sexual abuse, I made sure key people in the church knew about him. He was totally welcome and was afforded every opportunity to be part of the fellowship. As far as I'm concerned, it would have been inappropriate for me to not say something.

But as for you, brethren, do not grow weary in doing good. And if anyone does not obey our word in this epistle, note that person and do not keep company with him, that he may be ashamed. Yet do not count him as an enemy, but admonish him as a brother.
                                              —2 Thessalonians 3:13–15

Church should be a safe place to grow in our relationship with Jesus. We shouldn't have to fear being preyed upon. It's up to all of us to make sure it stays safe. At Calvary Chapel St. Paul we protect each other. It goes both ways. There have been women who have come to church only to find a mate. The mature sisters in our fellowship are on top of it. Sometimes new people just don't know better. We bring our baggage from the world into church with us. There have been numerous occasions where a visiting sister will want to hang out with the brothers. Usually a mature sister will show up to draw her away and minister to her. On occasion, the behavior didn't stop, so Matthew 18 had to be executed.

On a couple of occasions I've had sisters start to confess sin to me and seek my counsel. That's dangerous. Even Chik uses caution when ministering to sisters. I knew what to do. I stopped her, called a mature sister over, filled her in on the conversation, then politely excused myself.

On another occasion we were at a church retreat where there was live music at an outside stage. A couple of younger sisters were enjoying the music dancing in front of the stage. Only they were not appropriately dressed. It was awkward to say the least. I was about to remove myself from the event when I saw one of the mature sisters in our fellowship headed toward them. She pulled them aside and had a conversation. They left and came back in a few minutes wearing additional clothing. Thank you!

My phone rang. It was a sister serving at Sojourner's Café. "There's a guy in here hanging around the sisters. He's making us uncomfortable." "I'll be right there."

"Kevin, let's go. There is a brother we need to talk with." The assisting pastor snatched up the brother and we headed to a private place. "You've been told about not talking to . . . She asked you to leave her alone. Why did you think it would be appropriate to leave her a note telling her how you feel? This is your last warning. If it happens again you will have to leave." A couple of weeks later, he did it again. He's no longer with us.

After service one night, Chik called together half a dozen guys. He then began to confront one guy who had been acting very suspicious around the sisters and the children. First Chik cited the specific behaviors in question, then he said, "Everything about you looks like a pedophile. This is a church where you can get help if you want it. But as of right now you are on notice. You are not to talk to the sisters or children in this church. You get connected with the brothers. This is your chance. What you do is up to you." That was the last we saw of him.

I could go on and on with examples. By now you should get the point. Church should be a place where believers can deal with real problems. We need to get our hands dirty and protect each other.

This book scares me. The writing of this book is tantamount to committing social suicide. I've spent my entire life keeping these things secret. We are to live our lives in a fish bowl: open, honest, and transparent. But what I'm doing goes way beyond. The only people who see your fish bowl are those that you invite into your house. I'm building a public aquarium for all to see. What is on display is ugly. I'm among the modern-day untouchables, infected with social leprosy. It will take divine strength and conviction to live without fear.

Because the boundaries I've crossed violate the most liberal moral standards, many will reject me and dismiss my efforts to deal with sin. People will be watching; many will be waiting for me to fail. Then if I do fail, they'll cry out, "Once a pervert always a pervert. There is no cure. There is no hope." I'm not planning to fail. But that doesn't mean there won't be a struggle. No doubt the struggle will continue until the day I go to be with the Lord, and in that struggle there will be failures. Only I can never again allow myself to go to the depths of depravity found in this book. It would be better to end my life by my own hand—put a millstone around my neck and throw myself into the sea.[5]

---

[5] Matthew 18:6,7

So why write this book? Why put myself on display? Sexual sin is the proverbial white elephant. Perversion is everywhere. Just watch the news; not a day goes by without some account of sexual perversion. The church isn't immune. Believers are struggling and failing all the time, afraid to say anything. Someone has to start this dialogue, and the conversation has to include the offender. It's not going to get better by not talking about it. But until people can talk openly about these things without fear of reprisal, the bondage will continue. This is why I'm taking this step of faith. I'm starting the conversation . . . "There is a white elephant in our midst; what are we going to do about it?" Now it's up to others; actually it's up to you to keep the conversation going.

Are you a believer struggling with sin? There's hope. Whatever you do don't give up. Walk in the light. Fear God. Seek out a church that gets its hands dirty. Remember, repent and return every day. "Lord bring victory into these persons' lives. Wrap your arms around them and let them know how much they are loved. Bring them to a place of repentance, even if it means crushing them. Lord, don't let them waste their lives."

If you are not a believer in Jesus, I'm not sure why you're still reading this book. There's nothing here for you. You're reading someone else's mail. Become a believer, then we can talk. "Father, open the unbelievers' hearts and eyes to the truth. Draw them into the family. Don't let them have a moment of peace until they have accepted you into their life as Savior and Lord."

Are you a believer sitting in self-righteous judgment, as did the brother of the prodigal son?[6] If you find my life offensive, good, you should be offended by sin. But for the grace of God, it could have been you. It's great that your life has not been marred by gross sin. That's the greatest of testimonies. I'd be happy to trade life stories. Use your virtue to minister to others. Remember the father's words, *"It was right that we should make merry and be glad, for your brother was dead and is alive again, and was lost and is found"* (Luke 15:32). "Lord soften my brother or sister's heart. Teach them to hate the sin without hating the sinner. Let them use their virtue and moral

---

[6] Luke 15:25–32

integrity to minister to and strengthen us weaker vessels. May they rejoice with the repentant and mourn with the broken hearted."

> *Rejoice with those who rejoice, and weep with those who weep. Be of the same mind toward one another. Do not set your mind on high things, but associate with the humble. Do not be wise in your own opinion.*
>
> —Romans 12:15,16

To pastors, assisting pastors, church leaders and all who minister to God's people (which should include all believers). I'm a sheep. What would you do with me if I were in your church? Oh, and don't think I'm not in your church, or at least someone like me. Would I be welcome? Would I be allowed to participate in the work of ministry? We live in a lost and dying world that is plagued by gross sin. The people who come to church come out of this world. We can't keep our heads in the sand forever. It's time the church wakes up and fulfills its mandate to make disciples and feed sheep. It's time to get our hands dirty.

Finally, after all that has been said, I end with this simple Chikism, "What you do with this information is solely, wholly and totally dependent on you."

Appendix

CHIK'S LETTER

*B*y comparing the publication date of this book with the date of the letter, the reader will hopefully understand that God wrote this letter before this book was even a thought in the author's mind and heart. This letter is one of a kind. I have never before or since put my creditability on the line as a Pastor, Saint Paul Police Department Chaplain or Ramsey County Correction Facility Chaplain, as I have done here for this man and for his particular crimes. Everything in this letter is still very true to this day.

JANUARY 24, 2002

I am in receipt of your letter dated December 11, 2001 requesting my evaluation of Kevin. Specifically you asked whether Kevin is "curable," that is, whether he can overcome the problems that have led him to his current situation. My short answer is *yes*. As a pastor of seventeen years and an experienced counselor . . . it is my opinion that Kevin is absolutely "curable. . . ."

I have known Kevin and his family for over sixteen years . . . My first impression of Kevin was that he was aloof and not open with people, not even with his family. The best way I can describe Kevin would be fearful. He always seemed nervous and cautious about letting others get close to him. It seemed that he felt that he was not a very good person and was afraid that if someone knew too much about him they might not accept or love him. Therefore Kevin would not, or just could not, trust others . . .

I have found this attitude very common. The feeling that others are better or holier, that if anyone finds out that I'm not perfect, good, or sinless I will be rejected and unloved. The Bible makes it clear that we are *all* sinners in need of God's forgiveness. Yet in my experience just about everyone experiences these feelings at some time. Kevin, however, seemed particularly burdened. The Bible says Christians should be open and honest with one another. They are to ask for forgiveness, pray for each other, be accountable to each another and avoid sin. . . . This was something Kevin couldn't bring himself to do.

I tried to befriend Kevin as much as he would allow. It was difficult, but eventually we became friends. When I learned in the fall of 1990 that they were going to move to Winona, Minnesota I was very disappointed. I felt we were making great progress in our relationship and becoming good friends. Not only had their attendance at church become more regular, but they seemed to be functioning as a family. Kevin was growing in his faith, his family was coming together, and life had improved for all of them. Yet I continued to sense that Kevin felt he was not as good as others (and that if people knew the secret he was keeping he would be rejected or even kicked out of the church). Yet Kevin was gradually becoming more open about his life and daily struggles. I was convinced that given a little more time he would share with me whatever deep dark secret he was holding on to so I could help him through it.

By 1992 I was living in Saint Paul and pastoring Calvary Chapel of Saint Paul. About this time my family and I went to visit Kevin and his family in Winona. I was glad to see that they were continuing to grow in their relationship with God and with each other. As I reestablished our friendship, I continued to see hesitancy on Kevin's part to be totally open and transparent. I would press him, but he assured me that everything was fine and that maybe some day he would open up more to me.

Eventually Kevin and his family moved to Saint Paul and joined the church I am pastoring. In 1997 Kevin became a board member of the church and served a two-year term. During this time he also led our men's ministry. Again I felt there was something that Kevin was holding onto. Eventually I sensed he wanted to tell me about it. Finally he did. He told me how he had struggled with lust and pornography, how it had caused a great deal of trouble with his relationship with God and his family. He shared his feelings of guilt. I assured him that these feelings were common (they are), that many men deal with these issues, and that by confessing his sin, asking God for forgiveness, and being open and accountable to others he could overcome. I encouraged him to further confess this to his wife, which he later did.

Kevin had been struggling for a long time with feelings of moral failure. He was supposed to be good and holy, but he knew he wasn't. This led to secrecy, mistrust, and guilt. Kevin had been trying to be good and holy through his own efforts, by his own willpower. Willpower is like pushing a car without gasoline; it comes to a standstill as soon as it is left alone. Many Christians endeavor to drive themselves by willpower. The Christian life then becomes exhausting and bitter. Some force themselves to do "Christian things" that have no personal meaning because others do them. They force themselves to be what they are not . . .

There are two reasons why people use willpower to try to please God. First they have never given their lives to Jesus Christ; they do not have the new life Jesus gives to resist temptation and avoid sin. This was not Kevin; he had given his life to Jesus Christ. The second is that although they have this new life (are born again) they have not learned to trust in God and His Word. It is this lack of understanding and trust that results in habitual sin. Christians trapped in this cycle cease to believe in the possibility of anything better. It was this lack of understanding and trust and the ensuing guilt from moral failure that had plagued Kevin all these years.

While his confession and reconciliation with God and his family was a good first step, unfortunately Kevin did not come completely clean. Still expecting retribution, excommunication, or rejection, Kevin couched his admission in generalities and left out some of the things that caused him the greatest embarrassment and guilt. Again, Kevin was convinced that if people knew the thoughts he entertained in his mind and the sexual perversion he had experimented with, they would be repulsed and reject him. Therefore he was never completely clean and was not delivered from his self-destructive behavior.

In the spring of 2001, Kevin finally reached the bottom. It was evident to me that something had happened. He said he wanted to confess. I told him he needed to tell me *everything;* it needed to be all out in the open so we could really deal with his problems. Assuming he would shock and disgust me he said, "Fine, I will tell you everything, then you'll see!" But first he wanted to make a list so that he would not forget anything. This is the document found on Kevin's computer hard drive during the investigation.

Kevin confessed everything on the list. I told him that I had heard worse and that none of it was beyond God's forgiveness. We prayed, asked God for forgiveness and talked about the need to be completely open and honest. I told him that now he needed to confess all this to his wife . . .

Since this time, Kevin has been open and transparent, freed from deceitful patterns of behavior. Kevin has finally come completely clean with God, his wife, his family, and me. I know this cycle and pattern of self-abuse and self-destruction has come to an end. I'm convinced that if Kevin were going to continue in destructive behaviors, he would have done so by now.

Kevin is now "walking in the light" a phrase from the Bible found in 1 John 1:5–10 . . .

Walking in the light means more than being a good person. We are not perfect, and God knows that. Walking in the light is confessing your sin to God as well as to others around you. If we continue in sinful behavior without confession and repentance, we are living a lie (we are in darkness) and are not forgiven. Only by confession and repentance are we forgiven and able to overcome sin.

This is what Kevin needed to do all these years but was afraid because he thought he would be rejected and unloved . . .

It is clear that Kevin did not begin to walk in the light because he was in fear of the law. He was walking in the light well before he was arrested. He hit bottom in the spring of 2001 and his complete confession to me was on August 7. He confessed to his wife a week later. He also confessed much of his behavior (as appropriate) to his sons. A month and a half after his confession . . . the police first knocked on Kevin's door. I encouraged Kevin to be truthful and forthcoming with the police . . . The police commended him for his openness and how forthright he was with them. To my knowledge he has been completely honest during the entire investigation and I know he will continue to do so.

Kevin has finally realized that by walking in the light he is right where God wants him and will no longer be given over to sinful behaviors. . . . Kevin has finally found that by confessing his sin, being accountable to God, to me, and to others he can achieve victory in overcoming temptation. Thus it is by walking in the light of Jesus Christ that Kevin has found his cure.

In His grip!

Pastor Matthew (Chik) Chikeles
Senior Pastor, Calvary Chapel of Saint Paul
St. Paul Police Chaplain; Badge No. 9

RELAPSE PLAN

"How Kevin will continue to cease from sin."

In August 2001, prior to my knowing that I was under investigation, I took action to cease from sin. I confessed to my wife and longtime friend and pastor Matthew Chikeles. I took action to change my patterns of behavior. My motivation to change was not driven by the criminal charges. To some extent my motivation came from my being dissatisfied with my life and the distress sin had caused. My primary motivation, however, stemmed from my belief in God. I knew who He was, how much He loves me, and what He expects from me. I simply couldn't go on fighting against God. Admittedly my faith up to this point had not kept me from sin. That's because my life was full of unconfessed sin. I'm fully convinced that's why God allowed me to be charged. He wanted everything to be in the light.

Throughout the investigation and the court proceeding, I continued to be totally open and honest. I cooperated with the investigators. I was painfully honest for two different psychological evaluations and with my treatment counselor. I was open and transparent about my offense and my life with the men in my church; not just a few of them; all of them. At my pastor's request, I spoke to the entire congregation about my life and the offense at a mid-week service. Currently I am writing a book that deals with my life from a biblical perspective, also at the request of my pastor. There should be no question that there is true repentance in my life. The question is how will I insure continued success? The answer lies not in what I need to do differently, but how to stay motivated to continue on the current path.

Victory over sinful behavior begins with a right relationship with Jesus. The most verifiable events of human history are the life, death, and resurrection of Jesus. Jesus is who He said He was, "the Son of God." He came to reconcile man to God, to bring new life. *Therefore, if anyone is in Christ, he is a new creation; old things have passed away; behold, all things have become new* (2 Cor. 5:17). Any significant behavior changes I attempt apart from a personal, intimate relationship with Jesus will fail. To overcome sin in my life, I will have to remain close to Jesus.

Abide in Me, and I in you. As the branch cannot bear fruit of itself,
unless it abides in the vine, neither can you, unless you abide in Me.
I am the vine, you are the branches. He who abides in Me, and I in
him, bears much fruit; for without Me you can do nothing.
                                                    —John 15:4,5

Abiding in Jesus requires that I spend time with Him. I need to
talk to Him every day (prayer). I need to listen to His voice in my life
and be willing to obey His instruction. Jesus has to be more than just
my Savior. In order for me to overcome sinful behavior, Jesus has to
be my Lord. What I think and what I want are insignificant. All that
matters is what Jesus wants. I can trust Him. He is God. He knows
everything; he loved me enough to die for me.

"*The fear of the LORD is the beginning of wisdom . . .*" (Prov. 9:10).
The fear of God is a very healthy emotion. It inspires greatness,
produces obedience, and constrains evil. When I'm disobedient, I
should fear God's discipline as a young child would fear the discipline of a loving father. When I'm tempted to act out in extreme
rebellion (criminal), I need to be acutely aware that God will punish.
When I'm walking in obedience, my response to God should be one
of awe and respect.

In the fear of the LORD there is strong confidence, and His children
will have a place of refuge. The fear of the LORD is a fountain of life,
to turn one away from the snares of death.
                                                    —Proverbs 14:26,27

I need to nurture the fear of God in my life. The fear of God causes
me to stop and think before I act out on impulse or desire. Not fearing God has greatly contributed to past moral failures. It is easy for
me to lose sight of how great and awesome God is.

Do not be wise in your own eyes; fear the LORD and depart from evil.
It will be health to your flesh, and strength to your bones.
                                                    —Proverbs 3:7,8

The fear of the LORD is to hate evil;
                                                    —Proverbs 8:13

The Bible is the Word of God. Honest analysis of Scripture confirms its divine origin. The Bible contains everything I need to live a healthy and godly life. *All scripture is given by inspiration of God, and is profitable for doctrine, for reproof, for correction, for instruction in righteousness, that the man of God may be complete, thoroughly equipped for every good work* (2 Tim. 3:16). The Bible must be the first and greatest source of instruction guiding my life. All counsel and advice must be weighed against the truth of God's Word. Anything that contradicts God's instruction must be rejected.

It is critical that I maintain a regular diet of Scripture. It needs to be a part of my daily devotions. As I read God's Word, I need to look for inspiration and application, not just information. Staying motivated toward godliness is important. A devotional study of Scripture will keep me aware of who God is, the problems I face when I live for myself, and who I am in Christ.

The Bible contains instruction on godly disciplines that will enable me to achieve my goal to cease from sin (not relapse).

I beseech you therefore, brethren, by the mercies of God, that you present your bodies a living sacrifice, holy, acceptable to God, which is your reasonable service. And do not be conformed to this world, but be transformed by the renewing of your mind, that you may prove what is that good and acceptable and perfect will of God.
—Romans 12:1,2

But also for this very reason, giving all diligence, add to your faith virtue, to virtue knowledge, to knowledge self-control, to self-control perseverance, to perseverance godliness, to godliness brotherly kindness, and to brotherly kindness love. For if these things are yours and abound, you will be neither barren nor unfruitful in the knowledge of our Lord Jesus Christ. For he who lacks these things is shortsighted, even to blindness, and has forgotten that he was cleansed from his old sins.

Therefore, brethren, be even more diligent to make your call and election sure, for if you do these things you will never stumble . . .
—2 Peter 1:5–10

Fellowship with other believers—active participation in a healthy church—is essential. It is critical that I work at not isolating myself from others. This fellowship has to be more than just social. I have to exercise openness and honesty in these relationships.

> . . . *God is light and in Him is no darkness at all. If we say that we have fellowship with Him, and walk in darkness, we lie and do not practice the truth. But if we walk in the light as He is in the light, we have fellowship with one another, and the blood of Jesus Christ His Son cleanses us from all sin.*
>
> *If we say that we have no sin, we deceive ourselves, and the truth is not in us. If we confess our sins, He is faithful and just to forgive us our sins and to cleanse us from all unrighteousness.*
> —1 John 1:5–9

Spiritual health producing right thinking and good behavior can only be achieved through a personal relationship with Jesus. Since God is the Designer—Manufacturer—Creator of man, why not go to the Source? I've been a believer in Jesus most of my life and I've still failed miserably. My past moral failings are not a result of my faith; they stem from my lack of faith. God hasn't failed. God's Word hasn't failed. Kevin has failed to follow Jesus. Can Kevin fail again? You bet he can! But I don't have to fail, not if I stick to the plan. The biggest difference this time is the fellowship of other believers in my life. In the past I kept people at arm's length. In 2001 I came into the light. Everything was exposed. Today I continue to work at staying in the light. Most people in my church know about my failings and my weaknesses.

In summary:

- ➢ Spend time with Jesus, listen to Him, trust Him.
- ➢ Spend time in God's Word, let it inspire and instruct.
- ➢ *Fear God!*
- ➢ Exercise godly disciplines.
- ➢ Maintain fellowship.
- ➢ Walk in the light.
- ➢ Stick to the plan; it will save your life.